Life, Laughs and Football

LINEKER & BAKER

Life, Laughs and Football

arrow books

1 3 5 7 9 10 8 6 4 2

Arrow Books
20 Vauxhall Bridge Road
London SW1V 2SA

Arrow Books is part of the Penguin Random House group of companies
whose addresses can be found at global.penguinrandomhouse.com.

Penguin
Random House
UK

First published as *Behind Closed Doors* by Century in 2019
First published in paperback by Arrow Books in 2020

www.penguin.co.uk

A CIP catalogue record for this book is available from the British Library.

ISBN 9781787464230

Printed and bound in Great Britain by Clays Ltd, Elcograf S.p.A.

Penguin Random House is committed to a sustainable future
for our business, our readers and our planet. This book is made
from Forest Stewardship Council® certified paper.

MIX
Paper from
responsible sources
FSC® C018179

From Gary: To George, Harry, Tobias and Angus.

*From Danny: For Spud & Mickey, the Dockers and
the Chaps of Half-Way Line.*

CONTENTS

In which GARY reflects on his early days at Leicester City and considers the art of keeping it clean. Plus, some parenting issues, a quick phone call from Elton John, and why nothing will ever be better than the 2015–16 season (if you're a Leicester fan).

In which DANNY is awoken to his heritage and Millwall respond by immediately going on a 59-game unbeaten run. With further meditations on rosettes, pennants, building your own replica kit from spare parts, and arguing about geography with Sir Richard Attenborough.

CONTENTS

CONTENTS

CONTENTS

CONTENTS

FOREWORD

Football in Lockdown

It would be fair to say that *Behind Closed Doors*, the name that Danny Baker and I chose back in 2018 to christen our light-hearted and meandering football podcast recorded around my kitchen table, has taken on a different meaning for football in the age of COVID-19. At the time of writing, the Bundesliga has just restarted and is playing to empty stadiums. The sight of players – real players! – kicking a real football on a real pitch again has felt like watching a David Attenborough nature documentary. And it's done wonders for the soul after such a long break. In the opening game of the German league, the goals were flowing as Dortmund demolished rivals Shalke 4–0. But for all the players' talent and hard work, the atmosphere lacked, well, atmosphere, and the player celebrations were awkward, and just not that celebratory without the fans there alongside them. The game, like life itself, has been on hold, and we're only beginning to adjust to a new normal. We've never experienced anything like this in our lifetime. Football, it appears, will be played 'Behind Closed Doors' for the foreseeable future.

Obviously there are far more serious things to worry about at the moment than sport. I think we've all gained a sense of perspective from this pandemic by witnessing the bravery and sacrifice of so many frontline heroes working selflessly to help others. But sport does play a huge part in our lives, and I think it's OK to say that during this difficult period of lockdown and social distancing, we've missed football.

On a personal level, I've certainly missed presenting the highlights on *Match of the Day* and covering live Champions League football with BT. I've been lucky to continue working, albeit differently and without the excitement and thrill of watching current games. On *Match of the Day* we've managed to fill our slots on Saturday nights with a couple of programmes. A podcast with Alan Shearer and Ian Wright has been fun and has felt like we've contributed something at least, doing lists of Top 10s: goalkeepers, strikers, midfield players and all-time greats (oddly, I wasn't included). We had *Match of Their Day*, where we looked back on some classic games. Each of our pundits picked three games, two in which they played and one in which they didn't. It worked quite well and it's pleasing that some viewers have enjoyed it. But life is different and I miss the old *Match of the Day*, as much as I like working from home. Perhaps I'll get Shearer and Wrighty back around once live football starts again and we can record it from my front room.

But more than my job, what I miss the most, like millions of fans, is just watching sport. I always wondered what life was like for people that didn't enjoy sport, and now I realise. It's . . . boring. I mean, I know everyone's got different interests. But you can only read a book for so long (unless it's this one). You need that drama that sport uniquely gives us, and I can't wait till it fully comes back.

In writing this book – which aside from this foreword was written before the pandemic, I should point out – Danny and I have tried to celebrate everything we love about the beautiful game that perhaps isn't always spoken about by pundits: the behind-the-scenes, the personal, the profound, the hilarious, the trivial, the bizarre, the inspiring, the emotional and occasionally the transcendent. I hope the book can help transport you to a happier time that we will all return to soon – a time when football stadiums were packed to the rafters, when players hugged players in celebration without fear of breaking safety protocol, and when players could crouch on the pitch in the middle of a World Cup and relieve themselves in public live on television . . . Oh wait.

Before we begin, and in case you're interested in what else I've been doing during lockdown apart from eating bag after bag of delicious Walkers crisps, here is a quick lightning round of questions from my son Harry.

HARRY: Which professional footballer would you like to be self-isolating with?

GARY: That's easy. It would have to be Lionel Messi, wouldn't it? He could teach me a few skills in the garden. Note to readers: if you don't like Lionel Messi, you might want to stop reading this book now. More to come . . .

HARRY: Who would you rather self-isolate with and why – Danny Baker or Alan Shearer?

GARY: Oh good god! Probably Alan Shearer. Sorry, Danny, as hilarious as you are, I don't think I could cope with you for twenty-four hours a day.

HARRY: The government has advised self-distancing rules of six feet. If they enforced that rule in football during your playing days, would you have scored even more goals?

GARY: Well that's a yes, because if you're not marked then you're in space. I wouldn't even need to make any runs, so I think that's blindingly obvious.

HARRY: What has been your daily routine during lockdown? What are you cooking – any new lockdown recipes you can share?

GARY: I've managed to keep a mostly regular routine. It usually goes: get up, have a little workout, cook lunch, work if I have the BBC, cook dinner, read a bit, Twitter, watch a little TV – though I try to avoid too much news because it's obviously quite depressing at the moment. I've been doing a lot of cooking (note to reader: I like cooking. More to come à la Messi). There are lots of new recipes I've tried really, I don't know where to begin. It's been a great time to practise and I even did a bit of baking for the first time the other day. I cooked some butterscotch blondies, which were most enjoyable actually, but I'm not going to do too much baking or else I'll end up as fat as the house. Or I'll write another book called *Lineker and Baking* . . .

HARRY: On a more serious note, do you think footballers and football clubs have been thrown under the bus a bit, by being expected to forego salaries during the lockdown?

GARY: I think footballers were thrown under the bus, as they often are. They're easy targets, footballers, young men earning vast sums of money, which is fair enough. You would expect them to do their bit, but they did do their bit and more in a massively pleasing way with many great charitable donations. A lot of football clubs do a tremendous amount of good for the community, and they too have continued to do this during lockdown. But at the same time we've got to realise that Covid-19 is hugely damaging to football, financially, and a lot of clubs will fail to survive. It's not just about the wealthy giants; football's got many tiers, and players and clubs are going to find this very difficult. So I think footballers are an easy target, and for some awful reason I think there's something in the fact that because they're often working-class lads, society thinks that they shouldn't be seen as being too rich, whereas if it's bankers and CEOs earning millions, nobody seems to say anything. Footballers at least give the public entertainment for their money and provide pleasure and excitement to millions of people around the world. But it's the nature of it, and I think it's unfair to put the spotlight on footballers. I think putting the spotlight on the wealthy, and including everybody, would have been a much fairer thing.

HARRY: Do you think professional footballers can stay fit during lockdown? How do you think the delay in the professional game will affect players' fitness and game sharpness?

GARY: There are all sorts of problems. Yes, you can keep up a degree of fitness in your own house, and I'm sure most footballers have probably got a running machine or a bike and probably large gardens as well, so they can do a fair bit. But there's nothing like proper pre-season training, which they'll obviously need when they come back, because this is the longest break that most of them have had in their careers, aside from injuries. It's going to be very interesting to see how quickly they can get fit enough to start a game. I used to hate pre-season training, it's brutal and coaches take you to the edge of sickness mostly. So it's going to be especially hard for the players coming back because the break has been longer than anything before. I think generally players are in better shape nowadays, they live more healthily with better nutrition and that will help them, but it's still hard and they'll be dreading it.

HARRY: During lockdown, have you been doing the *P.E. with Joe Wicks* workout? If not, what exercises would you recommend from the Lineker 'Lean in 15' daily workout?

GARY: Sadly I haven't got a Lineker 'Lean in 15' daily workout, that's for sure, but I generally work out three to four times a week, although at the moment I'm probably working out five times a week. I'm lucky enough to have a little gym downstairs and I run on the running machine for a 15-minute warm-up, anything longer than that and my calf goes. Then I do quite a high-intensity workout, a mixture of heavy weights, press-ups, sit-ups, jump squats, all sorts of different exercises that you can easily do even if you haven't got any weights; you can use a couple of bags of sugar and things like that instead. There are a million workout videos out there, in fact I'm getting quite bored of seeing them all, so I don't want to force mine on everyone. If I'm going to offer anything, it will be a few recipes.

HARRY: What are your top comfort football matches (from any era) to watch during lockdown?

GARY: Old games are always good to watch, not as good as the real thing or live football of course, because you tend to know the result, which always takes the edge off things. But during lockdown I've looked back on the 2015–16 season, which has been particularly enjoyable, watching some of Leicester's triumphs, naturally. I've seen some of the football that the BBC has been showing, old World Cup footage, just to prove that football did indeed exist pre-Premier League. I've relived the bitter 'Hand of God' England game I played during the 1986 tournament against Argentina (more on that later in this book), and obviously Italia '90, where they showed both the quarter-final against Cameroon and the semi-final against West Germany, which brought back lots of memories that Danny and I will wax lyrical about later on in these pages.

HARRY: In your career in football, have you ever experienced anything like this – not the virus but football being put on hold? Does it remind you of missing tournaments for example?

GARY: We've never had anything like this, that's the thing; there's never been a long delay in football. It's incomparable. Personally, when I caught Hepatitis during the 1988 European Championships while playing for England, that was the only time I was out for any degree of time, at least until much later in my career when I left for Japan, when I had some extra problems with my foot. But I won't spoil those stories for now; read on for more (have you noticed a pattern recurring in my answers?).

HARRY: Finally, what is your view on the Premier League being suspended?

GARY: Of course the league had to be suspended. It had to stop. They had to flatten the curve of the virus, and they couldn't put the extra stress on the NHS. Perhaps we stopped playing games a bit too late? Only time will tell. But these are difficult times and difficult circumstances for those that make the decisions. At the time of my writing this new foreword, the Project Restart plans are afoot for the Premier League to start training and playing again safely behind closed doors. By the time you read this book, I hope you will have already been enjoying brand-new shiny football games for some time. Even just the thought of it lifts my spirts and makes me want to put on my boots. There are of course still so many questions, so many imponderables, and it's such a fluid situation that it's incredibly difficult to know what the right things will be to do. Or what happens in the immediate future for football's different leagues, tournaments and internationals over the coming year and years. This virus is going to have so many repercussions for all of us, not just football. All I know for certain is that for as long as I possibly can, I'll continue to watch and love and be delighted and infuriated by the sport that I first fell for as a lad from Leicester with big ears and even bigger dreams. So stay safe, everyone, stay alert (whatever that means) and let's begin.

Gary Lineker
May 2020

INTRODUCTION

'The teams are in the tunnel . . .'

GARY

Would a pre-match team-talk be useful to you at this point? A few uplifting words to take with you as you pull on the shirt, tie your boots, perform a few light stretches and generally try to get your head in the right place, ready to go out there and read this book? I ought to be able to help. I've sat in enough dressing rooms with enough football managers.

So, how about this one, from the late and revered Sir Bobby Robson? The scene is the Estadio Tecnológico in Monterrey, Mexico. The year is 1986. England are about to face Poland in our third and final match of the World Cup group stage. Thus far things have not exactly been running to plan. Indeed, 'disaster' would be one of the polite words for what has unfolded over this past fortnight in the dripping Mexican heat. We have managed to lose to Portugal and draw with relatively lowly Morocco, while scoring

11

precisely no goals. Meanwhile we have lost our captain, Bryan Robson, to a shoulder injury, and our vice-captain, Ray Wilkins, has been sent off and suspended for the unusual offence of throwing the ball at the referee.

To be fair, the ball didn't actually strike the referee; it arrived at his feet. But it arrived there pretty fast, flung by Ray in frustration after an offside decision that he didn't entirely agree with. And that, in a sense, merely further encapsulates the misery of this particular England campaign: even when we try to hit the referee from ten yards, we miss.

And now we face Poland, who have no reputation for being a pushover and who stand ominously between us and the worst of all World Cup ignominies – limping home in shame after the group phase. And, beyond that, the bravely borne but still painfully visible disappointment of our families and friends, the inevitable barracking in the tabloids, the season-long dog's abuse from the stands . . .

Some big words were called for, then, as Sir Bobby stood in front of his pretty demoralised troops – something resounding from the man in charge, with all of our reputations on the line, including his own.

Now, you won't find a player who worked under him who didn't respect Sir Bobby Robson and who didn't regard him as a profoundly wise man and a superb human being. But when it came to energising teams through the power of rhetoric alone . . . well, let's just say that even at the best of times Sir Bobby didn't exactly have a reputation for being football's Martin Luther King. Indeed, it was on the basis of his performances as a pre-match speaker that some of the players had taken to referring to him as 'Mogadon', in honour of the famous anti-insomnia tablets.

Generally speaking, when you gathered in front of Sir Bobby, you would be in for a lecture – long and detailed. Sir Bobby's favourite prop was the flip-chart – a giant pad of white paper on a stand which he would patiently prepare beforehand with diagrams and graphs and statistics, covering all eventualities for the game that lay ahead. These he would solemnly work through, turning those pages over, sheet after sheet, while we all sat there, pinching ourselves and trying to prevent sleep from setting in.

This much we all knew in advance, then. Moreover, as is often the case at this stage of a World Cup, the situation in the group, going into that game against Poland, was slightly complicated. A win would see us go through to the knock-out rounds, but a draw might also be enough, depending on what happened in the group's other remaining game, which was being played simultaneously. There were permutations, in other words. It was the kind of thing, one realised with sinking spirits, that would lend itself very well to some of Sir Bobby's famous flip-charts.

Yet, that day, in the dressing room, to everybody's surprise, the top page of the flip-chart was blank. Nothing was written on it at all.

Instead, Sir Bobby called for everybody's attention and

said: 'Lads, I could go through all the permutations of the results, but all of that is irrelevant if we do one thing: if we win. Win this match and we go through. It's that simple. Everything that's happened in the tournament up to now? None of that matters – if we win. And we *can* win. I know that – you know that. So let's go and do it. Here. Now. Against Poland. Let's smash them. Do it for the country. Turn it all around, make yourselves proud, make the nation proud.'

You could feel these words really beginning to get a hold on everyone. Redemption! A rewritten story! And ahead of us a fresh shot at glory. It was brilliant. Nothing complicated. Just a simple, direct appeal to the task in hand. Job done. We were on our feet – Terry Fenwick, Peter Reid, Terry Butcher. I could feel the adrenaline tingling in my system. People were shouting 'come on' and clapping and pumping their fists, utterly fired up. We felt unbeatable – like there was nobody who could stand in our way, Poland or anybody else for that matter. Let us at them!

And at that point, above the hubbub, rose the voice of Sir Bobby.

'But just before you go, lads . . .'

The blank sheet was whipped back and below it was the first of a series of further sheets on which Sir Bobby had painstakingly laid out the various alternative scenarios for the group. And these he duly talked us through ('Now, ninthly: if our game finishes in a high-scoring draw and Morocco win

14

by two clear goals against Portugal . . .') as we all gradually sat down again and as the energy left the room like the air from a paddling pool.

Anyway, the point is, thus inspired, and immediately uninspired again, we went out and crushed Poland 3–0. Frankly, I had been so peripheral and unimpressive in the first two matches that I had been quite surprised to find myself picked for this third one. But this time I scored a hat-trick, to which I added three more in the subsequent two knockout games and (I hope you won't mind me mentioning it) ended up becoming the first England player to win the Golden Boot, given to the tournament's top goal-scorer.

So much for pre-match team-talks, then. Some are good and some are bad, and some, like Sir Bobby's that time, are good at first and then eventually bad – and you still might end up getting the result you want. So maybe I won't waste your time by attempting a motivational speech at this point in the book. All the same, without wishing to get out a flip-chart of my own, perhaps I should try to explain the tactics, such as they are, behind the following pages.

These chapters arise from the conversations Danny and I started having on Monday lunchtimes in my kitchen for the *Behind Closed Doors* podcast. For those who haven't heard it, the set-up was a simple one: the two of us would get together in front of a couple of microphones and egg each other on to tell a few stories – me from my playing days, Danny from a lifetime of following the game, and both of us from a fair amount of time spent broadcasting about it. Along the way, often prompted by listeners, we would attempt to answer some frequently asked questions – such burning issues as, do players ever really 'hand in' a transfer request? Are goalkeepers truly different? And what's it actually like to share a bath with Paul Gascoigne? With me coming at it from the playing side, and Danny from the fan's side, we soon found ourselves travelling deep into football's most intimate recesses. Also, as the tales grew and the topics for discussion mounted up, we quickly realised that we had a surfeit of material. There were whole stories we didn't have time for, and there were other stories that we did have time for but which we were desperate to expand upon and add some flesh to. Hence this book.

Incidentally, when it came to finding a strike partner for this project, Danny was the first name down on the teamsheet once Sir David Attenborough had declared himself unavailable. (He'd picked up a niggle somewhere in the South Pacific, apparently.) Like Sir David, Danny is a broadcasting phenomenon. Unlike Sir David, he is a Millwall fan – and one of a very small number of Millwall fans to have sat in my kitchen. And he is one of an even smaller number of Millwall fans to have sat in my kitchen wearing a fez – wearing a different fez every week, in fact, from his extensive, globally-sourced collection. Above all, though, he is in possession of a formidable football-packed mind, and there is very little predicting the journey that football-packed mind will take you on, as we discovered during one session when Danny, without warning, brought up the little-discussed connection between Sheffield Wednesday and Salvador Dalí. The man is an absolute mine of information. One day some of it may even be useful.*

And now there's this volume – the fruit of our further discussions, in prose form. In order to impose some order on the anarchy, and to lend at least a semblance of the polished professionalism that you will be expecting from our unique double-act, we've arranged our tales chronologically so that, chapter by chapter, you can join us on the journeys our lives have taken through the football landscape – albeit with plenty of pauses to digress and pontificate on general issues arising. We'll delve back individually into the mists to analyse our childhood attachments to the game. We'll solemnly record our graduation to the first team (me) and to chief video operative on the hired coach taking Millwall fans to Portsmouth (Danny). Somewhere along the way, we'll head out to Italy for the 1990 World Cup with England (me) and as a hitch-hiker (Danny). We'll assess our experiences in the

---

* In 1969, Salvador Dalí designed the logo for Chupa Chups lollipops. The name Chupa Chups comes from the Spanish 'chupar', of course, meaning to suck. Thirty years later, Sheffield Wednesday entered a shirt-sponsorship arrangement with Chupa Chups, and thereby became the only British club in history to wear a kit partly designed by Salvador Dalí. Simple.

temples of the sport, from Wembley and the Nou Camp (me) to Bournemouth's Dean Court for Millwall's 1987–88 Second Division promotion decider (Danny). In summary, whether you're a player or a fan, or neither of those things, you'll find it all here – everything you always wanted to know about football, but didn't realise that you did, including the trials of the penalty shoot-out, the pluses and minuses of open-top bus parades and the things nobody tells you about shirt-swapping (me with Jean-Pierre Papin of France, Danny with Marc Bolan of T. Rex). There may even be one or two further adventures in motivational speaking with Sir Bobby Robson. And yes, I have an inkling Salvador Dalí will be sent to warm up at some point and then be brought off the bench for a cameo.

And if we really must have a pre-match team-talk . . . Well, how about: 'Just go out there and enjoy yourself.' Will that do?

DANNY

When the archaeologists of the future comb the soil in their quest to understand and tell the *Behind Closed Doors* origin story, no doubt the artefact for which they will be fighting each other with trowels will be the first text message that Gary sent me, marking the tentative dawn of what was to become a 21st-century media phenomenon.

It was just a simple, direct message, sent via the Twitter

social media platform, and it was, in truth, but seven words long. But, as history will be obliged to tell, they were seven words that were to shift the world of football-related story-telling on its axis.

Those seven words were: 'I'll take that as a no, then.'

Now, you will easily imagine my puzzlement as I stared at this cryptic communication on my desktop computer screen that evening in 2018 and wondered what it meant. It was startling enough for me to be getting a personal message out of the blue from a nationally-treasured England goal-scorer – the winner of the Golden Boot at the World Cup of 1986, though he doesn't like to talk about it. It was even more startling to find that nationally-treasured England goal-scorer immediately addressing me, without ceremony, in a frustrated and, if I may say, somewhat peevish tone.

Yet, although this was the first message I had seen from Gary Lineker, it was by no means the first message Gary Lineker had sent me. Actually, as I discovered when I scrolled back up the screen, it was about the sixth, the others being, roughly speaking, in reverse order:

'Was it something I said?'

'Do you never read your DMs?'

'Hello? Anybody there?'

'Did you have a chance to think about the above?'

(And finally) 'How do you fancy doing a podcast about football with me?'

Alas, the whole of this verbal volley had flown over my

head. I had been away on holiday, and blissfully removed from the wicked world and all its noises. Frankly, offers could have come in during that fortnight to lead voyages to entire other planets and I would have been too busy to notice or care.

But, fortunately, all was not lost. It was close, but the ticking time-bomb of Gary's patience had not entirely run out; my name had not been struck from the list; and Gary had not yet made an approach to what diary stories in *The Hollywood Reporter* were already touting as his second choice for the coveted role (Gwyneth Paltrow).

One shivers to think, though. Had my flight home been delayed by only a handful of hours – had I even dawdled a while in the last-chance chocolates and perfumes boutique, set like a fly-trap at the exit to the airport's baggage hall – *Lineker & Baker: Behind Closed Doors* might never have come to pass, the course of media history would have been irrevocably altered and the book you are holding would have been just so much untreated timber. Such are the fine margins and the chains of sheer happenstance on which the culture is built. Yes, a world without *Behind Closed Doors* seems unimaginable now, but in truth the show was merely the time it takes to buy a giant Toblerone and a 50ml bottle of Lancôme Midnight Rose from never happening at all.

Still, those perils are all in the past now. The project was duly born, and it grew and grew. It was a podcast, then it was a stage show, making its debut before an awestruck sell-out crowd at the New Wimbledon Theatre in April 2019. And now it's a book and, be assured, we shall not rest until it's a major movie franchise and a ride at Universal. I'm certainly in it for the long haul. What person with an interest in football wouldn't leap at the chance to help Gary Lineker crowbar open the dressing-room door and reveal what really happens in there? Not to mention revealing what happens in the tunnel and on the pitch and (with the appropriate pixellation) in the showers afterwards. Access all areas is the mission – and if that necessitates asking Gary whether, during his time in Japan, he was ever required to eat live octopus, then all the better.

And yes, it has also been our mutual duty to hit the game's major talking points head on – but let's be clear what we mean, in this context, by a major talking point. I'm rarely less overjoyed than when someone plonks themselves down next to me in a confined space and says: 'What about United, eh? Still two or three players away from seriously challenging for the title, wouldn't you say?' Now, I'm sure there are some brilliantly illuminating things to be said in this area, and maybe some fun to be had in saying them. Such things may even make suitable material for a book. But, when confronted by a question like that, I've got to confess: my blood pressure drops, my heart rate slows and something inside me quietly walks away to a dark corner to die. This, it seems to me, is how the media talk about the game – and fair play to

21

them, they've got their own racket to run. But it's not how the fans that I know talk about the game. And it's not how players talk about the game a lot of the time, either – except when they're talking to the media about it.

When I started the 606 Saturday evening phone-in on Radio 5 Live, my founding ambition was that the show would stand nobly apart from the first-thought news agenda prompted by what had no doubt been 'a busy day of action in the Premier League', and turn its eyes elsewhere: to the tangential things, the entirely mundane yet somehow glorious stuff off to the sides, the matters arising sometimes randomly from the game which amuse and preoccupy football supporters more than is generally acknowledged.

Accordingly, callers who basically wanted to moan about the lack of spending over the summer at their club would find themselves holding on for quite a long time. But people ringing in with first-hand reports of players whose heads actually steam in the winter cold . . . well, bearing such 24-carat bounty, these callers would be hurried on to the airwaves and given all the time they needed to share their treasures with the nation.

My idea of a properly curious journalistic mind is the man who stood up at a Q&A event featuring England's Sir Geoff Hurst. People had been taking the opportunity to ask the legendary goal-scorer the usual questions regarding the well-thumbed events of 1966 and soliciting his opinions about the England of the present and its chances going into whichever tournament was on the horizon. Eventually the microphone came to our man, who duly asked: 'Geoff, I'm asking footballers, if a turtle loses its shell, is it naked or homeless?' Alas, Sir Geoff's thoughts on this searching conundrum, if offered, have been long lost to the winds of time. But, sir, for considering this a reasonable forum in which to seek those thoughts, we salute you.

I brought much the same attitude to *Behind Closed Doors*. If, in addition to exposing what truly goes on during pre-season training, the pair of us could unlock an enthusiastic and informed debate regarding sightings of footballers at petrol stations, well then surely our debt to the national conversation was all but settled. As my portions of the following pages are bound to reflect, this just happens to be where my instincts and sympathies as a football supporter solidly lie. Sober meditations on the relative value of lining up 4–3–3 or going 5–3–1–1 with your number 10 playing just behind the striker in the hole . . . not so much. Eager reflections on the noise that footballs make when, having been booted over the stadium's roof, they bounce off bonnets in the car park . . . well, now, surely we've found something we can properly get our teeth into.

By the way, on the topic of getting your teeth into things, I should relate that the *Behind Closed Doors* conversations have habitually taken place over a lunch lovingly prepared by Gary himself. At least, so Gary always told me, though I have to confess that, in the early weeks, such was the

Michelin-starred quality of the food on offer, I did darkly suspect him of hiring staff from some top-notch West London eaterie and furtively hurrying them out the tradesman's entrance as I arrived, before answering the front door in a carefully spattered apron.

But no. It genuinely was Gary at the pans all along. And let me tell you, the man is a culinary master. From his lemon and asparagus risotto with gently sautéed lardons to his hearty sweet potato stew, the quality goes in before the name goes on. Trust me, you haven't eaten minestrone soup until you have eaten Gary Lineker's minestrone soup. Bursting with nutritious goodness? By my calculation it contains at least 17 of your five-a-day. We've thoughtfully included some of Gary's recipes as an appendix so that you can enjoy this book with friends over a light and healthy repast, in the convivial atmosphere in which these original stories were told. Our pleasure.

Meanwhile, your very best spread bets are warmly invited on how many pages will elapse before Gary mentions his Golden Boot.

What's that? He's already mentioned it? Good grief. And we haven't even started.

CHAPTER ONE

'And we're under way.'

In which GARY reflects on his early days at Leicester City
and considers the art of keeping it clean. Plus, some parenting
issues, a quick phone call from Elton John, and why
nothing will ever be better than the 2015–16
season (if you're a Leicester fan).

Two things I have in common with Roy of the Rovers.

1. In over 600 appearances for Melchester (with a short spell at rivals Walford, though that was a terrible mistake when Roy, as I think everyone now agrees, wasn't in a good place mentally), the most successful comic book hero ever to captain a football team was never booked. In 460 career appearances for Leicester, Everton, Barcelona, Tottenham Hotspur and Nagoya Grampus Eight, neither was I.

2. In over 600 and 460 career appearances respectively, Roy of the Rovers and I both released a record.

Indeed, we released a record with each other – a duet, no

less. The music world still trembles with awe at the memory of 'Europe United (Let's Work Together)' by Roy of the Rovers with Gary Lineker, released on seven-inch vinyl on the ACME label in 1990. Or it still trembles with something, anyway. The description of the record in the *Roy of the Rovers* comic as 'a hot rocking heavy metal rap with Gary Lineker and Roy on vocals and Roy on lead guitar' may have been slightly over-egging it, certainly in relation to my own contribution (and probably in relation to Roy's, too, without wishing to spoil anyone's dearly-held childhood illusions).

Rap? I prefer the polite description in a short and perhaps slightly shocked newspaper story published at the time: 'Lineker contributes a spoken section.' The lion's share of the rapping on the recording was done by Bruno Johnson – no relation, so far as I am aware, to Boris Johnson. My less bulky part was in the form of a short recorded message, asking England fans to behave themselves during Italia '90.

To quote: 'Ninety-nine per cent of the people who go to football matches deplore the actions of hooligans . . . Roy and I say, "Keep it friendly".'

Less Cypress Hill, then; more Jimmy Hill. Important sentiment, though, and the record-buying public seemed to agree. OK, 'Europe United (Let's Work Together)' didn't actually make it into the charts, but I just went on eBay and tried to find one of the original pressings for sale, preferably in its full colour seven-inch sleeve, but with no luck. Too precious to get rid of, clearly. Unless they are all in a landfill somewhere.

Still, I quote again from my 'spoken section':

Europe without England is like Rovers without Roy
Let's get Europe united
Over to you, Roy!

How freshly relevant all this now sounds, in ways we simply could not have foreseen in 1990. Perhaps they should rerelease the number as a unifying anthem for our divided times. On the other hand . . .

No bookings, though: that's a record that I'm even prouder to share with the legend that was Roy Race. I may have been kidnapped fewer times than he was (seven for Roy, none for me), and I may have been shot by fewer mystery gunmen who turned out later to be aggrieved TV soap stars (one for Roy, none for me). But never having done anything to attract a caution from a referee? We operate as equals on that level, Roy and I.

The closest I came to losing my unblemished record and getting a yellow card was very late in my time at Barcelona. I can't remember exactly what decision the referee had just made, but I can remember that I found it so wildly wrong that it made me laugh out loud. The referee did not share my amusement and, with a sinking of the heart (because obviously my completely clean licence had come to mean something to me by then), I watched his hand go to his pocket.

I was glad I had learned enough Spanish to be able to remonstrate with him. 'You can't book me for laughing, surely,' I said. The referee thought about it for a second and then his hand moved away from his pocket and the game went on. Record intact.

Where did this squeaky cleanness come from? It's possible that I can trace it back to my dad, and to a single moment on a football pitch in my childhood. As a kid I played youth football on Sunday mornings for Aylestone Park FC in Leicester. There was one match where I had already been ruled offside about four times – wrongly, of course. In every one of those four cases, the officials simply hadn't read the perfectly-timed nature of my run. Or that's the way I saw it. Anyway, it happened a fifth time and, in my frustration, I swore loudly at the referee. I can't remember clearly now, but most likely the expression I chose was, 'Fucking hell, ref,' although I may merely have accused his decision of being 'shit'.

Either way, it was too much for my dad. He took me off the pitch, gave me the most almighty dressing-down in front of everyone, and made it very clear to me that if I did something like that again, it would be the last time I played football. It was utterly mortifying: getting told off for swearing by your dad in front of the rest of the team, not to mention the opposition and the ref that you have just sworn at. But it obviously had an effect. I never swore at a referee again. I may have laughed at one or two. But I never swore at one.

At that time, in my early teens, I wasn't thinking I would

be a footballer. I really wanted to be one. I had been raised as a Leicester fan by my parents and grandad, went to games at Filbert Street, stuck pictures of Leicester players on my walls. I liked the *idea* of being a footballer. Who wouldn't? But I thought I had a better chance in cricket, which I was also quite good at and where relative size seemed to matter less. I was a small kid, late to grow and very late to reach puberty, which was an uncomfortable thing in dressing rooms in my teenage years, I probably don't need to say. There would be all these fully grown men, confidently striding around with no clothes on, and me, over in a corner, self-conscious as hell, carefully hiding myself in a towel. It was agony. I was about 17 when nature finally had mercy on me and I caught up.

I wasn't technically anywhere near as good as a lot of players, but I think my strongest traits were a) my speed and b) my head. I was an intelligent footballer, in the sense that I understood how the game worked, or certainly how it worked for strikers. But I was also mentally strong. Nothing would faze me. I was never nervous. The bigger the game the more I would look forward to it, the bigger the moment – for instance, taking penalties in World Cups, which is probably the maximum amount of individual pressure a footballer can know – the more I enjoyed it, in a way which, now I think about it, was almost masochistic. Taking those penalties for me wasn't something daunting: it was a chance to show off. A penalty in a shoot-out in a World Cup semi-final against West Germany? Bring it on.

I was also kind of mean-minded – and maybe you need a bit of that, too. When I was first called into the England squad, if I was sitting on the bench, I would be praying the striker on the pitch didn't score. I've had conversations with other strikers about this, and they were exactly the same: dead keen that a team-mate shouldn't do well. It's terrible, really – they're on your side. But at the same time you're thinking, 'OK, let's win 1–0, with an own goal.' That would be the best possible outcome: a victory for your side in which your rival for the striker's place hadn't done anything to cement his claim. I'll admit to it now, although at the time it would have felt like a risky thing to confess, so you masked those feelings. You would have been open to accusations of disloyalty – which wouldn't have been straightforwardly true because you never wanted the team to lose. You always wanted it to win. You just wanted it to win . . . in a certain way.

And it was amazing how many times it happened. I don't know whether this was as a result of me willing it to occur, but on numerous occasions the player ahead of me in the queue would have the anonymous match that I had quietly but desperately wished for him from the sidelines. And then I would get my chance and seize it. And even when you were established and you got injured and suddenly you were out of the picture temporarily, you were thinking, 'I hope he has a shocker and we win'. Because if the bloke in your place bangs in a hat-trick . . . well, that's the worst of all possible worlds.

I should also note that, when selected, I could be a first-class whinger. I was terrible for getting exasperated with other players and letting them know. Wingers bore the brunt of it: wingers who didn't see my run, wingers who hit the pass in too hard, wingers who knocked the ball over my head, wingers who checked back ... They would all hear it from me, something rotten. OK, I was also spoiled by playing with Chris Waddle and John Barnes – geniuses who knew where you were and could find you. Those two didn't hear so much from me in the way of irritation. But others certainly did.

And I was monumentally, perhaps even monstrously, focused on scoring goals. One year with Aylestone Park I made it into the local paper for scoring 161 goals in a season. I'm not sure even Ronaldo has scored 161 goals in a season. But quite simply, it never got boring. How could it? You'll see strikers these days earn heaps of praise for not celebrating when they score against their former clubs. Everybody commends them for their restraint, their respect for the old fans. I don't really get that at all. You're a striker: why wouldn't you celebrate a goal, any goal, scored anywhere? I scored for Tottenham against my former club, Everton, and I celebrated – without reservation, exactly as I would have done if it had been anybody else, and that's including Leicester. I never did score against my first club, as it happened. But it certainly wasn't for the want of trying. Would I have taken a penalty against them? You bet. Without any hesitation. Never miss a chance to score.

Where did that drivenness come from? Not from my father, who was incredibly supportive but never pushy. He drove me and the rest of Aylestone Park FC to matches in the van he used for his fruit and vegetable stall in Leicester Market. It made quite a team bus. No air conditioning, certainly. No TV screens. No music. In fact, no seats – or not in the back where we players were, sitting on the floor in the semi-dark with the odd empty orange crate or apple box sliding around. My dad put a lot of miles on the clock of that fruit van for the sake of my football playing. And when it came to supplying the oranges for half-time, he was, of course, unusually well-placed.

Incidentally, the ritual of the half-time orange segment exists only in the school and amateur game. I can report that not once in my professional career, neither at club nor international level, did I return to a dressing room at half-time to find a plate of orange segments waiting for me. Tea and water: yes. Fresh fruit, neatly quartered: no. I kind of missed it. Once a fruiterer's son . . .

My mum would always come and watch me, too, and also my grandad, who had been a good player and was offered the chance to turn professional, I think, but he turned it down in order to go into the family business, which probably seemed a better bet in terms of economic security in those days.

But none of them was remotely pushy, and certainly not my dad. That intervention after I swore at the ref was the only time he ever made his presence felt while I was playing, which was what made the moment so impactful. My dad was the last person I expected to hear from in the middle of a match, let alone to see arriving in front of me on the pitch. He was at the opposite end of the spectrum from those nightmare father figures that you hear about, and occasionally come across, who decide their children are going to be major sporting achievers and don't give them, or anyone else, a moment's peace until they are. You'll know the type: bawling from the touchline, giving the officials stick, coaching their kid, whether the actual coach likes it or not. My dad was the anti-dad in that respect, and I really came to appreciate him for it.

He offered the same quiet support when I decided to leave school at 16 and sign with Leicester City as an apprentice; which was fantastically exciting, of course, finding yourself behind the scenes at the club you supported, although it turns out there are some scenes you don't necessarily want to see behind. As an apprentice, I had to clean the Filbert Street dressing room for the first team after training – toilets and showers included. The first task, though, as soon as the players had vacated the place and gone home, was to pick their training kit off the floor and then carefully re-hang it on wire hangers on the pegs so that it would be ready for them when they came in to change the next day.

In those days, players didn't get a clean set of gear every day – not like nowadays. Nor did the kit even go to the laundry every day. It was sent off to be washed once a week, at the weekend. So the players wore that training kit anything up to five times in the course of the average week, which probably wasn't great for them, and certainly wasn't great for the apprentices. On Monday morning, your task of collecting and rearranging the dirty socks and shorts – and, of course, the undershorts – was something you could go about more or less cheerfully. By Wednesday or Thursday, though . . . well, some of that kit was so rank by then it was actually vibrating. Finally, on Friday, when, by rights, every apprentice should have been issued with a full-body hazmat suit at the dressing-room door, the kit would be bundled into a skip and dragged off, humming loudly, to the laundry. Some items practically walked there on their own.

Pretty soon, though, I had graduated to the first-team squad, and now it was me leaving my training kit all over the floor for the apprentices to sort out. A sweet turnaround. And almost straight away, at this extremely fragile moment in my young career, something historic occurred. Events conspired to mean I had a hand in Keith Weller's white tights.

Perhaps I should rephrase that.

I made my debut for Leicester on a frosty New Year's Day in 1979, at home to Oldham Athletic in League Division Two – the Championship as we would now say. There were three debutants in the Leicester side that day: Bobby Smith, who was a Leicester apprentice, David Buchanan, who had just joined from Hibernian, and me. Both of those two scored, and I didn't. In fact I had a shocker, which rather took the fun out of our 2–0 victory. Quite rightly, I was left out for the next game, which was a third-round FA Cup tie at home to Norwich. And in came, as my replacement, Keith Weller . . . in a pair of white tights.

Those tights have gone down in history, and they caused quite a stir at the time, too. Weller's choice of undergarment meant the gap between the top of his socks and the bottom of his shorts, where his thighs and knees would ordinarily have been, was now a vision in nylon – and bright white nylon, at that. Never before seen on British soil, this look earned high levels of derision, especially from the visiting Norwich supporters. Weller's response to that (the correct one) was to score in a 3–0 victory. Even so, *Match of the Day* that night concluded by showing Weller's goal set to ballet music. (It would never have happened on my watch.)

Later a scurrilous (and I should say totally unsubstantiated) joke emerged that Weller's wife had found those tights in the glove compartment of Weller's car and that Keith had explained them away as football-related, thereby obliging himself to back the story up in the nearest convenient cup tie against Norwich. In fairness to Weller, though, it was properly cold that day. Half the afternoon's matches had been entirely wiped out by the freezing weather, and Leicester v Norwich only narrowly survived. If ever there was a day for a footballer to wear tights, this was it.

Yet Weller was pilloried – not just for the whiteness of those tights (chosen, in fact, to conform with the white socks and shorts of Leicester's kit), but because he seemed to have broken an unwritten code of behaviour, set firmly against the very idea of wrapping up warm to play football. Players in 1979 just didn't wear extra items of clothing to combat the winter. It simply wasn't done. Even these days, when the use of additional layers gets a far easier ride, you will still hear people moaning about footballers who wear gloves, and accusing them of lacking bottle. Then there was that time not long ago when television cameras caught Michy Batshuayi, then on the bench for Chelsea, holding a hot water bottle to his face, and a minor scandal erupted. Some people apparently couldn't believe the levels of modern-age softness they were witnessing. Hot water bottles! On the bench! To which I thought: blimey, wait until they find out that the seats in the dugouts are made of leather and heated nowadays, like luxury car seats.

I know where I stand on this issue: entirely in favour of players keeping warm. I would have loved to wear gloves, if anybody else had done so and if the prevailing mood hadn't been so firmly set against them. Why suffer cold hands when there's an obvious and harmless remedy available? As it was, I used to put loads of Vaseline over my hands in the hope that a thick layer of grease would spare me the worst effects of the cold. Invisible gloves, if you like. It wasn't terribly successful.

But not much thought was given to these things. I can remember getting subbed off for Barcelona in a European tie in Moscow and spending the last 15 minutes of the match shivering on the bench without even a tracksuit top to put on. The temperature in Russia that night, I should point out, was minus ten. That wasn't good old-fashioned hardiness. That was straightforward neglect and health-endangerment.

Anyway, the point is, gloves or no gloves, if I had been any good on my debut against Oldham on 1 January, I would have retained my place in the side, Keith Weller wouldn't have got a look-in and the world of fashion might never have known that iconic moment. That, then, was my part in Keith Weller's white tights – though, again, perhaps I should phrase it another way.

So much about football is hereditary. There I was, playing for Leicester City, the club my parents had handed down to me, having inherited it from my grandparents. And I, in turn, would eventually pass Leicester on to my own sons. To three out of four of them, anyway. George asserted his rights in accordance with the terms of the Geneva Convention and decided to support Manchester United. Well, he always was a difficult child. He was certainly very good, as young children frequently are, at spotting a weakness in his father and carefully probing it.

'Wouldn't it be great to have David Beckham as your dad?' George once said to me.

'Why?'

'Because he's such a good footballer.'

Cheers, George.

Of course, all of them are far too young to remember me

playing and it gives them, shall we say, a different perspective on it all. The five of us watched a documentary about Italia '90 together and it was properly entertaining for them because they didn't know what happened at the end. The last time I saw the shirt that I got in a swap with Jean-Pierre Papin after a friendly for England against France at Wembley in 1992, it was on the back of Harry as he left the house bound for a rave.

The gift to them of Leicester might have looked a burdensome one from time to time down the years, but it paid off, of course, and spectacularly, in 2016 when Leicester won the Premier League. Who would have thought? Here's the truth: I would have given all my England caps, my Golden Boot and the medals that I won at Barcelona and Tottenham to have been a member of that Leicester title-winning side. All those years, all those games, all those goals – I would have sacrificed the whole job-lot in an instant. I mean – what a thing to have been part of. The night Spurs could only draw at Chelsea and Leicester's title was confirmed, I wept. And not just because I realised I would now have to present *Match of the Day* in my pants, as I had foolishly promised. I wept because it was Leicester and because, when all is said and done, that's my town and my club, and because it felt like some kind of implausible vindication and because of the miraculous, unmatchable, unrepeatable nature of it.

And somewhere in that weepy aftermath, Elton John phoned up. No, seriously. This was not something which regularly happened. My path and Elton's had crossed a tiny number of times down the years, perhaps most significantly when I was 20, and playing for Leicester at Watford and got caught on the follow-through by a defender, putting a long cut down the bottom of my leg which needed stitches, and from which I still bear the scar. Elton, who was then the Watford chairman, came to the dressing room after the match to check I was OK, which I always thought was very classy of him. Still, if you had told me back then that one day Elton John would ring me in my kitchen to congratulate me because Leicester City had just won the league . . . well, Lord only knows what state I might have agreed to present *Match of the Day* in.

I was so pleased my dad got to see it. He died a year later, in August 2017, and I spent a lot of time with him during those last days. I was going up and down to Leicester a lot, sorting things out, and we got the chance to have some conversations that we hadn't had. I'm very glad about that because I was able to thank him, and you realise how that exchange between a son and a father could easily never occur.

In one of those last conversations we were talking about football and my career and I said: 'You must have been surprised that it happened for me?'

He said: 'Eh?'

'Well, you couldn't really have thought that I was going to make it?'

'No,' he said, quite firmly. 'I always knew you would make it.'

'Really?'

'I always knew.'

'You never told me that.'

'No,' he said. 'I never told you that.'

He knew and he didn't say anything? It might have been nice to know . . . But I see now very clearly what he was doing and I don't have the means to convey my gratitude to him for the quiet way he played it.

This is the man who, in 1986, before the World Cup started (and without telling me he had done so) backed me to win the Golden Boot at odds of 14/1 – and made a tidy little sum when (in case I haven't mentioned it already) I duly went on and did so. And I can't imagine that anyone else in the entire country would have been interested in placing that bet.

Aylestone Park, incidentally, continues to thrive. I've been the club's president for 30 years. They have a 3G pitch and floodlights now, and when they built a new pavilion they said they would like to name it after me. I had been called many things by that point, especially on social media, but I had never been called a pavilion, so I was naturally delighted.

I went back to Aylestone at the beginning of 2019 when the club organised a party to celebrate its 50th year. As you get older, and your career as a player recedes into the mists, you get used to the change in the way people approach you. Once kids used to come up to you because they were fans. Then they start coming up to you and telling you that their parents were fans. But that's OK. Time passes, the game moves on and at least people are asking you for a selfie because 'my dad used to like you', which is far nicer than not asking you at all.

That day, though, at the 50th party for Aylestone Park, it changed slightly. A young lad came up to me and said: 'You're Gary Lineker, aren't you?'

'Yes,' I replied, brightly.

He said: 'My grandad used to play with you.'

Ouch.

* * *

But, you're bound to be asking, what about that promising cricket career that never was? Probably not an enormous loss for the English game, if I'm being honest, although you never know. I was good enough to captain Leicestershire Schools. I kept wicket and batted high up the order, and I continued to play a bit even after I had become a footballer. When I was at Tottenham and living in St John's Wood, I turned out occasionally, on days off, for the Cross Arrows, the team made up of employees of the MCC, who have the privilege of playing on the Nursery Ground at Lord's. I didn't keep wicket because it would have been a bit unprofessionally reckless of me to subject my leg muscles to all that crouching down. But I wasn't averse to having a bowl. What could possibly be the harm in it?

I found out what the harm could be the afternoon I came in, released the ball and felt a muscle go, high up in my back. It was as though somebody had just lumped me with a baseball bat. The following day I had to go wincing to Terry Venables' office and report what had happened.

'I'm afraid I picked up an injury yesterday.'

'How?'

'Playing cricket.'

'Oh, for fuck's sake . . .'

Terry was furious and wanted me to swear I wouldn't play cricket again. I was reluctant to give it up entirely, though. After all, as I pointed out, my contract explicitly prohibited me from riding motorbikes and going skiing. But it didn't say anything specifically about cricket.

'OK, then,' Terry said. 'But no bowling.'

Torn back muscles apart, I found cricket and football to be entirely compatible with one another. One day David English, who runs Bunbury Cricket Club, rang me up and asked if I would play in a charity game the next morning that he was struggling to fill a side for. I said I would have loved to, but there was no way I could make it because that night I was due to play a pre-season friendly for Spurs against West Ham – the final warm-up before the season started properly.

David said: 'Well, I could make sure the team bats first, and once you're out you'll be free to go . . .'

Turn up, bat and leave? Now, pre-season friendly or no pre-season friendly, that sounded like an ideal arrangement.

So I went along the following morning to a cricket ground in Finchley, north London and, just as David had promised, I was put in to bat straight away.

Opening the bowling for the opposition was a certain Courtney Walsh, who was still playing for the West Indies at the time. First ball, as I stood there slightly quivering in my pads, he came in like a freight train off what looked like a 17-mile run-up and sent down a bouncer, which sprung off the ground and shot about 20 feet over my head. Just his idea of a joke, of course. After that, he shaped up to take it easy on me and come in off a short, three-pace run.

But actually, watching him thunder in like that had pricked my interest. I realised I was curious to find out what it would feel like to face Courtney properly. I mean, how many times are you going to get the chance? So I asked him if he would at least give me the rest of the over in full flow.

'Are you sure?' he said.

I assured him that I was.

Well, the next ball was in the wicketkeeper's hands before I had even seen it. All I heard was a fizzing noise followed by the 'clop' of ball in glove. The third and fourth went the same way. Courtney was bowling outside my off-stump, which was nice of him because it meant he wasn't actively trying to endanger me physically. I felt Terry Venables would have thanked him for that gesture, had Terry had any idea that this reckless 'challenge Courtney' moment was going on, which, of course, he didn't.

The fifth ball from Courtney, though, I managed to play a forward defensive to, which was encouraging. So when the sixth and final ball of the over came, I decided I might as well at least have a go at it. The ball left Courtney's hand, I went down the wicket a little, smacked at it, felt it find the middle of the bat and watched it rattle away through the covers for four. A boundary off Courtney Walsh! What a sensation that was.

I was 112 not out at lunch, after which David, again true to his word, released me from further duties.

Then I went across to White Hart Lane and turned out for Spurs in the friendly, where I got a hat-trick.

A century and a hat-trick in the same day? Eat that, Roy of the Rovers.

Incidentally, when we were promoting that record of ours, I got to pose next to a life-sized cardboard cut-out of Roy for a photo-shoot. Nice guy, I thought. Didn't say much. Bit two-dimensional, maybe. Good player, though.

CHAPTER TWO

'If they can just keep it tight for the first 20 seconds . . .'

In which DANNY is awoken to his heritage and Millwall respond by immediately going on a 59-game unbeaten run. With further meditations on rosettes, pennants, building your own replica kit from spare parts, and arguing about geography with Sir Richard Attenborough.

That hoary old cliché about being able to see the floodlights of the ground from your childhood bedroom window – well, in my case, that bewhiskered saw is the exact and unexaggerated record of affairs. Sometimes, on school nights, I would go to bed at 9.30pm in our Debnams Road council maisonette and find the room I shared with my brother lit as though there had been a nuclear strike on our back garden. But this would be simply the glare from a Lions reserve game in progress – or perhaps speedway or greyhound racing, both

45

of which were also held on the track around the outside of the old Den.

In the school holidays, during the early sixties, I would go across to the ground and watch the players train. And sometimes we didn't even need to go to the ground because, some mornings, the players (to their immense delight, I'm sure) would be sent off into the streets on training runs that took them right through the estate. You would hear the clatter of boots getting louder, like the hooves of horses, and through they would come.

At this point, affectedly nonchalant exchanges would take place.

'Hello, boys,' one might pipe.

'All right, son?'

Just occasionally you would look up the street and notice some of those players stopping off at Hodges the Tobacconist for a packet of cigarettes, and then off they would clatter again. All of which must sound prehistoric now, I'm sure, and not just on account of the open and unashamed consumption by sportsmen of tobacco. But that's a community team, right there; one that runs through the streets where its fans live, and stops at the shop on the way past for its fags.

Legally speaking, it wasn't obligatory to support Millwall round our way. There were Chelsea supporters among us, Tottenham supporters. My best friend Tommy Hodges' brother supported Burnley: figure that out.

Then there was my mum, Betty, who, after many years of

declaring less than no interest whatsoever in football, looked up from her newspaper one night when *Match of the Day* was on, and said: 'That's West Ham, isn't it?'

'Yes,' I said, 'but why would you ask?'

'That's my team, that is,' said Mum.

I was aghast. West Ham? How? Why? Whence this affiliation with the enemy and for how long? And forged on what possible basis? Interrogation produced nothing of value. She was at a loss to explain it; it was just so.

Of course, we never spoke again. Once I had helped her finish packing her meagre belongings and closed the door behind her, we would only ever be in touch again through solicitors and then only because I needed to get the recipe for the magnificent parsley sauce she could whip up to accompany Conger eel.

Our family was Millwall. My grandfather watched Millwall in their first incarnation, when they played on the Isle of Dogs, before they moved to New Cross in 1910. My dad was born in Millwall, raised in Millwall and worked on the Millwall docks, so he could hardly have been more Millwall had he been named 'Millwall'. (In fact, he was named Frederick Joseph Baker and known to everyone as Spud.) My brother Mickey, six years older than me, was already off and going to games with his mates by the time I started. I would see him tumbling back home from this thing and be intrigued.

And soon it was my turn. I was initiated at the age of five, on a dank Saturday in March 1964, holding my dad's hand

and walking under the Victorian railway arches towards Cold Blow Lane, past the peanut seller and the rosette stand, proffering rosettes of all teams – Partick Thistle, even, if that's what you were looking for, as I suppose somebody must have been. (Possibly me, and the larger the better. A Cup Final rosette, the size of the Beatles' bass drum? Whack it on my lapel, Louie!) And then through the clattering turnstile – or rather, lifted above it, my dad asking the bloke at the gate if it was all right to 'put him over' and thereby avoid paying for me, which always seemed a legitimate option. And finally into the ground to see what it was, apart from my bedroom, that the floodlights illuminated.

Let's be clear, this was no gentle introduction to the football experience via the Family Enclosure. This was straight into the bear pit – Block B Row D Seat 26, next to my dad and among his docker mates, who would be worked into a snarling, profane froth the moment the 90 minutes of action began. Only twenty-four hours earlier, I had probably believed the plot of *The Woodentops* television series was the last word in excitement. But what *was* this? It was like being plugged into the mains – this alpha-male, unfiltered, deafening, full-on, 3D, all-swearing, all-smoking, hyper-animated Hogarth painting.

We beat Newport County 4–0 and my dad's question to me as we left was: 'Enjoy that, boy?' Lord, yes. I was shaking, and have continued to shake ever since.

Simon Inglis understood the place. In his estimable book

The Football Grounds of England and Wales, Inglis wrote: 'Cold Blow Lane on a cold wet night might be the perfect setting for a Jack the Ripper horror film.' The same author also noted how the ground and its environs 'resembled a huge trap'. Gloriously true. The area of wasteland adjoining the stadium was encased by high, soot-blackened brick walls and was arguably the last bit of London that looked like nowhere. Euston Films used it quite a bit in *The Sweeney* and, less playfully, the notoriously brutal Richardson crime gang availed themselves of lock-ups in the area for actual teeth-pulling activities. I've written before (in one of my three Pulitzer-sweeping volumes of autobiography, still available at the kiosk) about the evening when my dad walked me home and had to hurry me past a bottle-green Rover, parked up by the kerb in a dark street, with the interior light on, its driver motionless with his head tipped back, his mouth pouring blood. People think you lay this stuff on thick, like in Monty Python's 'Four Yorkshiremen' sketch, but that is the truth of it. Millwall was and remains to some extent just about the most proletarian football ground that England has ever produced. Even now, when the estate I grew up on has been converted into high-end apartments, gentrification struggles to take a convincing hold down by the Den, and it probably never will.

Of course, we move on. The Den went under the bulldozers after the Taylor Report, and the New Den replaced it in 1993, a quarter of a mile away. It's fine. But it's nobody's idea of a bear pit. These days pretty much all of us watch football in multiplexes and, of course, we're all comfortable and the view is great and I'm sure the standard of the catering has lifted 100-fold, like it mattered. But the last thing I wanted to hear was visiting supporters coming along to Millwall and saying: 'Isn't it a lovely ground? You can get five or six things to eat.' I wanted them to want to get out of there as quickly as they possibly could. That was what gave you a dark pride that supporting, say, Crystal Palace just wouldn't. Palace have got their own story, I assume, but nothing was like the old Den.

Millwall are a south London team and that matters. As South London as David Bowie, Michael Caine or Charlie Chaplin. For some reason East Enders strike people as more authentic, romantic even. I'm not having it.

In the 1990s, I happened to be interviewing Richard Attenborough on the set when he was making the film *Chaplin*. And he was talking to me about the story that he was trying to tell, and saying: 'In essence, you've got this guy from the East End, who . . .'

At this point, I heard myself interjecting – and, I might say, without preamble.

'Whoa! Whoa! Charlie Chaplin is not from the East End of London.'

Halted in mid-flow by this sudden explosion, the great director looked a little thrown.

'Oh, but he is.'

'No, no. Charlie Chaplin was from the Elephant and Castle, Walworth.'

'But that's the East End of London.'

'No, that's south London. It's the east part of south London, true enough. But it's south London. I don't mean to quibble, but I'm from that part of the world myself and it's a huge thing. A simply huge thing.'

'Goodness.' The great man had suddenly become thoughtful. After a moment of reflection, he called an assistant over and said: 'We've got a reference to east London in the cards at the start of the movie. We've got to change that.' And then he said to me: 'Bless you, bless you. You've saved me a lot of embarrassment.'

My pleasure, of course, to guide film-making royalty through this intricate geographical minefield. And had he got me started on the casual and gratingly ignorant mispronunciation by society at large of the word 'Millwall' (in the correct version the stress falls on the second syllable: not 'MILL-wall' but 'Mill-WALL'), we would possibly have been there all night.

Anyway, I owe Millwall to my dad, and much of what I know about Millwall I owe to him, too. For instance, we would have won the semi-final of the FA Cup in 1937 (we lost 2–1 to Sunderland) if the referee hadn't been drunk. Legless! Could barely hold the whistle in his lips. I carried that tale of scandalous injustice with me throughout my childhood and on into adulthood. It isn't even remotely true. Yet that is what my dad told me and secretly I still believe it.

Dad's 'second' team is Motherwell. I once asked him why. He said: 'Well, you have to have a second team, don't you?' I didn't realise that you did, in fact, but I said: 'Yes, but why Motherwell?'

'Well,' he said, 'Motherwell is like: is your mother well? Always liked that.'

And with that he would settle back in his chair with the *Daily Mirror*. 'Oh, and Bury, too,' he eventually threw in. 'Shortest name. Four letters. Don't mind Motherwell and Bury. All the rest can go fuck themselves.'

But however you came by your club in the mid-sixties, it wasn't as a result of television or advertising or some free-wheeling algorithm-driven branding operation. You weren't bombarded into submission that way, especially in the lower leagues. You practically never saw Millwall in the national press. I remember the *Daily Mirror* had a picture of our goal-keeper, Lawrie Leslie, taken from an angle that made the goal look extremely narrow. And the jocular caption read something like: 'Here's the reason Millwall have gone 52 home games without defeat.' Millwall in the paper! I cut it out and Sellotaped it to the bedroom wall next to Dusty Springfield.

No cigarette cards seemed to have our players on. No merchandising lured you in. The club once loudly announced that it would be putting a Millwall pennant on sale, and so novel was this shopping opportunity that we actually formed a queue on the day of release. It cost five shillings, and sales were strictly limited to one pennant per person. This extraordinary and, of course, entirely irrelevant item was fashioned from felt which was so unforgivingly thick you could have lagged a shed roof with it. Its face was divided into three segments for the roll of honours. In Millwall's case, this was always going to be a stretch, and so it proved. One segment contained the words 'Fourth Division Champions, 1962'. In another was written 'Third Division South Champions, 1938'. And the third contained the deathless boast 'Floodlights installed, 1953'. In lieu of greater triumphs we were reduced to trumpeting the arrival in our locale of electricity. Still, it went proudly on the wall with Dusty and Lawrie Leslie, and a terrific drawing I'd done of Steve Zodiac from *Fireball XL5*.

There was no Millwall replica kit on sale either, but that problem you could get around. One especially cherished Christmas, my parents cobbled together Millwall strips for my brother and me by imaginatively commandeering a Huddersfield shirt, Chelsea shorts and Tottenham socks – a monster creation, a Frankenkit. To achieve the required blue trim around the neck and cuffs of the shirt, my mother had gone to the trouble of stitching on short lengths of ribbon, an addition which became somewhat baggy after the first wash, a bit like a chorister's ruffle. My brother's shirt additionally boasted a Millwall badge, which my dad had somehow bullied the club into letting him buy. The badge was so stiff and unyielding you could use it as a chopping board – perhaps in the preparation of one of Gary's deliciously well-adjusted risottos, the recipe for which is exclusively vouchsafed to you in the back of this volume. But what bounty.

In a similar response to this massive dearth in the merchandising market, my brother Mickey spent a good term's-worth of school woodwork lessons building, painting and varnishing a football rattle in Millwall colours. A foot-long, indestructable thunder-maker, this solid piece of bespoke craftsmanship remains in my possession to this day and is still fully serviceable, if you're prepared to put your shoulder into it. It also bears the original blue and white paintwork, lovingly applied by Mickey, along with the legend he carefully inscribed in large white letters along the rattle's side:

'UP THE LOINS'

'What's that meant to say?' I said, when Mickey first brought this tremendous object home.

'Up The Lions, of course,' said Mickey, looking irked at my nit-picking slow-wittedness.

'Yeah, but you've written Loins,' I said, 'not Lions. Up The Loins.'

My reward for this astute but unwanted piece of literary criticism? He rattled his illiterate wooden creation right upside my head. My fault. Of course it was.

There was nothing much to buy or collect, but I had the floodlights shining into my bedroom and the ground a short step away, so what did I need? And then there were the autographs.

During the week, the ground would be open, so you could just wander in, walk down the terracing, take the seat of your choosing and watch Millwall train – to what particular end, from our point of view, I don't know, but the prospect of the team running up and down in tracksuits seemed to entertain us well enough. And eventually, when they were done, the players would go off to get changed and then head up to the clubhouse, which had a little bar in it, while a small bunch of us waited outside, frequently in the rain, to collect autographs.

Inevitably, the players grew used to us. 'What, you again? What you want it again for? You must have got it about 20 times by now.' And they were right. Twenty times was putting it lightly, actually. I had Len Julians' scribble on 31 programmes.

The only one who wouldn't comply was Eamon Dunphy. Dunphy was the sole international I saw play for us – he played for the Republic of Ireland, or Eire, as one then referred to it – and, whether as a consequence of his elevated status or otherwise, he declined autograph requests point-blank, and with a sternness that seemed to brook no further pleading. Consequently, this meant that, in the autograph-hunting jungle, Eamon Dunphy had become the collector's most lusted-after trophy, a kind of one-man Big Five. Clearly, in these circumstances, the person who could succeed in charming a scribble out of Dunphy would know glory unparalleled among his peers.

I took the decision that that person should be me.

One day, after morning training, when I must have been about nine or ten, I waited and waited and waited in the tipping rain. My mates had long since seen sense and gone home. All the other players had fairly quickly come out and left, but not Dunphy. The hours wore on, the rain continued to fall, and I, growing ever more sopping and bedraggled, continued to wait. What on earth could be detaining the great man? But I clung on. The storm raged ever harder and I pondered that the statistic about the human body being 60 per cent water was hopelessly conservative.

It must have been about three in the afternoon when the door opened and he finally emerged. A tall and somewhat forbidding figure, with a rather Bobby Moore-like head of light brown hair, Dunphy eyed with some incredulity the waterlogged urchin standing in front of him, proffering a rain-swept autograph book and a damp biro.

'Are you mad?' he enquired darkly.

It was a rhetorical question, I assumed, and I readied myself for the traditional Dunphy brush-off.

But no. The clouds abruptly parted, the scene was suddenly bathed from above in a golden light and, as a heavenly choir sang and a host of angels descended all around us,

Dunphy grunted 'Give it here' and removed the book and the pen from my trembling hands.

And with that, Eamon Dunphy signed.

His signature, when I got home to examine it, was unusual to say the least. As rendered for me on this particular occasion, it came in the form of a long series of loops, like a kid's drawing of smoke coming out of a chimney sideways, and bore very little visual relation to the words 'Eamon' or 'Dunphy', let alone to both those words at the same time. But no matter. One knew from long experience that many players left marks that mostly resembled one of those graph lines the Richter team produce after violent earthquakes. The crucial point was that this was the authentic work of Millwall's elusive number 8 shirt. The Grail was mine and all that remained now was to bask in the admiration and envy of the autograph-hunting world.

Of course, when I showed it to my mates, none of them would believe me. 'What, Dunphy? That? We're not all thick, you know. Yeah, right. YOU did that. Or your dog did.'

Five hours of patient stalking while stood beneath a solid torrent. And all I got was a reputation as a low-grade forger. Don't talk to me about Eamon Dunphy.

The Millwall that I found myself following were, it is fair to say, largely untroubled by major success. In the club song 'Let 'em Come', the line 'We'll only have to beat them again' has always been sung with ironic gusto. With almost as much ironic gusto, indeed, as the still more immortal line 'We've had our jellied eels and our glass of beer'. Although, in fairness, at the time this anthem was first popularised, there actually were shellfish stalls near the ground. (And, for the record, in the event that I were to be hanged in the morning, my last meal would be Conger eel with mashed potato, parsley sauce, crusty white bread and butter, and a vat of vinegar.)

Formidable at the Den, we were never much of an away threat. Routinely, either my dad or one of his mates would go out and buy the *Evening News* at some point on a Saturday evening and come back and say: 'Facking beat again. At Lincoln.' In a method of news distribution not so very far ahead of somebody on a horse with a rolled-up piece of parchment, the afternoon's football results would have been squeezed into the 'Late Extra' column, practically hand-stamped on to the final bit of the paper that went to press.

Hard to conceive, in this era of Jeff Stelling and goal alerts via text, but you could come out of a ground at the end of a match in the sixties and the paper seller would be shouting: 'All the half-times!' If I missed the BBC *Grandstand* teleprinter at 4.45pm and my dad was out, I sometimes had to wait until Sunday to find out how Millwall had got on.

Later, of course, in a mind-boggling leap forwards for technology, people would bring transistor radios to games and if you could get alongside someone tuned in to the BBC's *Sports Report* as you walked out, you would get your earliest access to the rest of the afternoon's results. Which only puts me in mind of what remains, in my opinion, one of the all-time great football-related practical jokes, as recounted to me by a caller to 606. The caller's friend had once, before the weekend's fixtures, used a small cassette recorder to record his own version of the football results. He then took the recorder to that weekend's game and played his tape back – loudly – as people left the ground.

'West Ham United 0 Everton 7. West Bromwich Albion 6 Arsenal 6. Manchester United 0 Tottenham Hotspur 8 . . .'

People crowded around him agog at these sensational scores. 'FACK! World's gone mad – you hearing this? Bet the telly's got the only nil nil!'

Anyhow, in the context of Millwall's general form, my own first months as a supporter were strangely charmed. Indeed, I seemed to have signed on with the Invincibles. I simply never saw Millwall get beaten. By some convenient piece of magic, between 1964 and 1967, the club went 59 home games without defeat, breaking a record held by Reading. My first game, against Newport, was the 18th win in that run, so another 41 loss-free home games stretched ahead, meaning that for the first nearly two years of my game-going life, I never knew defeat in person and struggled to conceive what that might feel like. It meant nothing to me to read in the paper that we had lost 2–1 at Bournemouth & Boscombe, as they were then. That was another Millwall, waging other battles in far distant lands. The Millwall that I saw always won or, at the very worst, drew.

But nothing lasts for ever. Eventually on 14 January 1967 we were beaten 2–1 at the Den by Plymouth Argyle, whom I have never forgiven. It was my first proper sight of defeat – quite dumbfounding, though it's fair to say that there have been one or two since. Still, in the meantime, in acknowledgment of their tremendous feat of stamina in putting that 59-game run together, each of our players received, with the best wishes of the FA, a gold cigarette lighter. 'Enjoy a stylish smoke on us,' was the evident message – one which is very unlikely to find much truck today. A gold FA vape any time soon? I suspect not.

What I eventually discovered, of course, is that perhaps the richest and densest of the emotions football can produce are to be found on the wrong end of a hiding, or even a simple setback. Certainly, the first time I heard my old man say the c-word was in a discussion about our defence. Millwall had lost 3–2 at Reading, my dad had gone along and, in the street a day or so later, a friend of his was asking him how it had been. My dad entered into a detailed and still clearly furious description of a hopeful Reading punt that had bounced twice and somehow ended up going over the Millwall goalkeeper, Alex Stepney.

'He's let it go over him,' I heard the old man say, 'and I thought: you c***, Stepney.'

This was new: an expression I had never heard my old man use, now rising freshly to his lips through the wonder of football. Clearly, there was so much to learn and I would learn it in the absence of trophies and titles and top-flight glamour ties and in the presence, instead, for the most part, of grubby reverses and lousy defending. For the sake of contrast and my broader education, my old man took me to see Manchester United at West Ham and at Chelsea, because he thought that I should see George Best play, and Bobby Charlton and Denis Law. The old man, incidentally, would have no qualms about supporting that Manchester United team vocally while sitting among Chelsea supporters. In fact, he'd relish it.

But he planned these excursions in entirely the same wild spirit that he took me sometimes to sit in the public gallery of the Old Bailey. He knew the ushers there and they would happily give him a steer on where the best morning's entertainment was likely to be found.

'Go in four, Spud. That's a good 'un.'

He would drink down these tales of crime and misdemeanour, occasionally roaring with laughter during them, to the point where he would attract the attention of the judge.

It was theatre to him, much in the way that Manchester United were theatre. Millwall, though, were something different. For Spud, Millwall weren't a hobby you chose or a pastime you casually attached yourself to. They were how you lived, what you were part of and, in his and my brother's cases, something you frequently fought for. You had no choice. From Spud's dad to him, him down to me, and now me to my son. We're Bakers. Lumbered. But wonderfully so.

I hear my old man's voice every time I watch football on television – hear his laugh, his loud complaints, recall his peculiar habits while fully immersed. If England got a corner, he would sit himself up on to the arm of the sofa. 'I've got to go up for it,' he would say, by way of explanation. It usually worked. Football was never a thing on paper to him. Not tactics, not formations. The result was all. 'Kick, bollock and bite' was how he liked to sum up matches he enjoyed. Just get out there, win the game, and then we all move on. All this I took from him. 'Let it go in off a defender's arse in injury time so long as we win. I don't care how we played. At all. We beat them.'

I am sure the diamond formation is a real and valid thing. But surely only maniacs watch the modern two-hour TV build-up before a game (no offence, Gary). My old man was not a scientist and happily football is not a science. It is chaos. It will not be tamed though, by God, those who regulate the circus are trying their best to make it behave.

And, of course, about other teams losing. For it is not enough that my team prospers: my enemies must suffer. Gary can't understand that at all. As long as Palace lose, as long as Chelsea lose, all supporters have their list and victory becomes slightly tarnished when you hear that certain other teams got one as well.

I impersonate my old man while watching football now

and I don't even realise I'm doing it. He harboured an explosive contempt for some of the commentators, and especially Kenneth Wolstenholme. It was Wolstenholme who, with England leading 2–1 near the end of regulation time in the 1966 World Cup final, declared: 'England are just one minute away from being world champions!' Whereupon West Germany equalised to take the game into extra-time, and my old man exploded with fury. He thought Wolstenholme had jinxed it. I seriously thought he was about to put the television through the window. Only nine at the time, I fled the house and missed England's third goal because I was on my way round to Tommy Hodges' place to watch the rest of the game there.

But flash forward a number of years. In 2008, Chelsea faced Manchester United in the Champions League final in Moscow. The game went to penalties and, in due course, John Terry departed the centre circle to walk down and take the penalty which would clinch Chelsea the biggest prize in club football.

The mere prospect was enough for me. Watch Chelsea lift the European Cup? I had travelled as far as I needed to come on this particular journey. I switched off the television in absolute fury – though others were still watching – and began striding upstairs to bed, loudly declaring my disgust.

The screams I heard once the set had been switched back on was the first I knew that John Terry had catastrophically slipped on to his arse in the tipping rain and poked his penalty against the outside edge of the post. My insane refusal to witness a bête noire success robbed me of what would have been an all-time golden memory. You had to be there. And I wasn't.

'Stick with it' was obviously the major footballing lesson for me to absorb here, but what are you going to do? We are sometimes the playthings of emotions we do not control, and, crucially, of our inheritance.

CHAPTER THREE

'It looked like he was shaping up to have a crack there.'

In which GARY contemplates giant-killings from the point of view of the killed giant, assesses the merits or otherwise of pre-season runs through sand dunes, and recalls the night he was pinned to the dressing-room wall by his manager.

Giant-killings? I've been on the end of one, and it's not an especially pleasant feeling, I have to say. This was in the 1979–80 season, when Leicester were drawn to play Harlow Town in the third round of the FA Cup. I would have been about 19 at the time – early in my career and in a period where I had made a couple of appearances but wasn't yet a regular. Harlow Town were in the Athenian Premier League at this point, many flights below Leicester, who were pushing for promotion from the old Second Division. Harlow was mostly notable at the time for having a dry ski slope, which was an extremely exotic amenity for a small town in

Essex. The place was less notable for producing sides which pushed deep into the major cup competitions, and I don't think many people were predicting that Leicester would have too much trouble going through, especially having been drawn at home.

So much for predictions. Harlow Town came to Filbert Street and drew 1–1, thanks to an 89th-minute equaliser, thereby earning a replay back at their place. I wasn't picked for that first tie. Instead, I watched it from the grandstand and I remember that the Leicester fans were sporting enough (or patronising enough) to applaud Harlow off at the end, which I thought was decent of them. Presumably they imagined we would win the replay easily enough.

I was part of the squad that travelled to Harlow ten days later, though, again, I wasn't expecting to play. Which was just as well because, sitting on the coach driving down the M1, I realised I was feeling absolutely terrible. I was hot and shivery and my throat felt like somebody had gone at it with a pan scourer – the clear early signs of tonsillitis, which I was annoyingly prone to as a kid.

Now, the obvious and sensible thing to have done in that circumstance would have been to report my symptoms immediately to the Leicester manager, Jock Wallace. But I didn't because . . . well . . . did you ever meet Jock Wallace?

Jock Wallace was a very forbidding man. If you were looking to cast a classic example of the no-nonsense, flint-hard, Scottish football manager, you wouldn't need to search much further. Jock had served in the Army with the King's Own Scottish Borderers, both in Northern Ireland and in the jungles of Malaysia, and those kinds of experiences will have an effect on your perspective. He was six-foot-three, well muscled and had a strong Scottish accent, so strong that it was at times impenetrable to soft, southern ears, although I certainly understood him clearly enough on my first face-to-face meeting with him. This was at half-time one evening during a Leicester reserve match in which I was playing. Jock had only just arrived at the club, having joined from Rangers where he had recently won the treble for the second time. And suddenly, randomly, on this Monday night, there he was, the new boss, walking entirely unannounced into the dressing room.

'You lazy, fucking wee English shit,' Jock shouted at me, by way of introduction. Then he walked over, picked me up by the throat of my shirt and pinned me against the wall.

'You're fucking lazy. You don't fucking run enough.'

I wouldn't have minded but we were 2–0 up at this point, and I'd scored both of them. Not that I felt particularly inclined to point that out to the manager – and certainly not from my position, smeared against the wall. I briefly wondered whether Jock was going to hang me up on a peg and leave me dangling there. Instead, he pressed his face in close and growled: 'My office. Nine-thirty tomorrow morning.' And with that, he set me back on the ground and left.

Needless to say, I was fairly distracted throughout the

second half and barely contributed anything at all. I continued to be distracted at home that night, hardly sleeping a wink and turning over in my mind the prospect of the next morning's meeting. I could only assume that Jock wanted to terminate my contract – that 'lazy, fucking wee English shits' had no place in his vision for Leicester City. Why else would he call me in to see him?

In the morning, I was in the corridor leading to the manager's room at least a quarter of an hour before the appointed time, sitting like a schoolboy outside the headmaster's office. Eventually I was summoned and I stood in front of Jock's desk, wincing in anticipation of the blistering and probably career-terminating dressing-down that was about to come my way.

'You were magnificent in that first half last night,' said Jock. 'Absolutely magnificent. I just want to keep your feet on the ground. Don't you ever rest on your laurels, laddie.'

Strange, I reflected, how Jock's method for keeping my feet on the ground had involved lifting me clean off the floor. Again, though, I wasn't about to quibble. It appeared I was still employed as a footballer, and that was an enormous relief.

One other detail about Jock: it was his habit, at the very beginning of pre-season training, by way of an opening session, to get his players running up and down in sand dunes. No better way to shake off the summer's lethargy and restore stamina, according to Jock. The method had worked very well for him at Rangers, apparently. But Glasgow was in striking distance of some actual sand dunes – the Gullane dunes in East Lothian, to be precise. Leicester, being solidly in the middle of the country, was not famous for its accessible and rugged coastline. That didn't stop Jock, though. He simply had us running up and down the mounds of sand and gravel in the Wanlip quarry near Birstall. He invited the press along to witness it, too. Which was clever of him because it kept us all on our toes, for fear of embarrassing ourselves in front of witnesses, and also allowed him to send a message out into the world that Leicester meant business this year. 'Look! They're running around in a gravel pit! That's how much business Leicester mean.'

I've got to say: that quarry-running session was among the most miserable experiences of my entire life, physically punishing and utterly thankless. Still, the terrain favoured us. At Gullane, apparently, the Rangers players would be passing out and throwing up and all sorts. So I guess we got lucky. Jock, of course, standing to one side and looking on at our struggles, loved it, and seemed to wear a quiet smile of satisfaction all day. My team-mate Dennis Rofe perhaps summed it up best that day when a radio reporter asked him how it was going under the new manager. Dennis, who had quite a squeaky voice, replied: 'I don't know, I can't understand a word he says. But when he says jump, you fucking jump.'

Bear all this in mind, then, as I ask you to consider whether this sounds like the kind of man whom you would happily approach on a team bus on the way to a match in order to say: 'I think I'm coming down with a touch of tonsillitis.' I assumed Jock regarded tonsillitis the same way he seemed to regard all other illnesses that didn't involve actual loss of limb – as something that could be run off. In any case, I wasn't going to be playing that night, thankfully, so it didn't matter to anybody else how lousy I was feeling. So I kept quiet, stared out the window and shivered in silence.

I was still shivering quietly to myself as we all sat in the tiny dressing room at Harlow, where Jock announced the team. 'And out on the right I'm going to play . . . Gary.' Had I heard him correctly? Please let this be an hallucination brought on by the fever . . . No, I had heard him right. Jock had picked me. And if there had been a right time to tell him about the tonsillitis, that time had surely passed.

It was a cold, misty January night. At Harlow's stadium, parts of the perimeter weren't built on and it had grass banks for terracing. I played exactly as you might expect somebody with tonsillitis to play – very badly. We went one down to a goal by John Mackenzie who, as the newspapers later enjoyed reporting, was actually a company accountant. We then spent most of the second half battering away for an equaliser, without success. The whistle blew, the Harlow fans slid all over the grass banks in their joy, and we slunk away to get an absolute caning from Jock Wallace and, in my case, to find a packet of Disprin and some throat pastilles.

Still, on the bright side, Brian Clough had predicted that no non-league teams would be in the draw for the fourth round. So at least we had the satisfaction of proving Brian Clough wrong. Harlow Town got Watford at Vicarage Road in the next round, fell 4–1 behind but kept on scrapping until it finished in a highly honourable 4–3 defeat. I believe those days are still spoken of in awe on and around the dry ski slope.

As for Jock, I owed him so much. Yes, he was formidable and he could strike the fear of God into you. And he was a ranter and a raver in the old-school style, which probably doesn't carry as much weight these days at the very top levels of the game, when players hold more power than they used to. In fact, Jock was such a ranter and a raver that he used to foam at the mouth – quite literally. He had a snarl, and when he got properly worked up, foam would appear at the corners of his mouth and occasionally fly out into the room. That's proper football management.

But you knew that he cared about you, too – that your welfare mattered to him. What I learned from him was invaluable to me – about commitment and effort and attitude and looking after yourself so that you were in a position to give your best. And I learned it all at a key time – when I was in my teens and could possibly have had my head turned and gone astray or perhaps, less dramatically, just lost focus and desire. He was always calling me into his office and talking to me about giving myself the best chance, living properly, doing all the rest of the stuff later. 'Don't go out drinking,' he would say, 'don't get distracted by women' – really old-fashioned stuff, I know. Yet I was so scared of him that I adhered to all of that. Go out on a Wednesday or a Thursday night before a game at the weekend? Under Jock Wallace? You must be kidding.

I picked up the way that he liked things done properly, in a certain way, and he's one of the reasons, I'm sure, that I had the disciplinary record that I had and that I didn't ultimately waste my career. Now, I can't deny that I've had better coaches in a strictly football-related sense. Jock was a goalkeeper and his team-talks and coaching sessions were all about blood and thunder and up and at 'em and hit it long . . . At Leicester, Gordon Milne came in after Jock, and he was much more flexible as a tactical coach. And before Jock I had a guy called George Dewis, who used to coach me as a kid, up until I was about 17. George had been a striker and he focused almost entirely on goal-scoring. Training with him was hour after hour of finishing, which was fine by me. That was practically all we did together – and it paid off.

But in the sense that he was the right influence at the right time in my life, I consider myself extremely fortunate to have been managed by Jock Wallace. Terrified, but extremely fortunate.

Jock died in 1996 and, sadly, contracted Parkinson's disease towards the end of his life, as did my grandfather so I knew a little about what that could mean. Nevertheless, when he was ill, the club held a golf day for Jock, which I went to, and it was very shocking to me to see him looking as withered and as frail as he did. For me he had always been this large, imposing figure who could never possibly be reduced. It makes you realise that however big someone's personality is, and however much of a giant they come to seem in your eyes, we're all fragile, really, and at the mercy of our health.

What a great man, though. Incidentally, when Jock took Leicester up to the First Division at the end of that 1979–80 season, he confidently announced to the press that we were going to win the title. And I thought to myself, 'Yeah, nice idea. But I'll go on telly in my underpants if that happens.'

CHAPTER FOUR

'Oh, that's schoolboy stuff, surely.'

*In which DANNY shows us his medals and reveals the
closely guarded hereditary secret behind his monumental
successes as a footballer. Plus, thoughts on the lost art
of toe-punting, how to play 'crab football', and full
instructions for your very own cut-out-and-keep
FA Cup tournament.*

So, Gary Lineker: he's got the caps, he's got the goals at the
highest levels, he's got the Golden Boot – England, Barcelona, Tottenham, et bleeding cetera. But here's the question:
does he actually have the footballing pedigree? This is what
I find myself asking. If you peel back the layers of history
and work your way carefully through the Lineker family
tree, is there evidence that representing his country at
football runs in Gary's blood, the way that it does in, for
example . . . mine?

For here's an exclusive. I've not revealed this before,

neither in print nor in podcast nor on any form of public airwave. But I am directly descended from a famous England football international.

And let me waste no time in telling you which one: Ivor Broadis.

Eat that, chef Lineker. Ivor Broadis was my dad's cousin on my grandmother's side of the family. Which means that he and I . . . why, we were practically twins.

I am aware that one or two millennials among you may need reminding who Ivor Broadis was. He played for Sunderland, Manchester City and Newcastle United. He earned 14 caps and scored eight goals for England, alongside such unquestioned legends as Stanley Matthews, Tom Finney and Billy Wright. When England were upended 7–1 by Ferenc Puskás and Hungary in May 1954, it was Broadis who scored England's goal. He played in the World Cup in Switzerland that year, when England reached the quarter-finals, and, in a 4–4 draw against Belgium, he became the first England player to score twice in a World Cup match. Which, I don't need to mention, was whole decades before Gary Lineker managed to fluke that.

Bill Shankly, no less, described Ivor Broadis as 'one of the strongest and most dangerous inside forwards that ever played'. That *ever* played, note. And to that ringing accolade I can add the further distinction that Ivor Broadis taught me everything I know about the game: about positional sense, about the way you carry yourself on the pitch, about working the channels, and a million other little bits of wisdom, those vital one-percenters that make the difference between the merely average player and the elite performer.

Although, of course, I never actually met him – or not so far as I'm aware. It's possible that he and I brushed past each other at a family wedding somewhere along the way. But if so I didn't realise and nobody said anything. And I certainly never saw him play.

But even so, blood is blood and family is family, and when I survey the extensive collection of medals from my years playing in Southwark Park in the five-a-side league, in the Sunday leagues for Loughborough, and as captain of the indomitable West Greenwich secondary school side in the early 1970s, I am content to think that I have done my best to honour the Broadis tradition.

I took those medals to Gary Lineker's house one day, just to let him know that he wasn't going to have it all his own way in this area. I'm not sure he knew whether he should howl with laughter or burst into tears of pity. But I like to think a point was made.

One of those medals from my school days had been presented to me, along with a firm hand on the shoulder, by none other than Eddie Firmani, then the manager of Charlton Athletic. Obviously, as impressionable kids just setting out in the game, we were overawed that someone from the professional ranks had taken the trouble to bless us with his inspirational presence. And yes, OK, maybe members of the Millwall quorum among us were muttering, as they stepped away: 'Charlton bastard. What did they want to get Eddie Firmani for?' But even so.

The medal collection ought to be bigger, too. I got given a wooden shield with a silver medal at the centre of it after some competition or other and my dad took it to be engraved with my name at a shop on the Old Kent Road. Every now and again over the ensuing weeks he would say: 'Must go and pick up that trophy from the engraver's.' One Saturday morning, he finally got around to it and I accompanied him there, keen to resume ownership of my prize. And, lo and behold, the place had closed down. No forwarding address, nothing. No real sign, frankly, that the engraver had ever been there in the first place, let alone that my precious embossed wooden shield had seen any action.

Which could mean that somewhere out there is a lost trophy possibly with my name on it. Let me know if you notice anything on eBay or at your local car-boot sale. Alternatively, it could mean that the trophy sits, even now, in an engraving shop somewhere, where, no doubt, if you went in and asked after it all these years later, they would tell you it will be ready in three weeks.

Ivor Broadis died in April 2019 at the great age of 96. Brian Glanville's eloquent obituary of him for the *Guardian* is detailed but somehow omits to mention his connection with the Bakers of Bermondsey. But it does mention Broadis's 'memorable partnership with the idiosyncratic Len Shackleton', while drawing attention to 'his pace, his adroit skills, his clever use of the ball and a strong right-footed shot'. So the family resemblance was clearly there to see. Ladies and gentlemen, I, too, am right-footed.

Did the Broadis blood flow as thickly in my dad's veins as it did in mine? I'm not sure. I have a team photo on my desk of my old man lining up with the Dock Labour Board side in 1947, so that's something. Not wishing to malign him, though, he would have been picked more for his feistiness than his finesse, I feel. Not much in the way of 'adroit skills' going on there. Then again, close examination of the photo reveals this to be, by all appearances, an absolute terror of a team, so maybe my dad blended right in.

The fact is, my old man couldn't really play at all. He toe-punted, a style of kick you just don't see any more in which the stub end of the foot does all the work, normally power-assisted by a heroically unbending leg, swung like a polo mallet. Indeed, my old man may well have been one of the last great toe-punters. Eventually coached into extinction at practically all layers of the game above the age of three, toe-punts scored highly for velocity but low for accuracy. If my dad was watching me play and the ball left the pitch and it somehow fell to him to kick it back, I would find my head descending into my shoulders in anticipation. The leg would swing, the toe would punt and the ball would rise quickly to a height of about three feet, level out, and fly three pitches away.

I used to go to pieces when he came to watch me – and not just on account of the potential for toe-punting. Trust me, there is no psycho-analytical work to be done here: my dad wasn't some touchline bully whose best hopes for me I was never going to be able to fulfil. There was nothing like that going on in any part of our relationship, football-related or otherwise. We got along wonderfully. But, after the first two games in which he watched me play were absolute stinkers for me, a sort of hex descended whenever he materialised thereafter.

When I came home with medals, he would always look hopeful and say: 'Well, you know, Ivor Broadis is part of the family, Danny.' But when he came to watch he was mostly puzzled and frustrated by the fact that I wouldn't, as he repeatedly put it, 'get stuck in'. He couldn't understand why I didn't 'upend' a few more players.

'Upend him in the first few minutes,' he would urge me, with regard to the biggest talent on the opposing side. 'He'll get the picture.'

As such I think my old man would have related very closely to my favourite ever piece of punditry, delivered to the viewers of Sky Sports by the great Graeme Souness. The occasion was a night of Champions League football in which an English side (it could have been Arsenal, or possibly Liverpool) had shown far more respect to their opponents than Souness evidently liked to see.

'You can't go into a game against Bayern Munich and let them play,' the notorious Scots strongman explained. 'What you do is, you go in hard in the first few minutes, and you stand over the guy and say: "This is how it's going to be tonight."'

Now, that was straight out of my old man's non-existent coaching manual. The rest of the Sky panel was appalled, but you have to say, there is something in that. And I speak as someone who has played in charity games and found himself kicked right up in the air within minutes by retired professional talents as diverse as David Webb and Martin Chivers. 'Let the media types know you're there,' has always been very much the watchword among pros on the charity circuit, and quite right too.

Still, they wouldn't have got near me in my prime. In my last year at Rotherhithe primary school I played right-back in a formidably slick outfit. We went on a mighty run that season. No one could touch us. Our magisterial form swept us to the quarter-finals of the Black Cup, and that coveted trophy was surely ours to lose – not least because the draw for the quarters had left us facing the no doubt negligible opposition represented by a fancy-pants private school in Kent.

Mind you, we couldn't believe what we saw when we got off the coach. It was like something out of Alastair Sim's

The Happiest Days of Your Life. Was this really a school? It looked more like a country estate. This place had its own pitch, within its leafy grounds. Sorry to play the prole card again, but at Rotherhithe we had an area of Tarmac at the back of the school, bounded by the metalwork and woodwork sheds. If you wanted a pitch, you had to get on a coach and drive up to Blackheath.

Moreover, in Kent, the whole school turned out to watch – hundreds of them, which seemed a bit intimidating. It was Toffs v Oiks, clearly, and I'm afraid to say we Oiks let the crowd and the occasion get to us. The Toffs crushed us 4–0 – 'poggered' us, to use the contemporary term. The shockwaves from this reversal were felt as far away as Lewisham.

It's hard to account in full the extent to which playing football dominated the waking hours of my childhood. Yes, other sports were available, but one barely noticed. There was cricket, of course, but I thought the ball was too hard, and I was by no means alone in thinking so. Variants of cricket in the street using a tennis ball I could more happily tolerate. There were stumps painted on the wall of the church opposite our house, at the centre of the goal that was also painted there, and they saw some use (though not as much as the goal, obviously). In cases where there were inevitable disputes over whether or not the ball had actually hit those painted stumps, the 'Three Blind Bowls' system would come into operation. Under the rubric of 'Three Blind Bowls', the batsman stood with his back to the bowler and his legs spread and swung the bat like a pendulum, to and fro across the gap between his knees. (The architects behind crazy golf courses would later borrow and adapt this principle in the creation of the typical 'rotating windmill' hole.)

Behind the batsman, the bowler had three shies at the stumps. If the ball got through between the legs and the swinging bat, you were out. Otherwise you turned round and batted on. My sense is that if the professional game had been this innovative down the years, it wouldn't be in anything like the trouble that it currently is.

Anyway, when I was at school there was clearly an urgent need to be playing some kind of football in any spare moment that presented itself. Condemned to the school hall in wet weather and unable to kick a ball around in the preferred manner, we would instead resort to playing the variation known as crab football. Regular five-a-side would have smashed the windows, but crab football presented a natural, glass-safe solution. You would turn two of the long benches on their sides at each end of the room for goals, and then assume the position. Think of the excised scene from the movie *The Exorcist* where Regan, who is at this point not entirely herself, comes down the stairs walking like an upturned spider. Basically, crab football required you to adopt a sitting position with your rump raised off the floor, and with your feet and hands, flat down, deployed to scurry you around. In this way a game of low-impact football could be made to happen and our insistent needs could be met.

And when football, for whatever reason, wasn't happening, we simply pretended that it was. In my case this would involve playing a game my brother taught me. You wrote the names of 64 teams on a piece of paper. Then you cut the names out and placed them in a box or some other convenient receptacle. And then you held a draw for your very own entirely imaginary FA Cup right there in your bedroom.

'Brighton . . . will play . . . Leeds! Ooh, that's a good tie. Exeter . . . will play . . . Manchester United! Tricky trip west for the Mancunians! And that, gentlemen, completes the draw for the third round of the FA Cup.'

With all of these match-ups carefully written down, you would then cut up further pieces of paper, this time with numbers written on them: five pieces showing zero, four pieces showing ones, three showing twos, two showing threes, one showing four. And then you would draw again to decide the ties.

'Brighton . . . 2 . . . Leeds . . . 0! Incredible upset!'

All this while making breathy noises that indicated crowds oohing or roaring in triumph. And thus would whole hours pass.

The shout would come: 'Your tea's ready!'

'Can I have it in me bedroom? I'm doing the FA Cup draw.'

'No, come down here!'

In due course, after many hours of excited paper shuffling,

you would arrive at the FA Cup final, and the chances are it would be, on the face of it, an absurd pairing: Wrexham going up against Shrewsbury, for instance. But it didn't matter. The fact was, these two unfancied teams had defied the odds and made it through to the tip of this extraordinary pyramid and who were we to dispute their right to be there on the basis of something as trivial as mere likelihood?

Incidentally, why is it, with the real FA Cup draw, that we are now routinely given a list of 'balls to look out for'? Why tell us in advance which numbers correspond with which teams? Come on, people: everybody knows that the whole show here is in the tense little gap between the declaration of the drawn ball by the special guest ('Number 34') and the announcement of the team by the compere ('Port Vale'). If you know the numbers in advance . . . well, talk about sucking the drama right out of it with an industrial pump. You might as well put the names of the teams on the balls, like in my bedroom version.

Having left Rotherhithe in a blaze of glory, I attended West Greenwich secondary school, and it was there that I made the natural shift from full-back into the number 10 role, where my Broadis-infused gifts could find their fuller expression. Our big rivals were South East London: one school was at the top of Deptford High Street and the other was at the bottom. So bitter was the rivalry that South East London were let out at 3.30 and West Greenwich at 4, so that the two tribes shouldn't collide and start hitting each other. But we often had punch-ups down the High Street in any case – not me, obviously, but those who enjoyed that kind of thing. It was quite traditional for the best fighter at West Greenwich to meet the best fighter at South East London in the park to sort a few things out. I don't know which of our two fine educational institutions held the upper hand in terms of scrapping, but I do know that in football the rivalry had been miserably uneven for many years. Few could even remember the last time West Greenwich had beaten South East London.

Imagine the commotion, then, when, under my captaincy, we once more faced the old foe at Coldharbour sports ground. The result? 10–0 to us. I scored four. The following morning's school assembly was bedlam and joy unbounded. I had to stand up and give a little report on the game and laid it on thick. I fancy my Churchillian tones evoked tears in some of the older masters.

It wasn't all glamour and popular acclaim, though. When you played on Blackheath, our 'home turf', you had to put the goals up. This would have been fine, except that, by some quirk of geography, whichever of the many pitches your match was appointed to, the shed containing the posts and crossbars always seemed a good two-day trek away. Lacking horses, we had to schlep it. And then we had to schlep it back again after the game. It's hard to evoke the full range of the suffering involved in carrying the posts back on your shoulder in the wake of a 5–0 hammering with the rain sheeting down. This, I belatedly realise, was my personal Golgotha, falling 13 times in the mud on my way to return the crossbar to its tin-roofed hangar.

As captain, it fell to me to pick the team – a starting XI plus one sub. Now, among the boons of being in the football team was that you would be excused from the last two lessons of the day in order to get up to the pitches and prepare everything, meaning that you effectively finished school at 2pm. And this was no secret. Consequently, I would find myself coming under immense pressure from the school's resident hard-cases, who, glimpsing the possibility of a cheap afternoon off, would approach me to say: 'Baker, put me in the team.'

Now, in many cases, although these hard-cases would be among your very first picks for a punch-up in Deptford High Street with South East London, they would be among the last people you wanted in your football team. To promote them ahead of better candidates would be to jeopardise the team's chances in a way which I, as captain, was not prepared to countenance. My solution (a diplomatic one, I like to think) was to establish a kind of 'hard-case rota', and nominate each of them in turn for the sacrificial role of sub. The anointed nut-job would then emerge from school with the rest of the team at 2pm, but immediately set off in completely the opposite direction and go and sit in a betting shop for two hours.

Now, I don't want to be constantly making the contrast, but I don't think Gary Lineker has ever been put in that position. To the extent that this arrangement limited the team in the event of an injury – and, of course, entirely removed the possibility of a game-changing 75th-minute substitution – I will grant that it was risky at a footballing level. But failing to keep the hard-nuts sweet wasn't without its risks either, so let's just call it a respectable compromise.

West Greenwich wore red and black halved shirts. When the television series *Cradle to Grave* was made, based on my first book, the producers recreated a match from this era, and I was moved to see that the wardrobe department had gone to the trouble of getting in the shirts accurately. Yes, they looked a little bit fresh by comparison with the over-laundered and always slightly musky-smelling ones that we used to pull out of the big net bag on match days. But my problem that day on the *Cradle to Grave* set was more, in fact, with the shorts and the socks – all white and all matching. I had to suggest an alteration here, because this quite simply never happened. The school supplied the shirts but the rest of it you had to bring yourselves, with the result that the team turned out in a whole medley of widely differing shorts and socks in the widest possible range of the typically available colours.

'Sounds like chaos,' said someone on the show.

'You're exactly right,' I said.

As for footwear, a few would play in plimsolls. Baseball boots were quite popular. But most of us had football boots. Boots, of course, weren't the high-churn industry that they are now. Tuf, more famously a shoe firm, made some – red and black, with red laces. They seemed to work well enough. My dad bought me a pair of Puma Tottenham one year, and he overestimated the size. 'You've got to grow into them,' he said. During the ensuing six-month wait for my feet to reach the appropriate length, I stuffed scrunched-up brown paper into the toes to fill them up. Of course, if you forgot your boots, the goalkeeper would lend you his and play in his street shoes. That was fine. He was a goal-keeper. A goalkeeper's need for boots is slight at best.

We played amid constant rumours of the presence of scouts. Out in the middle of the pitch, someone would nudge you and say: 'See those blokes over there? They're scouting for Brentford.' One time the whisper went round that the man in a mac on the touchline was from Charlton. I had a good game. As I left the pitch, I was thrilled to see the man in the mac heading towards me.

'You're pretty good,' he said. 'Are you signed anywhere?'

I said: 'No, I just play here, and a bit of five-a-side in the week.'

He said: 'Can I have a word?'

'Certainly.'

Seeing me taken aside, my team-mates were agog. 'Christ, Baker's cracked it here – that bloke's from Charlton!' As everyone else retreated to get changed, the scout and I went and sat on a bench, and a conversation began.

And let me just say that it became apparent after a very short while that this gentleman had little interest in football as such, and rather more interest in young boys in shorts.

I headed very quickly back to the changing room, where everyone gathered around excitedly.

'What did he say?'

And I replied: 'He wasn't a scout, I think he was a dirty old bastard.'

My team-mates for some reason seemed to find this inordinately amusing. It was as close as I came to being spotted by one of the big clubs.

People were always talking about 'going for trials'. And it always sounded impressive, but really it was such a routine thing. My brother Mickey went for trials all over the place: Fulham, Southend, Brentford. Millwall wouldn't give him one, for some reason, but almost everywhere else did. Mickey was a decent enough player, but there was probably a bit too much of my old man in him, if we're being honest, and he was always getting sent off. But that didn't mean he didn't 'go for trials'.

What would happen is that clubs would advertise that they were holding a trial at a sports ground somewhere – something like an open audition. Any kid could go along and maybe get ten minutes in an extended game. Thus the myths grew about 'having trials'. 'He had trials with

Brentford, you know.' It really didn't mean a lot. Most likely it simply meant that you had turned up out of choice, had your statutory ten minutes and then gone home, never to hear another word about it.

It may shock you to learn that I didn't 'go for trials' with any of the pro clubs, but I did have a trial for Greenwich Borough, which was a team that Ian Wright would eventually play for. Four of us from West Greenwich school were nominated and the trial took place one afternoon at Blackheath. It was quite a crowd scene – there were about 100 local kids there in total. But I wasn't worried about getting overlooked in the crush because I had thought this through and I had a sound plan to make myself stand out.

My idea was to make it graphically clear to the watching coaches that I was someone with a sophisticated footballing brain. To this end, while other kids got on with actually kicking the ball around, tackling each other, shooting etc, I spent my time finding what I thought were intelligent places to make myself available on the pitch. Then, when the player with the ball didn't find me in these oh so intelligent gaps, I would look across to the coaches on the sidelines and give them an intelligently frustrated expression designed to further underscore my footballing nous. Many minutes passed in this way, with me in my clever off-the-ball spaces, not getting a touch and then smiling knowingly. When the ball did eventually reach me, I tried to trap it, only to see it travel completely under my upraised boot and disappear behind me. I got eight more minutes and maybe one further touch and then I was pulled.

Mind you, my confidence in my footballing ability in those days (that old Ivor Broadis heritage again, I suppose) was fairly unassailable and I still felt optimistic. I mean, I was good, wasn't I? I had the medals and everything. How could they miss it?

Afterwards, everybody who had played gathered around and one of the coaching staff read out the list of the kids they wanted to see again. In the course of this roll-call, my three mates from West Greenwich were all mentioned, but my name was peculiarly slow to emerge. It would only be a matter of time, though, clearly.

'Thank all the rest of you for coming,' said the coach eventually.

What? Not selected?

I felt like piping up: 'I think you'll find you've missed someone. Could you tap that piece of paper and see if another name falls off it?'

It was a huge disappointment for me, yet also a formative moment. I think that little confrontation with reality was the point when I realised I wasn't interested any more in being Gary Lineker, as it were. That was the moment when I thought: OK, I'm not going to play for Greenwich Borough, I'm going to join Emerson, Lake & Palmer, or I'm going to be Rory Gallagher, or something similar.

That, in other words, was when rock music began to take

over and, soon enough, the twice-weekly football training sessions – running on the spot, charging round bins that the coaches had put out and all manner of other vaguely point-less exertions – began to pale in their appeal by comparison with, say, going to see Genesis at the Marquee. I guess, in the end, sharing the blood of Ivor Broadis could only do so much.

CHAPTER FIVE

'He'll be disappointed with that.'

In which DANNY leaps belatedly but spiritedly to the defence of Eileen Drewery, claiming it's just a matter of faith. And in which GARY strenuously denies being superstitious about anything, apart from his boots, his shirts, his hair, certain 'unlucky grounds', shooting during the warm-up . . .

DANNY

Football supporters are notorious humbugs. They radiate hypocrisy like Wi-Fi. Moreover, it's frequently the fuel for the dedicated fan's greatest flights of derision, and anybody in any doubt about this needs only to refer to the reaction generated by the arrival in English football of Eileen Drewery.

Eileen, you may well recall, was a spiritualist and healer – and one of a very small number of spiritualists and healers, so far as we are aware, to represent England at World Cup level. Glenn Hoddle had encountered her while playing for Tottenham and had been impressed by her services – so impressed that when he became manager of England he sought to make Eileen available to his players so that they, too, might know and benefit from the power of her direct line to the fourth dimension.

And, oh my – the hooting and honking that went up from football supporters of all stripes. A faith healer! In the England camp! What patently see-through bunkum. What cheaply bottled snake oil was this?

Now, it's fair to say that Glenn subscribed to a number of ideas for getting the best out of his team which you would have struggled to find in, say, a Jock Stein TED Talk, or Jeremy Clarkson's *My Wildest Notions*. Indeed, it's striking to reflect that, but for a few results here and there, and one notable moment of controversy, Glenn would have gone down in history as the triumphant and far-seeing pioneer of a whole raft of game-changing, alternative approaches to coaching – spiritual, astrological and otherwise.

For example, during the match against Argentina in France in the World Cup of 1998, Glenn is said to have dispatched backroom staff to walk around the pitch anti-clockwise in order to create some positive energy. Worth a try, I would suggest, given the stakes – although had I been one of the staff members dispatched to stomp around the touchline that day and thereby fruitfully manipulate the atmosphere, I guess I would have had one nagging question at the back of my mind: namely, why any positive energy generated by our anti-clockwise stomping would not also be felt by Argentina, with possibly unwelcome effects. But perhaps in the end this was one of those occasions when you just had to sit back, take the boss at his word, and simply accept that there are matters here which do not necessarily lend themselves straightforwardly to gimlet-eyed logic.

According to Gary Neville, whom one has few reasons to doubt, it was also Glenn's habit to pass among the players in the dressing room before a match and touch each of them briefly with his fingertips in the region of their heart. Whether this was a piece of important energy transference on Glenn's part, or just a warm and reassuringly fatherly pre-match gesture between a coach and his possibly anxious players, we on the outside must be content to remain unsure. Of course, less charitable observers would suggest that, in some cases, Glenn was just checking for a pulse, but that's a level of satire to which, thankfully, it is not our duty in this book to stoop.

Those entries, however, pale to nothing in Glenn Hoddle's ledger of perceived dishonour beside the one for Eileen Drewery – 'faith healer Eileen' as the tabloids like to refer to her – into whose presence Glenn seems to have ushered a number of the players in his charge. The famous story is that Ray Parlour sat compliantly in the curtained gloaming of Eileen's front room while she walked behind him and placed her hands on the back of his head, but then couldn't resist quipping: 'Short back and sides please, Eileen, while you're round there.' Legend adds that Ray duly paid for this act of ice-breaking insolence with his place in the England squad.

Again, we make no comment. We merely move on to note that Gareth Southgate, who would eventually succeed Glenn in the manager's office, later reported that, as a member of Glenn's squad in 1997, he felt largely bemused by Eileen's attempts to lift the hoodoo of his high-profile penalty miss in Euro '96 – a hoodoo that Eileen attributed to the continuing presence in Gareth of a negative female spirit whom, during their session together, Eileen had successfully identified and removed. But even Gareth, for all his polite scepticism, conceded that he definitely felt a bit better about it all afterwards.

It ill behoves any of us, then, to pour scorn. And it especially ill behoves those of us who support a football team. It must have struck Eileen as ironic, to say the least, that, at the peak of her public lambasting, she, a humble self-employed operative in the world of the occult, was getting stick from football fans. Of all people! Football fans, who believe in the power of lucky underpants. Football fans, who must always park in the same street and cross the road at the same traffic lights on their way to games, or else imperil their club's chances of success that afternoon. Football fans, who are rendered cosmically uneasy about what the fates may have in store for them if they fail to pat a police horse on its flank at some point on their walk to the ground. Football fans, who attribute the success of their side in a closely fought FA Cup tie to the presence in their coat pocket of an empty crisp packet – and who then solemnly carry that empty crisp packet with them to all ensuing games in the competition so that the team can continue to benefit from the silent but mighty powers that have somehow accrued to what would otherwise have been merely a piece of litter.

Yes, football fans, who, if the stadium has a digital clock and they glance at that digital clock during the game, cannot look away unless and until a 5 appears somewhere in the display. Sounds outlandish? I guarantee you it's true, because that particular football fan, my old corks, is me. Don't ask me why. It's just the case. There has to be a 5 showing when I look at the clock, and if there isn't, my eyes won't return to the pitch until there is. Indeed, the only time I failed in this (in order to see a seagull on the crossbar) Millwall were relegated just three seasons later.

I consider it a relation to the far more common habit, which I also share, of needing to get the price figures on the petrol pump perfectly aligned at a sum in whole pounds, at the expense of whatever amount of nudging and nurdling with the pump's trigger. This seemed a more or less logical ambition in the days of paying with actual money, when you were potentially sparing yourself from limping back to your car with two and a half pounds of loose change in your pocket. In the days of the credit card, however, it makes no sense whatsoever. And yet the practice continues. I've got a mate who has to bring up his house number in the pence column. If he goes past it, he's got to pump another quid's worth into the tank in order to get a second shot at it. He considers this perfectly regular behaviour, and so do I.

So, when football supporters flocked to berate Eileen Drewery in high style for her labours and dished it out in no small measure to Glenn Hoddle for encouraging her . . . well, what heavy-handed righteousness and what bare-faced hypocrisy was that? Let me be clear, ours is not to promote or condemn the practices of Eileen Drewery or those of a similar bent. Ours is merely to point out that, placed next to some of the superstitious behaviours of the supposedly ordinary football fan, Eileen Drewery and her spirit-hunting, aura-massaging hands were practically at the level of object-ive science. Anyway, the words 'Bristol Rovers' contain 13 letters. Weird, eh?

GARY

Superstitious? Me? Of course not. Perish the thought. Nothing so ridiculous. Besides, it's bad luck to talk about that kind of thing.

Oh, all right then, I'll admit it. As a player, I was superstitious. Highly so. It's quite unusual to find a footballer who isn't, to some degree, drawn to the power of certain habits and rituals, and who doesn't trust those habits and rituals to guard over them as they go about their business. In sport, so much is out of your control that, I guess, you grab at anything you feel you can control. But even among footballers, where I inevitably faced some stiff competition, I ranked highly for superstition.

Remember what Matt Goss so famously said, in that documentary about Bros? 'I made a conscious decision because of Stevie Wonder not to be superstitious.' Well, I heard that Stevie Wonder song, too, but I'm afraid it didn't seem to have quite the same effect on me. Indeed, I seem to have made a series of conscious decisions to be as superstitious as I possibly could.

Take the pre-match warm-up, for instance. I would never shoot during those warm-ups. Yes, I would pass to team-mates, dribble around with the ball a bit. But actually kick the ball in the direction of the goal in any manner which could be interpreted as 'taking a shot' and which risked the ball entering the goal and hitting the net? Absolutely not. Even now, the mere thought of doing that makes me slightly shiver.

You have to remember how unstructured the pre-match warm-up was in my time. We would basically come out in our tracksuit tops, run around for a few minutes and knock a few balls to each other. It was easy to get away with not taking a shot. These days the warm-up is a much more structured affair. It's all cones, bibs, games of two-touch, sets of specific exercises for the defenders, other exercises for the midfielders and the attackers ... And all of it is carefully monitored by coaching staff with stop-watches. There's always a dedicated shooting exercise, too, where the forwards are meant to get their eye in. Not sure what I would have done about that. Hidden behind the advertising hoardings, maybe, and only come out when they'd finished. Which, incidentally, would have been a variation on a tactic that served me very well on a cross-country training run under Terry Venables, but that's a story we'll come to in due course.

The point here is that I couldn't shoot during the warm-up. What if it went in? Then you would have wasted one. And you might, consequently, have diminished your chances of putting the ball in the net when it actually mattered – in the match. That was my logic here – assuming that logic was a part of it, which I probably have to concede it wasn't.

Then there was shirt-changing. You would usually have the option to change into a clean shirt in the dressing room at half-time if you wanted to – which, particularly if it was pouring with rain, would be most welcome. I was always happy to get out of a cold, wet shirt and pull on a fresh, dry one . . . unless, that is, I'd scored in the first half. If I'd scored in the first half, obviously I couldn't take off the shirt in which I'd done so. Because that shirt was clearly a good one. How could you abandon it now, after all it had just done for you? Even if the rain and mud had turned it into a sopping wet dish-cloth which now clung icily to your spine. I endured a lot of discomfort for the sake of this superstition. But it seemed important.

So important, in fact, that I'm not sure where it would have left me in relation to the vogue among today's players for swapping shirts at half-time, an activity which gets picked up on every now and again and always seems to attract scorn. I'm not sure that I have strong feelings about it either way, if I'm being honest. But what I do know for sure is that nobody would have been getting my shirt off me at half-time if I'd just scored in it. It wouldn't have mattered if Pelé himself had travelled through time to appear at my side as we left the field for the interval, smiling warmly and extending his yellow Brazil shirt as a token of our mutual sportsmanship. 'Not now, Pelé. You see, this one's a good one.'

I had an unlucky ground – Villa Park, where I never scored. And I had a lucky one – Selhurst Park, where I always did. Those kinds of things get into your head, definitely – along with a strong belief in the power of hairdressing. If you're slightly out of form and failing to score goals, try getting a haircut. It worked for me. I broke many a dry spell with a well-aimed trip to the barber. Stands to reason, doesn't it?

I believed in lucky boots, too. But in this case I had demonstrable proof. You, too, will believe in lucky boots after you have heard this story. Well, maybe . . .

It was the 1985–86 season. I was playing for Everton and we were having a terrific time: we'd made it to the FA Cup final and we were pushing Liverpool, the big rivals, for the league title in a really tight race that was (as they say) going right down to the wire. And, just to add to the fun, I was scoring lots of goals – 40 by the end of the season, in 57 games, which is not a bad strike rate.

And all of this, obviously, was owed to the pair of Adidas boots that I had been wearing since just before Christmas. What was so special about them? Well, nothing, ostensibly. These boots were black, a fact which would no doubt surprise and perhaps even bewilder younger readers, but what can I say? Black boots were very fashionable at the time, as outlandish as that may sound.

The chief difference was that I would ordinarily get through a number of pairs of boots in the course of a season. But I was scoring so fluidly in this particular pair, and right from the off in August, that I stayed with them. And here I was, still wearing the same pair of boots, right at the end of April, with the title now thrillingly within Everton's grasp. And yes, these boots were battered and stretched and bearing the signs of wear and tear which would ordinarily have seen me binning them whole months previously. But not in the case of these ones, because these ones were clearly delivering in a big way, as the league and the goal-scoring charts would both show. These boots were lucky.

This is how tight the situation was in the league, as April

ended. There were just three games to go – away at Oxford and then at home to Southampton and West Ham. And if we won them all, we would beat Liverpool to the title and have a shot at the Double in the FA Cup final, where, again, Liverpool would be our opponents – the first all-Merseyside final. If we dropped points, however, Liverpool would squeeze past us, and it would be Liverpool going for the Double at Wembley.

First stop Oxford, then, on a Wednesday night. Oxford were fighting to save themselves from relegation. On form, Everton would have been favourites to beat them, but the situation at the top and the bottom of the league added any amount of edge and unpredictability and we knew we'd need to be absolutely on it. So imagine my dismay, then, when the kit trunk came off the coach and into the dressing room, and was promptly revealed to be short of one particular item: my boots.

What an oversight. All of my major organs seemed to turn cold with horror: my boots were 170 miles away on Merseyside and there were no spares. The solution? Well, I'm aware that this is going to sound rather amateur and even a touch shambolic, given that we're talking about a professional club going for the biggest prize in English foot-ball. But I borrowed a pair. I don't now recall from which team-mate I borrowed them, but I can tell you that their feet were half a size bigger than mine. It may only have been half a size, but when I put those boots on, they seemed enormous. Perhaps it was the effect of the disappointment and the swelling levels of panic distorting my perceptions, but I felt at first like I was flapping around in clown shoes.

I tried to get a grip and put the whole thing out of my mind, but it was hard not to feel that there was something horribly ominous in this development. So many of the ingredients for an upset were present that night: a small, tightly packed stadium, a ravaged pitch with large patches devoid of grass, a defence ready to scrap for its First Division life against an under-pressure, title-seeking side whose striker is playing in borrowed footwear . . .

And sure enough: no lucky boots, no goals. And that was despite a number of really good chances, including one where I slid on to a cross in the six-yard box and somehow the goalkeeper got in the way – which he never would have done, obviously, if I'd been wearing the lucky boots. And then, of course, after loads of fruitless pressure from us, Oxford went up the other end and scored with a scruffy, headed goal 12 minutes from the end. You can find the video evidence for all this in a four-minute package on YouTube, should you be inclined to, although the chances are you will be scandalised, in those images, less by the largeness of my boots than by the smallness of my shorts, which are peak-eighties in their offering of minimal thigh coverage.

Look, I'm not saying that the absence of those boots cost Everton the league. At the same time, the following weekend, against West Ham, when I was reunited with the boots,

I promptly scored two goals in a 3–1 victory. I then scored a hat-trick when we beat Southampton 6–1 in the season's final game. Too late, though. The damage had been done at Oxford.

Having lost the league to Liverpool, it was no particular consolation to us to lose the FA Cup to them as well, 3–1 – even though I scored, thereby living the schoolboy dream of getting a goal in front of 98,000 people in a Wembley Cup Final, and simultaneously living the schoolboy nightmare of getting beaten to the trophy by your local rivals. And if that wasn't bad enough, in the immediate aftermath of all this, Everton were invited to join Liverpool on a rare unison open-top-bus tour of the streets of the city. Talk about the bus journey of shame. But that's a story of exceptional misery which I will get to later. Oxford, by the way, were in 20th place on the last day of the season and as good as sunk, only then to beat Arsenal 3–0 and escape from relegation. It was quite a season, all in all.

The lucky boots weren't finished, though. Understandably, given this late demonstration of their importance, I insisted on harnessing their very obvious goal-scoring powers for my country in that summer's World Cup in Mexico. So knackered were the boots by then that at one point they actually split and had to be packed off in a hurry to the nearest Adidas specialist to be repaired and rigged up for service again. And what eventually happened out there in Mexico? Well, I may have mentioned this before, but I won the Golden Boot, awarded to the tournament's top goal-scorer, thereby becoming the first English player to do so.

I owed it all to the boots, of course. Sadly, that really was the end of them, though. They finished the World Cup beyond economic repair. But they went to a respectable resting place: the Adidas museum in Munich, where I believe they continue to enjoy a happy retirement. (It was that, or going into the media.)

CHAPTER SIX

'All square at the interval.'

*In which GARY leaves home for Everton, but only after
a heart-rending custody battle. And in which he offers some
humble reflections on what it's like to achieve rock-star
levels of global fame.*

In 2019, a new film-length documentary about Maradona
came out. It was directed by the very brilliant Asif Kapadia,
who made *Senna*, about the racing driver Ayrton Senna,
and *Amy*, about the singer Amy Winehouse, and its opening sequence was literally a car chase – footage of Maradona
being driven through the streets of Naples on his way to
sign for Napoli from Barcelona in 1984, with huge numbers
of press and paparazzi in pursuit, the whole thing set to a
soundtrack of pumping dance music. Awarding the film
four stars, the reviewer in *The Times* wrote: 'You can't imagine a film about Gary Lineker doing that.'

Now, hang on a moment: what's the implication here? That my life has been somehow tame by comparison with the 24/7 tornado of wildness that seems to accompany Maradona as he goes about his business? I would have this reviewer know: I've had my share of paparazzi action. I know what it's like to have lenses poked in your direction, to attract more attention from photographers than you would ideally like to attract. Especially on beaches.

But . . . OK, on reflection, actual pursuit through European cities with packs of mopeds in attendance, not so much.

More typical, I guess, would be the time when our oldest two boys, George and Harry, were quite small, and Michelle and I went on holiday with them to Sardinia. We had just got ourselves settled beside the swimming pool when I noticed a big telephoto lens rise up over the bushes around the pool's perimeter. There were a few clicks, and it disappeared again. Then it re-emerged: click, click, click. Then it dropped down again. This wasn't exactly relaxing, or quite what we had come on holiday for.

Michelle said: 'What are we going to do about it?'

I said: 'Let's just sit tight, try and keep the kids out of the way and hopefully he'll get bored soon enough.'

He didn't get bored, though. The camera kept popping up above the leaves, clicking and popping down again. It was getting pretty wearing. Eventually, I realised that, if we were going to get any peace, I was going to have to say something. So I got up and began to walk towards the bushes.

And just as I was drawing breath to call out, I was over-taken by a guy in swimming trunks who came out of nowhere and stormed past me on the outside, going much faster than I was and seeming much angrier. When he got about three yards ahead of me, he shouted in the direction of the bushes: 'Hey! Stop taking pictures of my family, man.'

It was Jon Bon Jovi. The photographer wasn't taking pictures of me at all.

Close thing. If I'd left the sun-lounger even a split-second earlier, I could have found myself confronting this snapper and calling him out for his intrusiveness, only to hear him say: 'And . . . who exactly are you?' I guess it's always been about timing your run.

When the phone-hacking scandal hit British journalism in 2011 and issues around celebrities and privacy were in the air, I remember watching *Newsnight* and seeing an item about the press and surveillance. Some private investigator with experience in the field was talking about how it worked and what people like him were employed to do. He talked first about operations involving members of the royal family, and then he talked a bit about following David Beckham around. And then suddenly there was a picture of me, which rather startled me as I sat there in my armchair.

The private investigator seemed to be saying that I had been followed for around two years. But clearly I had been quite canny during that time because I never went anywhere that I shouldn't have done.

I thought, wait a second: canny? Followed for two years? I didn't have a clue about it. No idea it was going on. The *Newsnight* report even produced some video footage, taken from behind a bush, of me playing golf. Respectable swing, actually, now I came to look at it. But during a 24-month campaign of surveillance, someone had apparently been on my tail, even to the point of crawling around in the undergrowth while I was out on the golf course – and I was completely oblivious to it.

So, anyway: yes, unlike that Maradona documentary, a film of my life would probably lack sequences in which my decision to switch clubs triggered a car chase through a major Italian city. And it may explain why, the time I met Asif Kapadia (he introduced himself to me, much to my surprise and delight, when I was getting on a train in Manchester, and we talked very briefly about his Maradona project before he set off up the platform), he didn't say, at the end of the conversation: 'You know what? Scrap that plan. I'll do you instead.'

Oh well. I could at least have provided him with a bit of courtroom drama to open his movie. It would have to be a re-enactment because no footage of this event exists – or not unless that bloke on *Newsnight* was at it for even longer than he said. Nevertheless, a tense courtroom, defendants, plaintiffs, two clubs locked in a bitter battle for the custody of a young and innocent striker . . . it's all there, waiting to be exploited for movie purposes.

This was the summer of 1985 and I had decided to leave Leicester City – a huge wrench for me, I probably don't need to say. Leicester were my hometown team and the side I grew up supporting. Frank Worthington and Peter Shilton had been my schoolboy heroes. I stuck pictures of these people on my bedroom wall. And then, like something in the plot from a comic-book story, I ended up signing for the club. I overlapped with Worthington by six months when I was an apprentice, albeit that I kept a suitably awed distance in keeping with his status as a superstar and my status as, basically, the dressing-room floor cleaner. Shilton had left Leicester by then, but I went on to play with him for England and he became my room-mate on away trips. (Shilton was remarkable for many things, and longevity was one of them. I find it hard to get my head around this, but I watched Shilton at Filbert Street when I was eight years old – and somehow he was still playing when I retired. He preceded me and he outlasted me.)

My life was pretty cosy. I was earning £400 a week – no comparison with today's rates, clearly, but still a very comfortable wage – and I was still living with my parents. Never mind leaving Leicester, I hadn't even left home at this point.

However, sentiment and comfort have their limits, clearly. I was 24 and ambitious. At this time (well before those heady days when they bestrode the nation as Premier League champions), Leicester City were a yo-yo club – up and down between the old First Division and Second Division. If I wanted a chance to win things other than Second Division titles I would almost certainly need to be elsewhere. And if that meant I no longer had my mum to do my ironing . . . well, so be it. Those are the kinds of tough decisions that mark out the ambitious person.

I had had offers to leave a whole year earlier, in 1984. But at that stage I had one year left on my contract, and I had made a promise to myself that I would never break my deal with Leicester. I felt like I owed the club at least that much. So I played for one more season with Leicester, back in the top flight, and at the end of that I looked to move.

I could have gone to Liverpool. I had been the First Division's joint top goal-scorer, with Kerry Dixon of Chelsea, in that last season at Leicester, so my stock was high and both Everton and Liverpool made offers for me. They were the top two clubs in England at this time, remember. But Liverpool had Ian Rush as their striker and my impression was that Rush was a very similar kind of forward to me in terms of the way he operated: he was quick, relied on runs into the box, scored a lot of goals from close range. Also in that period it seemed to be Liverpool's habit to bring in players and keep them in the wings for a while. So I could easily see myself in a queue for a starting place behind Rush, and going to a new club and then being made to wait around would have defeated the point of moving, as far as I was concerned.

By contrast, at Everton, where they had just won the league, Andy Gray had recently been sold – a clear space for me to fill. So that's where I chose to go.

The problem was, Leicester and Everton couldn't agree on a price. I think Everton had made an offer of around £600,000; Leicester were holding out for something closer to £1 million. When transfer negotiations hit a deadlock like this, there was only ever one solution: the famous 'FA tribunal'.

This much I knew: an FA tribunal was the standard arbitration procedure when two clubs were at variance on the value of a player who was out of contract. An independent jury assembled by the Football Association would hear representations from both sides and then arrive at a transfer fee that they thought was fair. You heard about these things going on but the exact workings of them were utterly mysterious to me. Now I was going to take part in one.

Are you listening, Asif Kapadia?

A date was set at the FA's headquarters at Lancaster Gate in London. I wore a grey suit and a tie, exactly as though I was heading for a court appearance, which, in a sense, I was. Everyone else was wearing suits, too. Gordon Milne, who had taken over from Jock Wallace as manager, was representing Leicester. Howard Kendall, notionally my future boss, was representing Everton. Acting as judge and jury was a small panel of FA executives, who seemed very serious and rather unsmiling about their duties. The atmosphere around the table in what was essentially a municipal office was formal – intimidatingly so.

Gordon Milne opened. He gave a detailed account of my career at Leicester, pointing out that I had demonstrated over the course of the last two seasons that I was a guaranteed goalscorer, of enormous value to his team. Furthermore, Gordon added, it was patently obvious to anyone who had watched me recently that I had huge international prospects. He also testified on behalf of my good character and my highly professional attitude, defining me as an asset to my club.

I felt myself blush. Look how much Leicester loved me! Look how they believed in me! It was almost embarrassing that I wanted to leave them in these circumstances. It felt like a break-up, with me as the want-away party, causing all the hurt. I practically wanted to reach over to Gordon and say: 'It's not you – it's me.'

Then it was Howard Kendall's turn. His opening line rather surprised me. 'We're taking a big gamble here,' he said.

You what?

Howard's point was that, at this point, nothing whatsoever was certain about the kind of player I was likely to turn into. I was a relative youngster who just happened to have had a couple of good seasons recently – one of them, he reminded the jury, in the less pressurised setting of the Second Division. Howard additionally made the point that I had barely broken into the England set-up and that there was presently no guarantee I would flourish there, given the high calibre of the competition for places. He also made it very clear that he didn't expect me to be starting games for Everton very often – that, at most, he would be able to make limited use of me, coming off the bench, and that clearly any price Everton ended up paying would need to reflect this.

The longer Howard spoke, the more my heart sank and the lower I sat in my seat. I thought Everton were desperate to snap me up and that, as far as they were concerned, I was if not the finished item then certainly ready to use. Now, before I'd even got there, I was watching my prospective manager sucking his teeth and coming on like a builder giving an estimate – all pained expressions and 'Ooh . . . don't like the look of that . . . lot of work to be done here, you know' – while also setting out in crystal-clear terms why signing me was among the biggest risks he had ever taken, and possibly, on top of that, one of the worst ideas he had ever had.

I was thinking, 'I'm making a terrible mistake here.'

Eventually, Howard wrapped up the case against me and, having effectively written me off as any sensible person's vision of a top-class striker, sat down, and the people from the FA began their deliberations. I don't remember how long this part went on for; I was too busy licking my wounds to notice. However, the price eventually arrived at for my apparently indifferent services was, as commonly in these negotiations, pretty much smack in the middle of the two positions: £850,000. Sold to the reluctant bidder from Goodison Park.

We all trooped out, me feeling glum, Howard still looking like a troubled builder contemplating the massive job ahead of him. Once we were out in the street, though, and Gordon Milne and the Leicester delegation had disappeared round the corner, Howard's body language completely changed. His face abruptly lit up and he clapped me on the shoulder. 'Don't worry about any of that nonsense,' he said, smiling broadly. 'We're going to have a great season!'

I was confused and I must have looked it. The stuff about being an unfinished article? The stuff about being a major gamble for any club with serious aspirations? The stuff about being on the bench? I was apparently to file it all under 'Art of the Deal', or rather 'Art of the Tribunal'. Howard was clearly made up about the way it had all gone and the price Everton had managed to get me for.

Next thing I knew, my new manager was acquiring a couple of bottles of champagne from an off-licence on the way to the station and we were consuming them on the train from Euston back to Liverpool, where Howard then summoned a taxi and instructed it to take us to his favourite Chinese restaurant. Here the celebrations continued over a lavish banquet involving about 400 items off the menu, and a long chain of wine bottles, until, by the end of the evening, I was extremely full of egg-fried rice and completely plastered. (The Chinese restaurant, I was to discover, was Howard's traditional port of call in times of triumph for Everton, but also when the team was going through a bad spell and needed a boost. He clearly felt egg-fried rice had magical morale-boosting properties and he may well have been right. You would say this was generous of Howard, although I should point out that the bills for these banquets would be settled from the kitty made up of the players' various fines, for lateness or whatever. I suppose it was as good a way to recycle that money as any.)

So now I was an Everton player. I left my parents' house in Leicester and went to live in Southport, in an apartment that the club gave me. And then, about halfway through the season, I moved north-east of there to a little Lancashire village called Tarleton, where I lived in a converted barn, adapting as best I could, at long last, to looking after myself. And just five months after that I was off to Barcelona – but we'll come to that later.

Everton had a good team and I could feel the step up from Leicester in terms of quality, even in the training. There were some excellent players, all fiercely competitive among themselves. I'm not saying there hadn't been some excellent and competitive players at Leicester, too, but I could feel the jump to another level, an increased intensity. And that very quickly made me feel like I'd done the right thing.

However, before long the fixtures for the 1985–86 season came out and I discovered that my league debut for Everton would be . . . away at Leicester. It felt a little soon to be going back to Filbert Street. And it definitely felt a little too soon on the day. We went two goals behind in the first 45 minutes, both of them scored, somewhat gallingly, by my successor up front, Mark Bright. To cap it all, I left the pitch at half-time and, operating on auto-pilot, walked down the tunnel and straight into the Leicester dressing room. Which, of course, delighted my former team-mates enormously. Jeers and shouts of 'Fuck off!' duly filled the air.

In the second half, as I continued to fail to score, cho-ruses of 'What a waste of money' started coming from the Leicester fans. Do players hear what the fans sing? Oh yes. Very much so. Especially when they're the fans who used to sing your name. We ended up losing 3–1 – a disastrous start to the season and one that got a lot of attention because we were reigning champions. That night, hoping to put it all behind me, I went out with my family. So much for that. The piss-taking continued.

I was struggling to convince Everton fans, too. It didn't make it any easier that I was replacing a hero. Everton fans loved Andy Gray, my predecessor. He had only been with the club for two seasons but, in that time, they had won the league, the FA Cup and the European Cup Winners' Cup, with Gray scoring in both those finals, including that famously controversial goal at Wembley in 1984, when he headed the ball out of the hands of Watford's goalkeeper, Steve Sherwood. Yet Gray had been sold to Aston Villa, and now those fans were lumped with me, and they didn't seem to be particularly happy about it.

In midweek, a couple of days after the various embarrassments of the trip to Leicester, I made my home debut at Goodison Park and, as always, the team was read out over the PA.

'Number 6, Peter Reid!'

Huge cheer from the crowd.

'Number 7, Trevor Steven!'

Huge cheer.

'Number 8, Gary Lineker!'

At this point I heard a response which could have been the very definition of 'mixed' – a few cheers in there, yes, but definitely some boos, too. There may only have been a hundred boos in amongst a thousand cheers, but human nature being what it is, the boos are what you chiefly hear. I remember shrivelling inside a bit and thinking, 'Hmm, this is not so good.'

I didn't score that night, either. In fact, I didn't score in the first three games of the season and by now I was getting hammered in the *Liverpool Echo* – absolute pelters. Who was this useless upstart and why would Everton consider him a suitable replacement for the great Andy Gray?

But then, in the fourth game, we were away at Tottenham and I produced a diving header to win the game. A diving header will always cheer you up if you're a striker, and they will normally cheer up the fans, too. It's brave, it's flash, it tends to look great, and nobody doubts the commitment of a player who has just scored with a diving header.

And directly after that, we played Birmingham at Goodison Park and I managed to get a hat-trick, which settled some more nerves. And then, away at Sheffield Wednesday, I scored two more. So I had now scored six goals in six games and was the First Division's leading scorer, so I was finally able to stop lying awake in Southport thinking, 'What have I gone and done?' Even the *Liverpool Echo* calmed down a bit.

Years later, I talked to Peter Reid about that early rough patch and he said he had always known I would be OK. And the reason he thought so was not because he saw me score goals in training, or anything like that, but, on the contrary, because in my first pre-season friendly I had missed a couple of chances that I probably ought to have taken. And Peter said he had been struck by the extent to which it didn't seem to bother me, either there and then in the middle of the match or afterwards. There are clearly strikers who get upset by missing and let it get into their heads. And those are the kinds of strikers who, in a dry spell, often find the anxiety feeding on itself and building, with the result that they end up losing the ability to score for ages, until something goes right or their luck changes. I wasn't really like that, though. I guess it's down to having a certain kind of mental fortitude, the ability to blunder on regardless. Or 'stupidity', as it's sometimes called. Anyway, those initial days at Everton were as close as I came to feeling edgy and losing it.

So I went from being firmly a Leicester player to being firmly an Everton player. Supporters, I know, can never really understand how players can transfer their allegiances from one club to another. After all, it's famously what true fans don't do. Your club is your club for life. And, understandably, many fans assume that players who move around don't feel those bonds that fans feel. That's not entirely true. It's a different kind of relationship, certainly. But it's a weird thing: when you change clubs, you don't lose your feelings for your former team, but those feelings somehow automatically transfer to your new club. You start feeling things about its main rival – which was Liverpool, of course, when I was at Everton. You desperately care about the team doing well and about pleasing its fans. And then, not all that much later, I'm suddenly at Barcelona, and now it's Real Madrid that I'm in a rivalry with, and it's now Barcelona whom I desperately want to do well, and it's now Barcelona's fans that I'm trying to please. I'm sure it seems odd from the outside. But it's just what happens, and it feels perfectly natural. I know Maradona would tell you the same – assuming you could get to him through the tornado.

CHAPTER SEVEN

'They simply seem to want it
more at present.'

*In which DANNY is inducted into the life of the travelling
Millwall supporter and soon after is required to duck a hand
grenade – along with some profound reflections on witness-
tampering and pitch invasions by dogs, and with a full and
definitive explanation for the failure of 3D television.*

On the night of Friday 28 January 1966, an event occurred in
south London SE14 that was so unimaginably futuristic it
later made the climax of *Close Encounters of the Third Kind*
look as wondrous as the keycutting kiosk in Paddington
Station. Workington v. Millwall was beamed back via closed-
circuit TV to giant screens at the Den. LIVE! Oh, this was
TOMORROW calling!

When the news first broke we had a welter of questions,
not least among them: what did 'closed-circuit' mean? And
also, what did 'beam back' mean?

Remember, at this point we hadn't yet put a man on the moon (though several people had walked on Workington). But if a Third Division tie could be borne in its entirety 260 miles through the air to south London, then it was surely now only a matter of time before the British flag stood upon the lunar surface.

It wasn't quite the first football 'beam-back' – not untypically, the ever-pioneering Jimmy Hill, manager at the time of Coventry City, had got ahead with the idea a few months earlier, arranging to have a game at Cardiff packaged up and sent home down the wires. But we weren't fussy. It was still a rare and improbably exotic prospect – exotic enough to inspire one of the newspapers, during the build-up, to print a cartoon of footballers having make-up applied via oversized powder-puffs in order to look good for the cameras. Imagine! Players succumbing to vanity!

At the Den, before a (it has to be said) largely sceptical crowd – many of whom repeatedly asked if there was to be a B picture in support and whether tonight's attraction was a comedy – three giant screens and a pile of PA speakers had been erected on the pitch. This field day for the terrace wits continued as talk of 'outdoor aerials' and 'shillings in the meter' rang around the cheap seats.

And just to bring a further whiff of Hollywood to events, the evening was hosted at the Den by broadcasting star Pete *Six Five Special* Murray, fresh from MCing that year's NME Poll Winners' Concert at Wembley, where the Beatles and the Stones had topped the bill. That he brought equal brio and vim to our big night just goes to show what a true professional Pete was.

Now they do say the sixties was the decade when everything went technicolour, but I have to say that this rainbow world took a little longer to arrive in Football League Third Division. The pictures we saw that night were in black and white. Or rather, grey and a slightly different shade of grey. When I later read there had been commentary by Peter Lloyd of ITV, along with Ken Jones from the *Daily Mirror*, I was stunned. The noise inside the Den was admittedly every bit as raucous as a proper home game, but nobody heard a peep out of the piped-in match PA system. As comedians often remark, 'Is this thing on?'

And what a scorching match it turned out to be. Final score: Workington 0 Millwall 0. Perhaps unsurprisingly, I bear little recollection of the game itself, though I know many about us echoed my dad's précis, 'Well, what a fuckin' waste of time, that was'. One image I can recall was that, come half-time, the camera simply sagged down to show the touchline, presumably while the cameraman went off to have a brown ale. And that's where it stayed for the next ten minutes. When it bobbed up into life again it got the biggest cheer of the night.

The next day, I felt that Millwall should have been awarded the points. Attendance at Borough Park in Workington that evening was 4,323 while the Lions pulled in

9,134 fans just to watch what was basically a silent movie. Sadly, this ratings victory went unrecognised.

Our primitive experiment was never repeated. But, from this distance, I am reminded of those advertisements, much later, for Sky's seemingly doomed experiment with 3D television. 'Imagine your football in 3D,' the ads purred. To which the only sensible riposte, surely, was: 'Yeah, go to a game. That's 3D guaranteed. 4D if the ball actually hits you.'

Incidentally, I have a theory about the failure of 3D football on telly, and it comes down to the glasses. Wearing those special picture-transforming frames is, I would argue, all very well in the darkness of a cinema, or even at home while watching, say, *Cloudy with a Chance of Meatballs 2*. But those glasses do not betoken seriousness on the part of the wearer. Indeed, to don them is to make an open declaration that, for the following 90 minutes, you are a happy thrill-seeker, wrapping yourself indulgently in a fantastical amusement. And football is absolutely not a fantastical amusement. Only a television executive with no real experience of football could even begin to think that it was. End of 3D football.

Clearly, despite the hopeful claims of closed-circuit beam-backs and 3D TV, there is no substitute, in the end, for being there. And just five months after my first game at the Den, my old man was scooping me off to Gillingham and setting the stage for more than a quarter of a century of entertainment as a travelling Millwall supporter.

Now, Millwall fans were famous for not behaving themselves away from home. They were famous for not particularly behaving themselves at home, either, now we mention it. In the 1970s, fans weren't above expressing their displeasure to the chairman, Mickey Purser, by putting the windows through in the VW car dealership he owned on the Old Kent Road. Disciplinary ground closures weave through the tapestry of Millwall's history the way that European Cups weave through the tapestry of Liverpool's. The ground was closed for a fortnight after missiles were aimed at Newport County's goalkeeper, who apparently went over the barrier to confront the fans who were doing the aiming, and was knocked over. The date of this worrying mayhem? 1920.

The ground was closed again in 1934 (crowd trouble) and in 1947 (more crowd trouble). And it was closed yet again in 1950 after fans attacked the referee. In 1978, there was unusually deep trouble at an FA Cup tie against Ipswich. Sentence: a fortnight's ground closure. I mention this merely to point out that, whatever else you want to say about it, this stuff is not 'a modern sickness'. Indeed, a quick appraisal of the figures would suggest that Millwall's ground has been closed, in total, longer than MK Dons' stadium has been open.

So this was the milieu into which my dad formally introduced me. He himself, I should insist, was no pack-hunting trouble-seeker. Far from it. He was just, individually, wildly protective of his club and sometimes overly so, which got him into trouble. And he was not a small man, so the trouble that he got into tended to look a little . . . outsized.

For instance, quite early on in my supporting life, he took me to Queens Park Rangers where, for some reason or other, our tickets placed us among the home supporters. This was not, in and of itself, a major problem because QPR fans tend in the main to be polite and Loftus Road has never been a notorious trouble zone. However, on this occasion Millwall took the lead, only for QPR to quickly equalise. Everyone around us jumped in exultation – not having noticed what my old man had seen, which was the linesman's flag raised on the far side of the pitch to indicate an offside. My dad took a gleeful pleasure in bringing the neighbourhood roundly up to date.

'Offside!' he crowed. 'A mile offside. Siddown! Siddown!'

Later QPR equalised, this time legitimately. Then they scored again. And again. And again. And again . . . 6–1 the score got to. At this point, the bloke sitting directly behind us, a suburban-looking man in a corduroy hat, tapped my dad on the shoulder and said: 'Where's your offside now, my friend?'

My old man's response to this was to stand up, turn around, draw his arm back like Popeye and knock his interlocutor high up into the air. My response to my old man's response was to burst into tears. 'Now look what you've done to him!' bellowed Dad, and promptly sent the chap up into orbit. The stewards swiftly escorted Spud from the ground, with me trailing tearfully behind.

It would be by no means the only time I knew the misery and alarm of seeing my old man wrestled from the premises by stewards or policemen and realising that the afternoon's entertainment was over. It happened at Oxford, at Southend, at Gillingham and at least twice at Crystal Palace's Selhurst Park, until I grew kind of used to it.

Of course, these incidents would come to seem quaintly sepia-tinged and almost bucolic by comparison with scenes I later witnessed following Millwall around the country during the peak period for high anarchy which was the 1970s and 1980s – with my old man still beside me a lot of the time, because he continued to travel to games with us. Indeed, he was funny and more popular than me among my mates and, on the days when he didn't fancy the trip and I rounded the corner without him, all those already on the coaches would make their disappointment loudly clear.

But, in his company and out of it, I ended up seeing some shocking stuff, and not least of all at Luton on the quickly notorious night of the FA Cup quarter-final in 1985. Yes, I was there. Thousands of fans were let through into this tiny area of the ground. This was pre-Hillsborough of course but, looking back, you see how aspects of that horrific disaster were grimly foreshadowed here.

I remember the crush outside the ground, and how it was tight enough to lift me clean off my feet. We were shouting 'Open the other gates', but nobody seemed to be listening. Inside, the terrace was soon dangerously crowded and people began to climb out into the third-full stand next door, simply to get nicked for doing so, or shoved back among us. Millwall was criticised afterwards by the FA. To cap it all, the police held us in the ground long after the game. Some of us responded by going on the pitch, others by tearing up the stand. Again, this is not by way of offering excuses or an alternative explanatory version of events, but reports of the night tended to misrepresent key aspects of it, and omit the extent to which the anger had been fomented.

Now, two things I will happily confess that I have never done: 1) smoked weed. 2) hit anybody. I was never a fighter, nor remotely tempted to become one, and my tactics when war broke out around me, as they did at Luton, and also in Southampton and, frankly, in many other places, are probably best summarised by the expression 'interested onlooker'. But my brother Mickey did get in a few scrapes, most notoriously in Portsmouth, where he got laid out by a lump of rock. The rock, alas, had been thrown by a Millwall fan, but Mickey was so far ahead of the pack that it pole-axed him. And then, as he was coming to, he got hauled off by the police.

My old man accompanied Mickey back to Portsmouth

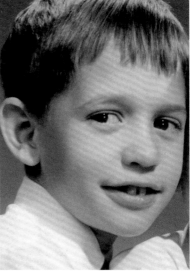

Danny: Christmas Day, 1965. My 'Frankenstein' Millwall kit: Huddersfield shirt, Chelsea shorts, Spurs socks. Note also that I was a more handsome kid than Gary Lineker.

Gary: I was a small kid, late to grow and very late to reach puberty, which – it probably goes without saying – was an uncomfortable thing in dressing rooms in my teenage years.

Danny: Here I am in another not-quite-Millwall shirt, 54 years on, recording an episode of *Behind Closed Doors* in Gary's kitchen.

TOP LEFT
Gary: I made my debut for Leicester on a frosty New Year's Day in 1979. (*Getty/Mark Leech/Offside*)

TOP RIGHT
Gary: In action for Everton during the 1986 FA Cup final against Liverpool. (*Getty/David Cannon*)

ABOVE
Gary: At Barca with Terry Venables and Mark Hughes. Terry is one of the best coaches that I ever played for. (*Getty/Bob Thomas*)

LEFT
Gary: On the road to Spurs' 1991 FA Cup victory. Here I am, seconds after scoring against Arsenal in the semi-final at Wembley Stadium. (*Getty/Paul Popper/Popperfoto*)

Gary: In many ways, Mexico '86 was a life-changing tournament for me. Having scored no England goals in eight months, I managed to score three by half-time against Poland in our World Cup finals match. (*Getty/Bob Thomas*)

Gary: Italia '90. Celebrating after scoring the equaliser against West Germany in the World Cup semi-final. Before the fateful penalty shoot-out. (*Getty/Simon Bruty*)

Gary: You may be surprised to learn that in 1986 I became the first England player to win the Golden Boot at a World Cup with six goals scored. I don't talk about it much. (*Getty/Bob Thomas*)

LEFT

Danny: The Den entry gates at Cold Blow Lane, through which I walked ten thousand times. Note the exquisite craftsmanship of the finely tooled letters. 'This Is Anfield?' Pah!

LEFT

Danny: My dad would often say, 'Don't go to school today, boy, come racing with me.' This is Fontwell Park. I am holding a Russian made cine-camera recently liberated by Dad from a shipment at the docks.

BELOW

Danny: The rattle my brilliant brother made. MADE. Note the paint scraped away where it had originally said, 'UP THE LOINS'.

Danny: One of my favourite examples of football graffiti. Later someone added after it: 'Yes. And WE BITE!' Touché.

LEFT
Danny: The London Dock Labour Board team 1944. My dad is on the far left, back row. Not the most finessed of players, Spud was an expert toe-punter. And not just of the ball.

Danny: Three generations of Baker boys: Spud, me and my Sonny at Wembley for the Auto Windscreens final v. Wigan. Lost 1–0 in the last minute. Hooray!

ABOVE

Gary: My favourite boys: my four sons and Lionel Messi. I love them equally. Almost. My sons understand.

LEFT

Gary: Little known fact: England did win a World Cup. I know this, because I made it myself.

Danny: Another away game, another pub en route. Players may get all the glory but supporters have the better days out. As Keats wrote in Ode to a Second Leg: 'Win or lose, we'll have a booze. (If it's a draw we'll booze a bit more.)'

ABOVE, LEFT, BELOW LEFT

Gary: I spent two wonderful, injury-plagued years playing for Nagoya Grampus Eight in the newly launched J-League. There, all 5 ft 10 of me was respected for my heading prowess in defensive situations. My second son, Harry, was born there and I still think of it as a happy time. Just one without much football in it.

Danny: Meanwhile, the crowd on match day outside Millwall.

Gary: What a tournament…the 2018 World Cup in Russia. The BBC was given England's quarter-final match against Sweden and it was clear that the audience at home was going to be massive. And, well, you know the rest . . .

LEFT
Danny: Recording *Behind Closed Doors*. Here I am explaining how exciting the game is now we have the wondrous VAR to finally educate us fans and calm us all down.

Gary: It's not all fast cars – but sometimes it is. Me with Alan Hansen, Ian Wright and a beautiful Ferrari.

Gary: The Bafta award-winning BBC 2018 World Cup Russia team. Almost a decent 11-a-side team, too.

for the ensuing court hearing, which was one of a long series of cases of minor affray relating to that particular match, for his perceived part in which Mickey was at risk of being fined. The hearing went on and on through the morning, without my brother being called, and eventually they broke for lunch, with lots of people stepping out to the pub across the road.

I don't think my brother noticed anything untoward going on in the pub over that lunch hour, and I think both he and my old man were a bit startled to hear the judge open the afternoon session by asking, 'Is there a Frederick Baker present?'

My old man identified himself.

'Mr Baker,' said the judge. 'It is alleged that you approached the father of a witness in the Golden Hind during recess. And it is further alleged that you said to this father of a witness – and I quote: "If this comes on top for my boy I'm going to drop you on your fucking head." Did you say this, Mr Baker?'

Dad tried to recollect such an exchange but couldn't be sure. Sadly, a second witness could. So my brother ended up getting fined £50 for his claimed part in the original post-match ructions, and my dad, who had gone along merely to chaperone him, ended up getting fined £150 on the spot.

But let me not paint a picture here of permanent lawlessness and antisocial behaviour on these away trips, because, for one thing, Millwall hardly need their reputation in that area underscored and, for another, truly, it was not always so. And let me stress also: the hand grenades in the upcoming tale were only ever dummy hand grenades.

I refer here to a story that I harboured for many years, and yet which, in due course, under the terms of any sober analysis, seemed so utterly implausible that I started to wonder whether I had actually invented it, or whether, like the 'drunk' referee in the 1937 FA Cup semi-final mentioned in an earlier chapter, it was just one of those great oral myths passed down through the ages, bearing no relation to actual events.

Part of the problem was that this tale had at its heart Chic Brodie, the Brentford goalkeeper, whose place in the game's wider folklore is already cemented as a consequence of suffering a career-ending injury in, of all things, a collision with a stray dog. Which, you would have to say, doesn't often happen. Indeed, interruptions of any kind by dogs are rare nowadays, contemporary stadium architecture generally militating against freelance incursions by the four-leggers. The game is the poorer for it. What we have gained in aesthetics we have lost in belly laughs.

On a recent *Behind Closed Doors* Gary and I drifted into a shared nostalgia for days when football matches could boast stray dogs on the running order. This led me to wonder how police horses get into a ground or on to the pitch. They just seem to emerge from nowhere at the end of matches. Do they come out of the tunnel like players? Hereford once had a live bull as a mascot – did they keep it in the changing rooms?

Anyway, back to the story of bombs on the pitch. Could this bizarre file in my memory banks simply be some kind of fantasy or half-recalled shaggy-dog story concocted beneath a full moon? For surely a player already at the centre of a tale involving a terminal dog-to-knee coincidence couldn't also be caught up in a narrative involving a hand grenade on the pitch. Could he?

He could. A friend eventually alerted me to a clipping from the old *Daily Sketch* fully substantiating the episode in my mind and referring in no uncertain terms to 'the hand grenade that shocked British soccer'.

So it genuinely had happened, then. A Millwall fan had thrown a hand grenade on to the pitch in front of my actual schoolboy eyes. And, almost equally shockingly, nobody had run away.

This was November 1965 – the day after Bonfire Night, appropriately enough – and Millwall were playing at Brentford. The traditional winding up of Chic Brodie in the Brentford goal by the away fans behind him took, at first, entirely conventional forms. But it then escalated dramatically with the arrival in the mud in his goalmouth of a perfectly authentic-looking, World War Two-period hand grenade. The rumour was that one of our number had found it up by the railway lines, whereupon his very first thought was: 'Ah – the very thing with which to tease Chic Brodie of Brentford.' So the grenade had been smuggled out west to Griffin Park, and now here it was, landing with a soft thud (but, as yet, nothing louder) in the Brentford penalty area.

Now, some accounts of this tale have Brodie either legging it or heroically diving on the grenade, before casually lobbing it out of harm's way into the back of his goal, presumably on the grounds that it could be dealt with later. That's not my recollection. In my version, the goalkeeper pretty quickly alerted the referee to the fact that what was quite possibly a live bomb had just landed on the pitch. Certainly, I recall the referee stopping the game and taking the players down to the other end of the pitch while everybody weighed their options.

An immediate and complete evacuation of the ground must have been among the possible courses of action, and would almost certainly be considered the sensible way forward today. But these were clearly less flighty or less organised times because what actually happened was that, in due course, with everyone in the ground still solemnly looking on, a policeman walked out carrying a bucket of sand. As he neared the rogue bomb, this policeman's pace slowed, his steps became a little lighter and his legs went kind of single file, as if he believed a stealthy approach to be the wisest. All this, I hardly need add, was soundtracked by Millwall fans behind the goal shouting 'Bang!'

We may smirk now about the bucket of sand, but it was a tactic used with sick in school corridors since time immemorial, so why not with unexploded World War Two ordnance? However, instead of tipping the sand on the grenade, the policeman gingerly lifted the grenade from the grass and placed it on top of the sand in the bucket. Clearly, we were now all perfectly safe. The bucket was carried away around the perimeter of the ground, amid a mixture of ironic cheering and genuinely grateful applause and, with a stout blast on the whistle, the game resumed.

Millwall went on to win 2–1. Indeed, no further grenades interrupted play at any other match I went to, win, lose or draw. And, as I mentioned, even this grenade was later examined and found to be entirely dud. Still, as the strapline above the story in the *Daily Sketch* thunderously asked: 'A harmless grenade this time, but what next?' Indeed. They might have put that question to Chic Brodie. 'A ruinously clumsy dog v. Colchester,' would have been the answer.

Between 1988 and 1990, Millwall, for the first and still the last time in their history, spent two seasons in what was then Division One and, recognising the likely rarity of this invitation to dine at football's so-called top table, we went to every game, home and away. We all knew Millwall's presence in the division was a liberty, an outrage, a swashbuckling punk-rock party. We couldn't have been happier. It came to be my role to make three-hour VHS tapes to show on the coach. This would occupy me at home for ages in the week. I would fill those tapes with bits of comedy shows and cartoons and pop videos taken from the telly, as well as all manner of off-colour things, including unlicensed amateur boxing bouts, such as Roy 'Pretty Boy' Shaw fighting Mad Dog Lenny McLean – properly raw stuff. We would sit there and watch all of that going away to, say, Anfield.

Kevin Nixon, one of our number, had developed an irrational hatred for Steve Wood, the Millwall defender – the kind of irrational hatred for a footballer that you can only carry for one of your own. Hatred for an opponent is casual, almost reflexive. Hatred for one of your own, though . . . that's deep, that's personal, that is the truest of hatreds. Indeed, it may be the most profound and most genuine of the football emotions. Anyway, Kevin would spend a large portion of games shouting 'Fuck off, Wood' – to the point where he had become quite famous for it. 'Fuck off, Wood' he would scream in annoyance, as another pass went astray, another tackle was missed, another move broke down. 'Fuck off, Wood.'

I took a video camera to Millwall's training ground, down at Sidcup. I had enough clout at the time to be allowed in and to take Kevin Nixon's least favourite player aside and say 'Do me a favour, Steve . . .' He was possibly a little confused, but he happily complied and I left with a personal and intimate recorded message, delivered to camera and directed at the fan most famous for shouting 'Fuck off, Wood'. This personalised whizz-bang I buried halfway through one of my compilation tapes, with the result that it screened, unannounced, on the next coach trip.

A cartoon ended and up I popped on the screen saying: 'And now, a message from Millwall's Steve Wood.'

And then up came Millwall's Steve Wood himself.

'No, *you* fuck off, Nixon!' he bellowed down the coach.

And just like that, Kevin Nixon's jaw was on the floor.

Something I quickly learned and filed away: people don't sit on coaches bound for football matches and say, in the manner of pundits on the telly, 'I think he's playing him out too wide' or 'Why aren't we getting men forward and exploiting the channels more?' Not the people around me, anyway. Nor did those people sit in the grounds and speak in such a way. The game was not the all-involving, all-consuming, agenda-driving obsession of media myth. You'd have your back to it sometimes, and be talking about the boxing that had been on the telly that week. This seemed important to me, and increasingly overlooked as the media's grimly tame and tedious template for intense 'footy' discussions began increasingly to become the norm.

Something else I learned: it's quite hard to get a drink in a pub as a travelling Millwall fan. Publicans, it may not surprise you to hear, don't always like coaches pulling into their car parks and disgorging 52 Millwall supporters. Even establishments without a declared 'No Coach Party' policy would very rapidly declare one, even as the airbrakes on our bus were still sighing notice of our arrival.

So we evolved a system where we would send in my old man as an advance negotiating party. He was 15–20 years older than the average member of our party, and probably, if we had been judging this by his record of getting tossed out of grounds, the biggest troublemaker among us, in fact. But mature appearances unquestionably count for something, so in he would go, in an ambassadorial role. More often than not, he would then re-emerge, sorrowfully reboard the bus and announce: 'They won't have it, boys.'

Well, that was understandable. Millwall's reputation not unreasonably went ahead of us, and charm and diplomacy have their limits – every ambassador knows this. What were we to expect?

As the pubs went by, though, we began to get suspicious of the time it was taking my old man to complete these peace missions. The simple act of entering the pub and engaging the landlord or landlady in a conversation designed to sell them on the prospect of admitting 51 further Millwall fans seemed to absorb more minutes than one might have imagined, given that what was essentially being proffered here was a simple question requiring the answer 'yes' or 'no'.

Our suspicions were further aroused when it eventually came to our attention that, nearly every time he came out of the pub and began to return across the car park to the bus in order to impart the usual bad news, Dad would, for some reason as yet unexplained, be wiping the corner of his mouth . . .

It eventually struck us that the old git was having a drink in every one of these putative venues – meaning, of course, that he would have had five, six or seven away before he got lucky and found a pub that would take us. 'Well, be sensible, it wouldn't be right to go in and not buy a drink,' the old man brazenly explained when his solo crawl was rumbled.

His assumed benign status as a senior actually caused him to be offended at Bournemouth one glorious evening late in the season in 1988. This was the point where Millwall were in reach of the title and promotion to the First Division, and, against the backdrop of these heightened stakes, the prospect of our arrival on the genteel south coast – the English Riviera, if you will – seemed to induce a lengthy outbreak of pearl-clutching. First of all Bournemouth tried to get the game played at 5pm on a Thursday, the assumption being that Millwall fans with jobs wouldn't be able to make it. But then they realised that quite a lot of their own fans with jobs wouldn't be able to make it, either, so 5pm notionally became 6pm.

Then they floated the imaginative scheme of charging visiting supporters £20 for entry, instead of £5 as usual – but giving you back £15 if there wasn't any trouble. A 300 per cent deposit against the possibility of breakages? Not even the most heartlessly conniving of landlords would try and pull a stunt like that. This plan, too, was quickly quashed.

Millwall, for their part, organised a Workington-style

beam-back so the game could be seen at the Den, thereby quietly discouraging travellers. Note how the glorious innovation witnessed in January 1966 was now being wielded as proxy crowd-control. From the future of entertainment to surrogate policing tool in just a couple of decades. This has been the story of technology from the beginning.

In the end, Bournemouth settled for a 7.30pm kick-off, a police presence so enormous that in certain places there appeared to be three policemen and a dog for every Millwall fan, and a security cordon around the stadium so tight that it suggested the imminent arrival of an American president. The frisking at the turnstiles, I hardly need add, was obligatory and detailed.

My old man, who would have been about 60 at this point, was with us, and one by one we all submitted ourselves for a patting-down. Then it was my dad's turn. But as he assumed the position, the steward casually said, 'Ha-ha, you don't need it, Pops – in you go,' and waved him in.

My old man was absolutely appalled.

'Pops? Pops?' he shouted, as affronted as I had ever seen him. 'You saucy bastard! I *demand* to be searched!'

We went 2–0 up in the first 20 minutes, including a strike of the very purest thunder from Terry Hurlock. Time for my favoured football stand battle-cry: 'Nothing can go wrong now!' But then, of course, not long into the second half it becomes 2–1 and then, in the dying seconds, there's a panicked handball in the penalty area and Bournemouth have a penalty. That, Dan, is what can go wrong now.

Incredibly, Brian Horne dived to his left and smothered it. We all went wild in the stand behind him, and the Bournemouth police probably heaved a sigh of relief, too. The title would be won two weeks later in the grandeur of Hull City's Boothferry Park, a game which has taken on the status among Millwall fans of the Sex Pistols' last UK performance at Ivanhoe's in Huddersfield in 1977. In both cases, if you gathered everyone who claims to have been there at the time, you would have enough people to fill the venue many times over.

Well, I wasn't in Huddersfield for the Sex Pistols. But I was in Hull for the title. A huge thunderstorm rumbled around the edges of the ground for most of the first half, the rise of Millwall apparently having angered Thor, and it caused many of us to believe the game would be called off. It wasn't, though, and we eventually got the penalty which decided it.

Was it even true? Had we actually won the title? People were asking the question even then – not out of giddy disbelief, but with perfectly sound reason and on the basis of sobering experience. Back in April 1972, Millwall were beating Preston 2–0 at the Den when, entirely unrelated to the play, an outbreak of cheering began in one corner of the ground and spread until the whole place was shouting and jumping for joy. It could only have meant one thing: that Birmingham were losing at Sheffield Wednesday, which would in turn mean Millwall were about to be promoted to the First Division for the first time ever.

As the final whistle neared, the crowd readied itself at the touchlines. When the referee blew, at least half the 20,000 people present swarmed on to the pitch to celebrate. The players, breaking for the dressing room, had their backs royally slapped and their hair vigorously ruffled and a couple of them even had their shirts ripped from them in the excitement. Millwall were going up!

Except we weren't. Benny Fenton, the manager, on the touchline knew. The people in the press box knew. For them, the reaction of the crowd was entirely mystifying. Birmingham weren't losing at all and Millwall weren't going anywhere – not unless Birmingham lost against Orient in midweek. Fenton had to go and break it to the players in the dressing room. The PA, meanwhile, broke it to the crowd. The atmosphere popped like a pricked balloon and everybody sheepishly evacuated the pitch and headed for the exits. (Birmingham didn't lose to Orient in midweek. Of course they didn't. Bleeding Birmingham.)

So, a phantom promotion celebration, caused by a false rumour or somebody's idea of a joke, or who knows what? It was the emotional equivalent of being jilted. And that whole narrative was in play again 16 years later in Hull, albeit mostly in the form of a rich line in gallows humour, with people asking: 'Has anyone checked the fucking Birmingham score?'

This time, though, there was nothing even Birmingham could do to soak the crisps. Cue 20 minutes of celebrating on the pitch by our players, while around me many big men were in floods of tears, not just for the title but for the dads, the uncles, the friends long gone who didn't get to see it, which I think is what these moments chiefly bring home to you and why people weep. My old man and I, there and then, dedicated this miracle to the memory of my brother Mickey, who died at 29. There were no tears from us, though: our DNA was too phlegmatic for that, and the pair of us were too steeped in the darker varieties of humour to find ourselves going theatrical on a football terrace in Humberside.

However, what did make us feel surprisingly emotional was the way that, as the long line of coaches and cars departed for London, the people of Hull came out of their houses and lined the streets in great numbers to applaud us as we passed. This we were not accustomed to, and it was impossible not to be touched by such a display of vicarious pleasure in the triumph of your foe. We duly applauded them back. See how respect breeds respect?

It was only when we were well down the motorway that we figured they had probably been dancing in the streets to see the backs of 6,000 Millwall supporters, heading home.

We were up! Arriving back from Boothferry Park, we piled into a Bermondsey pub that was thumbing its nose at the licensing laws and staying open for the night. It is in these moments, and the following few days, in which promotion is still sweet and untainted for unlikely sides such as ours. Yet even as we try to process the idea of top-flight football, just hours after its confirmation, a sort of panic sets in.

Someone will start talking about next season's fixture list, saying vulgar things like 'Manchester United', 'Arsenal' and 'Liverpool', and you look towards a mate from the corners of your eyes, swallow something hard and jagged and, through a rictus grin, mutter, 'Oh fuck . . .'

CHAPTER EIGHT

'Ordinarily you'd be expecting him to bury that.'

In which GARY gets a ticket for the bus ride from hell.

Poor old Norwich City. The specially painted canary-yellow open-top bus, with 'We Are Premier League' written proudly down its sides, was all ready to carry the players and staff through the streets of Norwich and receive the acclaim of the fans after winning the 2018–19 Championship title . . . and it wouldn't start.

'Who hired Leeds' coach?' asked somebody on Twitter. Some of the Norwich players, celebratory bottles already in hand, were seen going round the back end to give it a shove. Typical: you wait years for an open-top bus to come along – and you end up push-starting it.

And even that didn't work. Eventually someone rang around in a panic and got hold of one of the city's sight-seeing buses – red, unfortunately, not canary-yellow, but it would have to do – and the players bundled upstairs on that instead. Whether they got the tour guide's commentary on the way round is not reported.

That's nothing, though. Epic open-top bus fails? Beat this. I once had to go through the streets on the top of a bus with the team that had just lost the FA Cup final, having finished second in the league. Yes, a losers' open-top bus parade. But it was worse than that. The bus was obliged to trail through the city behind the open-top bus carrying the team that it had just lost out to in both the FA Cup final and the league, and whose fans were waiting on the pavements to celebrate.

So, a double losers' open-top bus parade in the direct wake of a double winners' open-top bus parade . . . If you were looking for a definition of open-top bus misery, then maybe you have just found it.

This was in 1986, at the end of my first and only season at Everton. It was, by any measure, a good season – spoiled only by the fact that Liverpool had a slightly better one. The two rival clubs had been in a tight fight for the league, with Everton holding a slim advantage until a slip-up at Oxford in the 'Night of the Missing Boots', which I write about elsewhere in these pages. Liverpool eventually took the title on the final day.

Meanwhile, both clubs had made it to the FA Cup final – the 'Merseyside final', as it was being called. As soon as Liverpool won the league, a decision was taken that, no matter which of us won the FA Cup, there should be a dual parade, featuring both teams, to mark what was objectively an amazing time for the city.

I'm not sure in whose office this twin-bus notion first surfaced, but it's easy to see why it would have found some traction with the Football Association. It was only a year since the Heysel Stadium disaster, where 39 spectators died when a perimeter wall collapsed during a crowd disturbance at the 1985 European Cup final between Liverpool and Juventus. English teams were indefinitely banned from European competition (and wouldn't be allowed back, in fact, until 1990). Anything that sent out into the world a positive message about English football and the community of its fans at this particular juncture was likely to be thought a good idea.

Point taken about the bigger picture, obviously. Yet, with the advantage of hindsight, may I beg to differ? This was an absolutely terrible plan – or certainly from an Everton player's point of view.

The misery began down in London. We lost the final 3–1, after I had put us ahead in the first half, thereby realising the childhood dream of scoring a goal in the FA Cup final at Wembley, shortly before realising the childhood nightmare of losing the final in which you have scored. Talk about a roller-coaster of emotions. I was utterly drained afterwards. There was a low-key dinner after the game at Wembley, about which I recall almost nothing, having spent it in a kind of dazed trance, and the following morning it was decided that, in a grand show of unity, the two teams would share a plane back to Liverpool. That was horrendous in itself. The Liverpool players were all up the back, partying, and we were sitting quietly at the front, staring out the windows and pretending not to notice.

Then, at Liverpool airport, we were met by the buses. My team-mate Peter Reid straight up refused to get on. Allegedly he told Howard Kendall, the manager, that he wasn't doing it, and Howard told him that he would be fined two weeks' wages if he didn't, and Peter said 'Deal'. He watched the parade on television from a pub somewhere near his home. I only wish I'd had Reidy's nerve.

Instead, along with the rest, I meekly trooped on board and climbed up to the top deck and off we went. It was like some kind of torture. The streets were packed and, though I know there were blue scarves there, my abiding memory is of a heaving mass of red ones. Up ahead were Liverpool, revelling in their glory, and fumbling along behind were us, still trying to digest the fact that we had come out of the season with nothing. We just felt embarrassed – publicly embarrassed. Dragged through the streets in our shame. Surely this was the kind of barbaric thing that would have happened in medieval times, had they had open-top buses back then.

Of course, from the Liverpool fans' point of view, it represented a fantastic two-for-one offer – probably the best one seen in that area since Danny Baker was last in town with his boxes of washing powder. Not only could those fans cheer their players, they were also granted a golden opportunity simultaneously to gloat over their defeated rivals. In that sense, it's probably a good job we were in Liverpool. Indeed, that was possibly the only English city in which this two-bus idea could even have been attempted. The rivalry between the two Liverpool clubs is unbelievably intense sometimes, but it feels different to other city rivalries – friendlier, more familial. I still vividly remember driving to Wembley for that FA Cup final, looking out of the bus window and seeing thousands of people going to the game, a sea of red and blue all mixed together. And there was a dad with a red scarf carrying a kid on his shoulders in a blue scarf. I thought that was incredible – and unique. You certainly don't see that so much with, say, Tottenham and Arsenal. And certainly not with Barcelona and Real Madrid. So maybe we got off lightly on our losers' bus parade.

For the sake of balance, I should point out that open-top buses can be very nice if you have won something. The one after winning the cup with Tottenham in 1991 was particularly enjoyable, as I recall, and I had a couple of good ones with Barcelona, too, particularly after the final of the European Cup Winners' Cup in 1989. That match was played in Bern at the brilliantly named Wankdorf Stadium – long since demolished and replaced by the no less brilliantly named Stade de Suisse, Wankdorf. We won 2–0 against Sampdoria of Italy, who had Gianluca Vialli and Roberto Mancini in their side. I remember after the match we were driven back to the hotel, all extremely happy and pleased with ourselves and expecting a party of some kind – only to find that nothing had been laid on. Apparently the club had taken a decision, three years earlier, in 1986, not to get ahead of itself with the celebrations. That was the year Barcelona, under Terry Venables, faced Steaua Bucharest of Romania in the European Cup final. Nobody gave Steaua a chance. They were the far weaker side on paper, and Barcelona were smashing everybody that year. Plus, the final was in Spain – in Seville. It was all set up for an historic Barça victory – their first ever in that competition. Back at the hotel, the champagne and canapes were piled high in preparation.

And, of course, the game finished 0–0 and went to penalties, whereupon, unthinkably, every single Barcelona penalty-taker missed. The first two Steaua takers missed, too, so the shoot-out ended 2–0 – perhaps the most feeble penalty shoot-out in history, and certainly the most feeble penalty shoot-out in the history of the European Cup. Anyway, the pre-ordered cakes and jellies looked a little foolish after that, and the club's catering department resolved never again to be quite so presumptuous.

Which is why, in 1989, returning in triumph to our Bern hotel, we found not so much as a bowl of complimentary peanuts waiting for us. By that point, it was after 10pm and everything was shut. There was nowhere to go, so we all went to bed. Switzerland, folks.

However, we landed in Barcelona the next day and an open-top bus was waiting for us on the Tarmac, and it took us gently down to the seafront in the sunshine where there were tens of thousands of people out to greet us . . . Glorious. That was the most fun I ever had on an open-top bus.

Even then, though, forgive me for mentioning it (and I realise that I may sound a touch ungrateful here), but the format of the open-top bus parade does have, in my experience, an in-built fault. The fact is, the bus goes so slowly and, after about ten minutes up there on the top deck, you've kind of done your whole routine. How much waving and smiling can one person do? It's charming and gratifying, obviously, but . . . well, first world problems and all that, but it does go on a bit.

And it especially goes on a bit if you have lost. Now, if that Everton bus in 1986 hadn't started, like Norwich's all those years later, it would have been a result. And I can assure you: none of us would have lifted so much as a finger to get it going.

CHAPTER NINE

'That's not the cleanest of connections but it's somehow gone in.'

In which DANNY creates the 606 phone-in and conversations about football are, quite simply, never the same again. With deep meditations regarding Alan Ball's fruit bowl, the secret diabolic life of Brian Kilcline and the wisdom of asking Frank Sinatra to come in and review the papers.

Before Radio 5 Live, the rolling sports and news station as we now understand it, there was something called, simply, Radio 5. And Radio 5 was a bit of a jumble. The BBC seemed to have opened a station without thinking too hard about what it might be – a good thing, in my opinion. The result was a kind of jamboree bag – a bunch of shows with no fixed identity that had to feel towards one as they went along. I was asked to do a phone-in sports quiz show called *Sportscall*, which went out at midday on Saturdays. This was essentially a sports-only pub quiz on which it was possible to win really quite substantial prizes, such as tickets to tennis finals and big European football matches.

Sportscall was a palpable hit, possibly Radio 5's first glimpse of such a thing, and it led to me being asked to take over the channel's moribund breakfast show, *Morning Edition*. This also seemed to go with a swing for a while, causing my star to ascend gloriously at the station and handing me a reputation for a Midas touch unseen at the corporation since David Attenborough burst through the door with mud on his boots. In 1991, with this tsunami of approbation rolling onwards, the controller of Radio 5 said to me: 'We're thinking of launching a sports phone-in show. But we want it to go out at 6pm on a Saturday and you go to Millwall, don't you? Well, if we got a car to bring you to the studio straight after games, would that work?'

I thought it would work very well. Nobody had thought of a title when the show appeared in *Radio Times* next to its designated time slot as '6.06: Sports Phone-in'. And 606 is what it became.

I should point out that this was long before that sort of thing was everywhere, and long before such a programme would be considered a natural extension of Radio 5's output. We used to pick up from a half-hour current affairs show and then, an hour later, hand over to a pre-recorded look at the European pop charts. Think on that and weep, Robbie Savage. The show was in splendid isolation within an absolute patchwork, to put it politely. The audience had to *find* you. And audiences like that.

On the very first show, which, true to my usual practices, had been very few minutes indeed in the planning (turn up, turn on and go has long been my fundamental approach to these things), I promoted for general consideration the topic: 'Exactly how crooked are referees?' Now, if I'm being perfectly honest, this question wasn't aimed at actual professional footballers, fresh from the showers. It was aimed at listening fans, in the hope of encouraging far-fetched gossip or well-augmented legend, relating most probably to the running of amateur games on playing fields, which are, of course, football's Wild West. Yet, to my immense surprise, who should be almost instantly on Line One but Andy Townsend, then of Chelsea.

'You wanted examples of bent referees,' Andy opened. 'I've just been in a game with one.'

This was manna unlooked-for. Barely had we opened for business and here was a well-known international player, fuelled with indignation about the way his afternoon had gone, and making startling, and we should say ultimately groundless, allegations about the impartiality of a top-flight referee. It was a fit of pique for which Andy eventually paid in actual pounds. (He was fined by the FA.) But it was also a fit of pique for which I will be forever grateful to him. The following day's papers lapped up the story and 606, which couldn't have designed a multi-platform publicity strategy this transcendent had it employed every advertising brain in Manhattan, was well afloat.

Not that Andy's enraged and tabloid-friendly call would turn out to be typical of the show's tenor. Then, as now, I stood in firm opposition to the sappy and patronising way the media treats football supporters, and even more shamelessly the way that advertising treats them – blokes on sofas punching the air and eating Doritos. This is not normal, until it becomes normal by a process of saturation and brainwashing. In the meantime, people don't sit there saying: 'If we played Hoggins instead of Coggins with Boggins in the hole . . .' The media really think people talk like that. They don't. Media people do. Regular people sit there asking each other: 'What was that ground we were at when the ball hit that bloke and his wig flew off?' To be honest, it takes a heart of stone not to feel for those poor studio pundits, condemned to talk about the night's game for more than an hour after it has finished. TV execs need to visit pubs after a televised game. The coverage might still be on. But nobody is listening to it.

If 606 was founded on an essential truth, it was that football supporters couldn't care less about other clubs and their fans. However, the equal truth is that we all agree to declare a truce for the sake of comedy. And, accordingly, 606 would do its utmost to establish the conditions for that truce and ensure that it held for at least an hour. To this end, tiresome rants about the inefficiency of your team's back four that afternoon at Reading were actively discouraged. If, by contrast, you had something to contribute on the theme of 'things you have seen at a footballer's house', we were listening, and listening closely.

That particular topic was essentially an invitation to delivery people or maybe handymen who had found themselves with privileged access to the homes of the stars to share their exclusive observations. And lo and behold, one caller had been impressed to note, in the house of 1966 World Cup-winner Alan Ball, a bowl containing fruit.

And not just any old fruit: limes.

These were the first limes this caller had ever set eyes on. Fair enough, limes did not always enjoy the casual association with the British fruit bowl that they eventually assumed. Indeed, connecting the green lime-flavoured Opal Fruit with an actual organic object was for many years a challenge which defeated all but the most widely travelled of users. But not Alan Ball, clearly. Alan Ball was right out in front in the citrus fruit revolution.

This thread grew apace with news of a visit to Brian Kilcline's house, and the tremendous observation that the former Coventry City captain had, in his hallway, three or four mannequins. Just that: an assortment of mannequins of the kind you might see in a clothes shop window. Now, here was bare material ripe for development. Was something dark afoot? It sounded like it. Or it could certainly be made to sound like it, if I embroidered the scene elaborately enough. Very soon Brian Kilcline's mannequins were dressed in 17th-century costume and forming a tableau around a pentangle, while incense burned thickly in the light cast by a red candle. Very shortly after that, we were positing the rumour that Brian Kilcline never shakes hands before games for fear of revealing his cloven hoof.

And then, and hat way off here, Brian Kilcline himself started getting in touch and confirming all this. I was so grateful to him for jumping in and going along with it. And not just going along with it, in fact; towing the whole thing forwards at exciting new speeds. It was Brian himself who now soberly contacted us to suggest that we should rename the show '666'. He even grew a goatee, which made him look like Robert Plant at the time of Led Zep III. Thanks in no small measure to Brian himself, 'The diabolic private life of Brian Kilcline' was a real runner for a while, and I would argue that all of our lives were richer for it.

We heard, too, from Pat Nevin regarding his struggles to read the *New Musical Express* as a Chelsea player. Pat's team-mates believed that one of their number had no business reading this counter-cultural rag and would seek out Pat's *NME*, rip it up and throw it in the showers. Consequently, Pat took to buying two copies every week. One he would place near the top of his kitbag for his team-mates to find and destroy. The second copy he would conceal at the bottom of the bag where it would go unlocated, meaning that Pat could eventually sit in his car in the car park and enjoy it. This sudden shaft of light, abruptly illuminating a hitherto dark corner in the daily lives of familiar football-ers, seemed to me to offer far more to get your teeth into, ultimately, than any match report.

With the advent of squad numbers, and the likelihood that any starting line-up would include a 15, a 27 and pos-sibly even a 33, we invited listeners to apply the shirt numbers from their team's most recent outing to their local Chinese take-away menu and see what they came up with. Thus people would ring in and solemnly relate how they had prawn crackers in goal, with curried corn on the cob at centre-back. This ran for some weeks, with other menus and lists coming into operation, reaching the peak, or cer-tainly the point of no return, when a listener decided to use a catalogue of Danish porn to form a team made up from the terrible punning titles of adult films. Apparently, at left-back that afternoon, making his first appearance after six weeks out, was *Romancing the Bone*. That was the apogee – stupid, off-colour but, man, it was good radio.

At other times, we concentrated on the awesome destruc-tive power of the ball. Everyone who has ever played in a public space is familiar with the moment when your shoul-ders rise up to your earlobes in horror as the ball flies towards a woman walking a pushchair, and I once witnessed a shot on Blackheath that carried far enough to strike the top of a double-decker bus with a satisfying 'clonk'. Resounding

cheers – though, disappointingly, no damage. In the programme we learned of somebody in a park game who had
hit a shot which collided with a funeral cortège and shat-
tered the floral arrangement spelling 'DAD'. What on earth
was a person to do in such a situation? (The answer, it
seemed to me, was to try to keep your head over the ball at
the point of impact and thereby retain greater control of its
direction.) Someone else had passed a ball through the service window of a parked ice cream van and out the other
side – a surely never-to-be-repeated feat, even with 10,000
further hours of practice. And yet another correspondent
was able to report knocking a ball over the wall and into
Wormwood Scrubs. Immediate dilemma: should they now
knock at the prison's giant oak door and say: 'Can we have
our ball back please?'

The show staged avid discussions about footballers who
most resembled female pop stars. In this category, the more
than superficial similarities between Emerson of Middlesbrough and Donna Summer did not go unnoticed. If there
was a 100-yard sprint for players with big noses, who would
get over the line first? Betting without Ian Rush, of course.
And then there was the Alphabet Soup challenge: two
people with bowls of the popular canned dish and spoons,
and the first to fish out letters spelling the name of an actual
footballer scores – 1–0. Letters back in, give it a good stir
and go again. Which is, of course, indefensible nonsense,
but it gives you your coach journey home.

There are two labels posthumously applied to 606 which I resist. The first places the show within the then prevalent 1990s 'lad' culture, which it had nothing to do with. It was always more fly than that, and had no connection that I can discern with Britpop or getting drunk or lairy. The second label, not unrelatedly, suggests that my role in all this was as some kind of 'shock jock'. True, I was frequently hot-foot from the latest ineptitude at Millwall and a certain amount of ire would frequently accompany me into the studio and work its way out of my system in the course of the hour. Consequently, I think it's legitimate to say that Bruce Rioch, Millwall's manager at the time, probably tuned into Classic FM on his post-match drive home.

It's possibly also the case that I marginally overstepped the mark by urging Spurs fans to boycott their club's merchandising, including programmes, on the grounds that nothing was likely to get the chairman Alan Sugar's attention like not receiving 30,000 people's money on a Saturday afternoon. Then I instructed them to take back the stuff they already owned and put it on the pitch. At this, Lord Sugar pointed out to me that he may have to look at the legal side of all this and, collar felt, I shut up. Lord Sugar and I married in 2002.

But far more common to the show was a spirit of cheerfully mischievous low-key disruption. During a long-running series on the unlikeliest items ever confiscated at the turnstiles (I think a breast milk pump probably swept the awards), it emerged that a steward at Torquay had removed from a home supporter a paperback book. What did they think he was going to do with it? Start an unruly book club? So I encouraged people to take a paperback to the next Torquay home game, in the hope of bringing an uncontainable flood of literature to the gates, and about 2,000 fans did so.

We would discuss ways to get into grounds for nothing, thereby hearing from a bloke who had acquired a Standard Liège tie and would write to clubs on his homemade Standard Liège headed notepaper, claiming that he and his mate were scouts for the Belgian side and could they have a pair together for the upcoming game? Nobody knocked them back and up they would rock, with the caller offering his club tie as his sole bona fides. Aston Villa rolled out the red carpet, saying they had a couple of youth team players that might be of interest and offering to screen them some videos. Similarly, when news broke of a fence down at Leeds we encouraged people to gather there and avail themselves of the free entry. Some of this, needless to say, did not go down well with the clubs in question.

606 gave birth to further similarly motivated adventures in broadcasting, across other platforms, with my great friend and cohort Danny Kelly, and the show also directly spawned the *Own Goals & Gaffs* video compilations, which allowed me to buy the solid gold library from which I type these words. Those videos arose from what seemed to me a fairly

obvious realisation that we care about good football, certainly, but not quite as much as we care about bad football. And by bad, I mean hopeless, inept howlers that still give their perpetrators nightmares. So, one Saturday, I casually floated the notion that all these 'Best of' and '100 greatest' videos were missing a trick. I was contacted the following Monday by Virgin Video. Boom time: the ensuing *Own Goals & Gaffs* videos sold by the cartload, along with their spin-off, *Freak Football*, a compilation of outlandish football turn-ups, such as QPR going 5–0 up against Newcastle by half-time, only for Newcastle to score five goals in the second half and then hit the bar in injury-time.

606 won awards and spawned imitators and when people talk about the evolution of football coverage in this country, I don't mind saying that I cough quietly and point at my chest. It was piratical and unrehearsed and in free-flow, as well as being, at times, wilfully unhinged and proudly unbalanced. In the halcyon period at the station, mentioned above, when my clout was at its maximum, an exec at the station had a conversation with my breakfast show producers, Ollie and Nick, wanting to make sure I was happy.

'Is there anything more we could be doing?' the controller asked. 'Is he getting all the guests he wants?'

The producers replied that, so far as they were aware, I was happy enough with the guests.

'Well, who would be his ideal guest?' asked the controller.

Now, at this point we are perhaps to imagine Ollie gently kicking Nick under the desk.

'I don't know,' said Ollie. 'He loves Frank Sinatra?'

'Are we getting him?' asked the controller, earnestly.

'Well, I don't think Sinatra is doing any press,' suggested Ollie, 'and certainly not the breakfast shows.'

'Well, has anyone put in the call?' said the controller.

'Really?' said Ollie. 'But what would we be wanting from him?'

And this is no word of a lie, the man said to my producers: 'I don't know, maybe he could come in and do the papers.'

Seriously. Can you imagine?

'So, time for our regular look at what's making the headlines this morning. And I'm pleased to say I'm joined in the studio by multi-platinum-selling showbusiness legend, Hoboken's very own Frank Sinatra. Frank, what's caught your eye this morning?'

'Well, there's this story in the *Express* about a pig that's rearing a litter of kittens . . .'

In some ways, of course, it would have been a coup if we could have swung it. At the same time, you would have to say this exchange took some beating.

But what could you do? The slogan had become 'Have your say'. In radio, 'have your say' means 'have your say, but only once it's been carefully filtered through the call-screeners, the executive producers, the producers and, ultimately, the presenter, who has somebody whispering in his ear who will have strong views about the direction this conversation containing your "say" should be taking'. And this, surely, you already know, because if it *is* 'your say', then they're picking some of the dullest people in the world. In practically every case, if the callers to 606 were sitting behind you on a train, you would get up and move.

Beware of the radio show that claims to be your show, and whose presenters insist they are like you and that it's your programme. Pure oil and moonshine. Surely that's your only duty as a broadcaster, as a writer, as an entertainer: to be not like everyone else. Otherwise, why are you there?

I think of my old man, who was always most affronted when someone on the radio said: 'It's your show, we want to hear from you.' My old man would call out in the direction of the speaker: 'Yeah? Well, you're the only fucker getting paid for it.' True dat, Dad.

CHAPTER TEN

'You have to say that's magnificent.'

In which GARY unpacks 1986 and all that: from the hand
(and shirt) of God to the shoulder of Bryan Robson,
and all points in between. Plus, some handy tips for
playing golf against presidents.

Mexico, 1986. The World Cup quarter-final, England v
Argentina, six minutes into the second half. Steve Hodge,
under pressure, hits a looping back pass into our penalty area,
not having noticed the run of Diego Maradona, who jumps
with Peter Shilton and, before you can say 'Hang on, that
was his hand, wasn't it?' the ball is in the back of our net.

I didn't see it. I was hanging around somewhere on the
halfway line and I had no proper view of the incident at
all – I can only recall the ball going in, the noise of the
crowd, and Maradona running out towards the right-hand
corner flag in exultation, because a phoney goal needs a

convincing celebration, clearly. As for the second goal he scored that day – the one often said to show the other, purer side of Maradona's character – if you had seen the state of the pitch, you would have known that he had no business scoring it. The turf at the Azteca Stadium was freshly relaid in small strips, with the result that the earth literally moved under your feet as you went about the place. It was like trying to change direction on a running machine. Making a run like the one Maradona made, for 40 yards, riding multiple challenges and retaining control of the ball while the ground slipped like an untethered stair carpet underneath him . . . there was some major-league sorcery going on there, most definitely.

Maradona himself now makes jokes about the 'Hand of God' goal. It's become a routine for him, a shtick – literally a punch-line. Some of my team-mates, on the other hand – Peter Shilton, Terry Butcher, Kenny Sansom – are still apoplectic. They still hate him for it, and the anger will never leave them.

Steve Hodge was angry about it, too, yet he swapped shirts with Maradona after the match. 'Awks', as the kids say these days. Hodge had stayed on the pitch doing a television interview and he found himself walking back down the tunnel at the same time as Maradona, and he couldn't resist. He made the universally understood 'care to swap?' gesture, Maradona peeled off his shirt, and the deal was done.

Hodge got a lot of flak from some of the team, coming

into the dressing room with that blue garment scrunched up in his hand – the robe of the devil. 'How could you? That cheating bastard!' However, current estimates put the value of the 'Hand of God' shirt at £250,000, so maybe Steve was right to take the longer view. The shirt is now on display in the National Football Museum in Manchester, credited to 'The Steve Hodge Collection'. Before that it was in Nottingham Castle alongside Torvill and Dean's Bolero costumes from 1984 – which are not from the Steve Hodge Collection, so far as I am aware.

The big question, though, is whether Steve Hodge's shirt is still in the Diego Maradona Collection. Perhaps we'll never know.

Anyway, I'm not one of those who is still angry. Obviously, I would much rather Maradona hadn't done what he did – hadn't punched us out of a World Cup that we might well have gone on to win. (I will never be persuaded that the 1986 World Cup was not winnable by England.) At the same time, he got away with it – so, to a certain extent, congratulations to him, I guess. If anything, I was more angry with the officials than with Maradona. All these years later, I think the linesman saw it – and I think the linesman bottled it. There was no way the referee could have seen what happened. The linesman, though? I reckon he could see it, and I reckon he did see it. But he didn't have the courage to put up his flag.

Ah, well. It was never going to end conventionally, somehow. Mexico '86 was a tournament in which misfortune, slapstick and moments of dark comedy seemed to follow us all the way. Much went right along the journey – but an awful lot went wrong.

I should have recognised that this was not going to be a straightforward campaign when my World Cup nearly ended during a warm-up game in Vancouver. The team had been flown out to America, in advance of the tournament, to train for altitude and then for extreme heat, in anticipation of the fact that we would be playing in temperatures in the low 40s. We went to Colorado and exercised in giant steam rooms, doing press-ups and all sorts with a hot Bobby Robson shouting at us. Then we flew up to Vancouver to play Canada in one last friendly before the tournament, during which I managed to fall over and bring my whole weight down on my wrist. There was pain like I had never known. I had to be given gas and air and if you had given me the option to end it then and there, I might well have taken it. Given the amount of pain I was in, I thought there was no way I hadn't completely broken it. In which case, that was it: I was out. Fortunately, the hospital scan showed only a small fracture and not a proper break, but it still meant I would now be wearing a thin plastic cast during the tournament, wrapped with a bandage. The cast couldn't be plaster of Paris or anything more substantial because of the risk I would injure other players with it. Even so, it was just what you needed in 40-degree heat – an extra coating of bandage. Also, the pain didn't leave. In a full-on sprint, the pressure of the wind against the cast would cause the wrist to hurt, and falling down on it, which I did regularly in the course of the tournament, would set it right off again. I played through a lot of pain in that World Cup. Still, better a hand than a foot, I guess.

All this happened very soon after Bryan Robson, our captain, dislocated his shoulder – something which seemed to be a bit of a hobby for him around this time. He had done so early in the previous season, in a game for Manchester United, when Bryan had the unusual misfortune of injuring himself by falling on to the electrics box that powered Old Trafford's undersoil heating. Who put that there? He then dislocated it for a second time in a fifth-round FA Cup tie at West Ham. This was only three months before the World Cup and at that point there were real doubts about whether he would be able to travel to Mexico at all. Back he came, though, and all seemed well until the warm-up game against Mexico in Los Angeles, when Bryan made a sliding tackle and his shoulder elected not to slide with him. That time the physio pushed it straight back in and soon after Bryan was reporting no ill-effects.

When we got to Mexico, Bryan's shoulder was still in its socket where it ought to be, but he fell heavily during the opening defeat to Portugal, and we all held our breath for a moment. Again, though, he seemed to be unscathed. However, nearing half-time in the second of the group stage games, against Morocco, he attempted to go around a defender and got pulled back by the arm, and out popped the shoulder again. This time there was no quick fix. He left the pitch in tears of frustration, his World Cup over before it had really started.

There's an air of unreality about any World Cup – a sense that you've crossed over into some kind of parallel universe, operating according to its own laws. And that was especially the case in Mexico, where the team was taken everywhere with an armed guard, not just in an accompanying vehicle, but actually on board the bus. Simple Minds' 'Alive and Kicking' (our appointed theme song) would be playing through the speakers, the squad would be sitting in their various groups and blithely playing cards, and a Mexican with a huge machine gun would be standing in the aisle. This just came to seem normal.

We stayed at a hotel in Saltillo, chosen for its proximity to the training ground, but, that convenience aside, a rather blank-faced and unlovely place at that time. It also had a wide range of non-flushing lavatories and a hot water supply which went from patchy to non-existent. There is a famous photograph of Bobby Robson on one of the hotel's balconies, after we lost that opening game, with his head clamped in his hands, staring down in the direction of the swimming pool with a distant expression on his face. It was used widely in the press to suggest that the England manager was already in a state of despair – the 'fool on the hill', as one writer dismissively described him.

A tortured man? Alone with his darkest thoughts? The truth is, at that exact moment, Bobby was pressing the headphones of a Walkman to his ears and listening to a recording of himself on *Desert Island Discs* – specifically the point in the programme, he would later relate, where he requested 'The Girl from Ipanema', sung by Astrud Gilberto. Which, in so many ways, would have been a better story for the papers. But never mind.

Two games in, on the brink of elimination, with only one point on the board, with Bryan Robson injured and with Ray Wilkins suspended following the out-of-character ball-throwing incident that I mentioned earlier, Bobby Robson clearly had to change something. The partnership up front between Mark Hateley and myself hadn't produced a single goal in the tournament. Indeed, I hadn't scored for England since October 1985. At that point, it could so easily have been me who got the chop. Instead, he took out Mark and brought in Peter Beardsley. It all changed after that. Beardsley supplied some of the spark and invention which we had lacked and, playing for our lives against Poland, having scored no England goals in eight months, I had scored three goals by half-time. In many ways, Mexico '86 was a life-changing tournament for me: it established me as an England player and on the global scene, and was the catalyst for so much of what went on to happen in my career. Yet in another version of the story, not so far removed from the reality, I don't make it beyond the second game. Such are the margins.

Having pulled it together and made our way out of the group stage, we moved into Mexico City. But the slapstick continued. There was an indoor tennis court beside the hotel where Chelsea's Kerry Dixon, in a four with John Barnes, Chris Waddle and Chris Woods, somehow managed to smack himself in the face with his own racket, opening a wound between his eyebrows that needed stitches. From then on Kerry had to wear a gauze dressing over the wound, which he was under strict instruction not to get wet. This made washing his hair a bit complicated. It's touching to relate, however, that members of the squad helped out by washing it for him. I'm not sure whether Kerry remotely imagined, when he set out for Mexico with the England squad, that he would one day get a shampoo from Ray Wilkins, but clearly dreams do come true.

In the middle of all this I was tapped up by Barcelona. There had been some whispers about this possibly happening. Howard Kendall at Everton had taken me aside, in the closing stages of the season, and mentioned that Barça, who were managed by Terry Venables, had been showing some interest. Which was obviously exciting to hear, although I felt I'd only really just arrived at Everton and it was possibly a little soon to be thinking about moving again. Whatever, it all went quiet, and then the World Cup came around. At that point I told my agent, Jon Holmes, that I didn't want to be distracted at all and that he was to fend off calls until the tournament was over, whoever those calls were from.

Then, one afternoon, out in Monterrey, I was summoned to the phone in the hotel reception. This was the pre-mobile age, and also the age in which phoning abroad from a hotel was ruinously expensive. Accordingly, the rule was that you were allowed one phone call home per week and could receive one incoming call – like being in the army or at boarding school or something. Anyway, on this occasion, it was my agent. 'I know you said that I wasn't to disturb you,' Jon said, 'but Barcelona are saying that they want you. However, you have to agree to sign with them now, or they're going to walk away.'

Obviously, this was great news, in a sense – but great news at altogether the wrong time. I was in the middle of a World Cup, playing for England. I didn't want to be thinking about next season. I certainly didn't want to be weighing up the pros and cons of moving, or thinking about the logistics of starting a new life in another country. I couldn't have had all that in my head. I wanted to be able to concentrate absolutely on the job in hand. So I told Jon to explain to Barcelona that I wasn't in a position to consider their offer at the moment. I said: 'If they want me now, they'll still want me at the end of the World Cup.' And then I hung up, hoping I was right.

We beat Paraguay 3–0 in the first of the knockout rounds. I got two goals and an elbow in the throat in an off-the-ball, hit-and-run incident involving a Paraguayan midfielder which the referee didn't pick up on. And after that it was the quarter-finals, and Argentina. Even at this stage the possibility of chaos always seemed to be present. For some reason we weren't given permission to train at the Azteca Stadium the day before the match, which was the conventional courtesy. Instead we were relocated to a nearby club ground. This would have been fine, except that all the changing rooms at this particular ground were locked, presumably because nobody had been given notice of our arrival. We ended up getting changed outside on the pitch. Here we were, on the eve of the national side's biggest game in 16 years, and we felt like a park side on a Sunday morning when the groundsman hasn't shown up with the keys.

Still, in all honesty, there was probably no amount of careful preparation that could have helped us cope with Maradona that day. Maybe Bobby Robson should have tried the Brian Clough method for handling him. Clough was in charge of Nottingham Forest in 1983 when they came up against Barcelona in a pre-season friendly. Maradona was in the Barcelona team at the Nou Camp that night and, according to Steve Hodge, who was part of that Nottingham Forest side, Clough approached the Argentinian when the teams were lined up in the tunnel, looked him up and down and said: 'You might be able to play a bit, but I can still grab you by the balls.' Whereupon Clough reached down and did just that, before turning and heading on out to the pitch.

Well, whatever works. Then again, in the 28th minute

of that game, clearly unaffected by Clough's manhandling, Maradona slalomed through most of the Forest defence to score a goal which, with hindsight, looks eerily like some kind of dress rehearsal for the wonder goal he scored against England three years later. Barcelona ended up winning 2–0 and the only conclusion one can draw is that there is more to this management lark than the odd bit of intimidation in the tunnel.

In that quarter-final in Mexico, I pulled one back for 2–1, from a cross by John Barnes, who had been sent on as a sub. We were criticised for playing within ourselves and for only really coming out and giving it a go once we were 2–0 down. But at the risk of stating the obvious, it's easier to play like you've got nothing to lose when you've got nothing to lose. Throwing ourselves forward, we almost equalised in the 87th minute – another cross from Barnes, right to the back post that I managed to get to, but could only head into the back of Julio Olarticoechea, the Argentina defender. A few minutes later we were out.

In the process of going for that last chance, I fell forward and collided with the post, injuring my knee – the medial ligament, to be technical about it. The perfect ending, really. Nothing was ever said about this, but the fact is, even if we had advanced, I wouldn't have been able to play any further part in the tournament. I would have been replaced in the semi-final, most likely by Mark Hateley. Hateley didn't know I was injured and probably won't know, unless he reads this, that he could have played in a World Cup semi-final – and, who knows, given that our opponents in that semi would have been Belgium, who were not the force they later became, maybe he would have ended up playing in a final, too.

As it was, I flew back to London and had my first dabble in a BBC television World Cup studio, with Des Lynam, Terry Venables, Lawrie McMenemy and a variety of decorative pot plants. (Add your own joke here.) Nothing was finalised, but rumours that I might be leaving Everton to join Terry at Barcelona were now quite widespread and Des did his journalistic duty by asking the pair of us, live on air, what was going on there. McMenemy, rather magnificently, got the hump at this, insisting that we were all 'out of order' for having the conversation, and adding that the person to whom Lynam really ought to be addressing questions about my future was Howard Kendall, the Everton manager. What I managed to say to Des was: 'I shall be playing for the team I want to be playing for next season.' What a diplomat!

Anyway, the point of me being in the studio was to watch the final, hoping that Maradona wouldn't score so that I would win the Golden Boot. And he didn't. And I did. Which I may have mentioned . . .

Since then I must have forgiven Maradona for 1986 to some extent because I have made two films about him for the BBC, one more successful than the other. The first time around, he proved somewhat elusive. I had flown over to

Argentina for three days on a promise of an interview with him for a programme we were doing about Golden Boot winners, but there was no sign of it coming together. On the downside: no Maradona. On the upside: I got invited to play golf with the President of Argentina, Carlos Menem, which doesn't happen to me very often. So off I went, to a very chic course, where I was put in a foursome in which the President partnered an ex-professional and I teamed up with one of the President's friends.

And, of course, it was fascinating. Menem had been imprisoned during the 1976 coup and had been in jail in 1978, when Argentina hosted the tournament and beat Holland in the final, and when Mario Kempes won the Golden Boot, and we talked about all of that on the way round. Then, somewhere around the eighth hole, he asked me whether I had yet managed to speak to Maradona for my programme, and I conceded that, in fact, it wasn't working out too well and that, as yet, we hadn't been able to reach him. Whereupon the President of Argentina said: 'Let me call him for you.' Without further ado, he took out his phone and dialled a number. 'Diego!' he said, and a short conversation ensued in Spanish, at the end of which the President snapped his phone shut, turned to me and said: 'He'll do it.'

I thought, this is brilliant. This is how you get an interview with Maradona: by being the President of Argentina.

The round of golf continued, and I might as well tell

you what happened at the end of it because this, too, is an interesting study in the way power works. Eventually, with the scores all square, I found myself getting ready to tee off at the 18th. As I was taking a few practice swings, my partner, the President's friend, stepped across and quietly said: 'We don't win this hole.'

'Sorry?'

'We don't win this hole,' he repeated. 'The President never loses.'

Ah, I got it: protocol. You hear about this kind of thing on the golf course. Powerful people must be deferred to. Presidents must be kept happy. Well, OK. I was a guest, after all. Looking down the fairway, I saw that there was a large water hazard off to the left, well within reach. If I could stick the ball in there, my diplomatic duty would be done.

So once again I got ready to play my ball, planning the shot which would convincingly land me off the fairway for the President's benefit. I may even have been drawing the club back, getting ready to swing, when the thought suddenly popped into my head: hang on . . . what? No, screw that. Lose deliberately? This is golf. I'm not doing that.

I drew the club back and sent the ball as close to plumb down the middle of the fairway as I could manage. My playing partner was discreetly incensed. 'What are you doing?' he hissed. I could only wince and shrug, as if to say 'Look, I was trying to find the water . . .'

We ended up halving the hole and tying the match, and I must admit, as the President walked across the green at the end to shake my hand, I did slightly wonder about the wisdom of what I had just done, at the geopolitical level. Maybe he would regretfully inform me that the battle for the Falklands was back on. Far from it, in fact. 'Thank you for trying,' he said, as if true competition was something he had been secretly longing for, but which nobody around him would permit him to have.

The next day in Buenos Aires was spent doing some more filming, after which I went to bed. I didn't think much more about the President's urgent call-out from the green to Maradona. At around three o'clock in the morning, though, I was woken up by the phone ringing in my hotel room. It was President Menem. 'Diego will do an interview with you now if you can get to . . .' And he mentioned the name of what was evidently some nightclub in the centre of Buenos Aires.

But what could I do? It was three in the morning. I would have had to scramble the crew together, get all our gear over to this nightclub . . . It would have been past dawn by the time we all got there, by which point who knew whether Maradona would still be in the building. I found myself thanking the President for his efforts on our behalf, but conceding that an interview for our purposes might not be entirely possible at this time. Fame keeps its own hours, clearly. And so do presidents, it would seem.

The last time I saw Maradona was in Moscow at the draw for the 2018 World Cup finals. I was presenting it and he was attending as a guest, one of eight star players representing the victorious World Cup nations. This was an unusually tough presenting job from my point of view because there were so many possible permutations at every stage. A computer was hard at work in the background, and I had a voice in my ear relating why certain things meant that other things would now have to happen so I could pass that information on to the viewers . . . We must have spent about three days rehearsing it, trying to get all the eventualities covered.

In fact, as it happened, the draw went off fairly simply and, through the luck of the numbers, most of the truly complicated scenarios requiring further explanation didn't arise. Even so, I felt quite relieved afterwards to have got through the event unscathed and I was quite proud of the job that I had done. When I went behind the scenes, Maradona came up and gave me one of the huge hugs that he goes in for, and he complimented me on getting through the complexities of the draw without falling on my face.

'You know what?' he said. 'You were all right as a footballer. But as a TV host, you might almost have been as good as me.'

Thanks for that, Diego.

CHAPTER ELEVEN

'They're looking the more likely at the moment.'

In which DANNY and GARY attempt in vain to solve the 5,000-piece puzzle that is Paul Gascoigne.

DANNY

We come at last, in this compendium of marvels, to what is arguably the story that has everything. It is certainly the story that has Paul Gascoigne, a cage full of hungry tigers and a horse's head, so if you've got all three of those on the card in front of you, now is the time to rocket from your seat and claim bingo.

Return in your mind, if you will, to the year 2003, and transport yourself as best your imagination can to the city of Lanzhou, the capital of Gansu province in China, the setting for our tale. It is not, perhaps, the most romantic or glamorous of settings, being a largely industrial city on the edge of a featureless desert and not altogether the Western tourist's first choice of likely Chinese hotspots. Lanzhou is twinned with Chorley in Lancashire, although we can draw no especially helpful conclusions from that. But it is also, critically for our story, a city which boasts a good-sized and amply stocked zoo – unlike Chorley, as it happens, whose residents, a review of the map reveals, are obliged to go to Chester or Blackpool for their captive tiger needs.

This was in the brief period when Gazza, fast approaching the end of his playing career, was living in China, having made the pioneering but eventually ill-starred decision to sign for Gansu Tianma. It was also a period – it was evident from talking to him about it – when Gazza was monumentally bored. And when we say Gazza was bored, we are, let's be clear, speaking about someone who has always had a world-leading need to guard himself against inactivity. Gazza's boredom threshold was so tiny that it was invisible to the naked eye and, indeed, the scientific instrument will probably never be invented that could accurately register it. In the days when he and I knocked about together he was beset by a constantly questing need to fill the blank moment, to occupy time – to make life just that little bit more interesting at any point than life was automatically making itself. It was the aspect of his character which, in my warmly cherished experience, made him such electric and extraordinarily good company and which has also no doubt contributed significantly to his well-documented troubles.

China, however, was a particular challenge to Gazza. His agent appears to have kept him company some of the time but, for the most part, his friends were thousands of miles away, in a different time zone. The culture was spectacularly alien to him. And there were, inevitably, after training and his duties to his football club were completed, long afternoons and evenings to fill. It was an obvious recipe for disaster, in a way, although, at the same time, the period drove him to perhaps some of his greatest feats of ingenuity.

For instance, there happened to be an ornamental pond in front of the hotel where Gazza was billeted, containing a host of koi carp. Most people wouldn't have thought too much about it. But one day, in need, as ever, of something to do, Gazza found a stick of bamboo in the hotel grounds, used his hotel room's complimentary sewing pack to furnish himself with some thread and a needle, which he carefully bent, and brought these materials together to fashion a primitive fishing rod. And thus equipped, he went and sat by that ornamental pond and fished for its koi carp.

Keep your fly fishing for salmon in the River Tay; here was sport of the highest order. Gazza successfully hooked one, too. His bait? Another imaginatively repurposed item from the hotel's complimentary offerings: a biscuit. More specifically, the Chinese equivalent, Gazza recounted, of the biscuit known to the Western world as a Jammie Dodger. Ornamental koi carp can't get enough of Jammie Dodgers, apparently. All the fishing magazines will tell you so.

On other days, though, when, for whatever reason, the ornamental carp weren't biting, Gazza would find himself filling an idle hour at the Lanzhou zoo. He would go there frequently, apparently, and especially enjoyed being there, as people do, for feeding time. And what Gazza particularly liked was feeding time for the tigers. And why not? A hungry tiger is a sight to behold, and when the zookeeper arrived outside the tiger cage to toss meat from a plastic tub into the pen, and the tigers within grew agitated and noisy in anticipation, Gazza would be a regular and enthusiastic spectator.

In fact, such a regular was Gazza that he got to know the zookeeper a little bit and to engage with him in conversation, as much as was possible across one of the world's bigger language barriers. One thing Gazza was keen to know was exactly what it was that the tigers were finding so delicious from the zookeeper's plastic tub. The zookeeper was able to furnish Gazza with this piece of information. The answer was: lumps of raw horsemeat.

In due course, though, watching the tigers get fed was not enough for Gazza. He conceived a desire to do the feeding himself. Flinging offal over a fence to hungry and dangerous zoo animals? Who doesn't have that on their literal bucket list of life's must-dos? Gazza certainly did, and he now embarked on a campaign of pleading with his new friend the zookeeper to be allowed to serve the meal. No doubt in accordance with the strict regulations regarding public tiger feeding, the zookeeper was initially reluctant to let him. But Gazza, typically, was both persistent and charming and eventually the zookeeper relented, agreeing, one afternoon, to allow Gazza the opportunity that he so clearly craved to lob one of his pieces of horse tiger-wards.

So, a delighted Gazza went to the tub to choose his weapon. Now, it probably goes without saying that your tiger, even in captivity, doesn't need his or her luncheon pre-cut into bite-sized portions. Not for them the dainty 'minced morsel' of dog-food legend. They like a serving on the bone that they can properly work on, something more in keeping with conditions in the wild. Consequently, it probably shouldn't unduly surprise us that, as Gazza ruminatively browsed the zookeeper's tub that day, he discovered that, among the various large joints of gristly offal prepared for the tigers' delectation (flanks and thighs and God knows what else), was an entire horse's head. Or, as Gazza's Geordie accent had it, in his gleeful retelling of this tale, 'a horse's heed'.

For Gazza, as a novice tiger-feeder, this seemed to be the perfect cut and he duly lifted it from the tub. It was wet, Gazza reported, and slightly slimy, and a little hard to hold. Nevertheless, it definitely looked like the business to the hungry tigers, who began to approach the bars of their cage excitedly, slavering at the very sight of it. Their enthusiasm inspired Gazza to protract the moment for a while by holding the meat towards the cage but out of reach. Thus taunted, the hungry tigers would roar and paw the bars – which only inspired Gazza to continue with the taunting, jabbing the horse's head at the bars and, for good measure, doing some roaring of his own, by way of giving as good as he was getting. This teasing went on for some time – the tigers pawing and roaring, Gazza prodding and also roaring – until the zookeeper eventually stepped in to urge Gazza to put the animals out of their misery and send the meat over.

It goes without saying that the head was quite heavy and Gazza realised he would need to give it a fair old hoick in order to clear the bars. So he stepped back and, holding the head in two hands, with arms extended, as you might hold a heavy sack, began to swing it, twisting at the hips, gathering momentum and getting ready to put his shoulders into it at the point of release.

Calamity! As Gazza swung the meat back for the last time, and at the extreme limit of his two-handed backswing, the slipperiness of the meaty missile got the better of him. He entirely lost his grip, the 'horse's heed' flew behind him, in the exact opposite of its intended direction, travelled through the air over a nearby wall and came to rest with a soft thud in the penguin enclosure.

Is Gazza the only England player in history to have fed raw horsemeat to penguins, inadvertently or otherwise? Without even consulting the record books, or checking the exact wording on the plaques on Gary Lineker's extensive range of commemorative trophies, I hazard that he is – and, furthermore, that this distinction may long outlive him as history further unfolds. But oh, to have been present that day and to have witnessed these scenes in Lanzhou zoo – a moment of golden slapstick with the power, surely, to cheer up even the most downcast of on-looking pandas.

Of course, with Gazza, the scrapes and the pranks are legion – an industry, frankly. Like the one where Middlesbrough buy an expensive new coach and as part of the deal the players all have to put their suits on and be photographed in front of it. And while everyone is getting ready, Gazza nips out and persuades the driver to let him drive the coach around the corner and park it out of sight, so that when everybody emerged for the photo session, it would look as though the coach had been stolen. All good, harmless fun. Except that, as he gets to the corner, Gazza misjudges the turn slightly and wipes one side of the brand new coach on a bollard. Massive bollockings ensue.

Or there's the one where Alan Shearer is outside filming an interview for *Football Focus*, blithely unaware that Gazza has stationed himself on a nearby balcony with a bullhorn. And thus Shearer's piece to camera is interrupted by a very familiar crackly voice, saying: 'Shearer: stop pretending you're educated. You're just a thick fucking Geordie like me.'

Prank upon prank, scrape upon scrape, and all of it born of the cosmic boredom which was at once Gazza's greatest boon and his sorest affliction. I've seen him tire of sitting in a London traffic jam, jump from the taxi that was carrying us both and persuade a workman in the adjacent roadworks (health and safety people, look away now) to let him have a go with his pneumatic drill. A small section of London's pavement enthusiastically, if needlessly, pummelled, Gazza then rejoined me in the taxi, another dull moment filled.

Or there were the more carefully considered, more slowly matured bits – the set-pieces, if you will. My friend Danny Kelly and I used to do our Saturday night radio show in central London and then, when it finished at 7pm, adjourn to a nearby pub – frequently the Nellie Dean. And one evening we were in there as usual, just sitting in the corner, chatting. I think Danny went to the bar first, and came back with the drinks, and in due course, I went up to order a second round. As I stood waiting for the barman to finish pouring, the bloke next to me, sitting on a stool, hunched over his pint, said: 'Here, you're on the telly ain't you, mate?'

I turned to the figure who had spoken. He was wearing someone's jacket that was too big for him and somebody else's glasses and the grin of someone still further who was exceptionally pleased with himself. It was Gazza – Gazza in thin disguise. Knowing we would eventually arrive, he had inserted himself in the pub before 7 and then, no doubt chortling inwardly the while, had remained 'in character' even as Danny and I sat just a few feet away and drank and talked. Gazza must have been on that stool, in that jacket and those glasses, for more than an hour – which, whatever else you want to say about it, demonstrated an extremely high level of dedication to the gag.

The first time I met him was in the summer of 1990, when we were brought together to make a video, *Gazza: The Real Me!* – a media mission which, incidentally, saw me bound effortlessly into the car park at Tottenham's training ground with a microphone in hand to interview a fresh-faced Gary Lineker. As I didn't say to the Golden Boot-winning England striker that morning: 'One day they will invent podcasting and you and I will gather in your kitchen to create history and reflect fondly on this germinal moment of togetherness.'

Gazza, though? The popular label, courtesy of Bobby Robson originally, was 'daft as a brush'. Well, yes, you could see why it took hold. But the Gazza I knew was also smart as a whip. If he felt under pressure to do so, he would give people what they appeared to want: he would do the silly faces and the burping into the microphones and the plastic tits on the top of the bus. But that was so far from being the whole story.

He had a trophy room at his house – four shelves from the ground upwards, heaving with silverware. But, when you looked at them closely, only about a third of these cups and medals and statuettes were for football. The rest were for table tennis, running, snooker . . . He was patently a sporting prodigy – a kind of Rainman of sport. It all seemed to come easily to him. Even now, when he plays people at snooker, he has to use the thick end of the cue. When he plays people at table tennis, he has to use his hands, rather than the bat. When he plays people at darts, he has to throw with the sharp end pointing at his nose. These handicaps have to be introduced to keep it alive, or else there is no challenge to it. In some sense – and, in the end, dangerously – that's his whole approach to life.

I introduced him to Chris Evans and the three of us had some enlivening nights out and a lot of fun – some of the best fun I've ever had, in truth, in a life that has not been short of it. At the same time, all that stuff about 'The Three Muske-Beers' that the newspapers drummed up out of our social alliance was such nonsense. The problem was that, feeling we had nothing to hide, we chose to go openly to pubs, rather than sneak into secluded hotel bars or secrete ourselves in off-limits media dens like the Groucho Club. And then we would get papped and the impression would very easily be given by the more piratical quarters of the press that we had been in there all day. To be fair, in Chris's case that might occasionally have been true, for this was a period in Chris's life when he could certainly tie one on. Gazza, though, was, at that stage, an utterly hopeless drinker who would switch to Cokes as soon as the company would tolerate it. Beer? Maybe. Spirits? Forget it. Bear in mind that he was part of a culture where hard drinking was the norm and, to some extent, the measure of you. It troubled him that he couldn't do it, that he wasn't keeping up. People would ply him, of course, generously standing him unasked-for shorts to accompany his pint, but he had perfected the technique of reaching below the table and surreptitiously emptying his glass into the carpet.

Nevertheless, the story flew. 'There they go – the lads on the lash.' It was a legend that I certainly found amusing, at the age of 32 with two kids. Twenty-four-hour benders? I couldn't do that when I was 16, let alone at 32 with a school run to complete most mornings. To some extent, I found it flattering. I was perfectly happy with the growing myth that we were the new Burton, O'Toole and Harris. But a myth is exactly what it was and our evenings together were not the bottle-heavy orgies of unbridled self-indulgence that the media, with its own agenda, made them seem.

There's the one photograph in particular, which, heaven knows, has now been picked over and scrutinised for tell-tale details more thoroughly than the Zapruder footage of the Kennedy assassination. It's the three of us – me, Gazza and Chris – together at a 'London bash', as the newspaper captions like to describe it, and the concise message this widely distributed image most immediately conveys (I can't deny this) is: pissheads.

Bear with me, though. The picture is taken shortly after midday. None of us is drunk, nor even a fraction of a sheet to the wind. I am in a duffel coat, because there had been talk that the three of us might spend the afternoon at the races. Instead we have diverted, through thick London traffic, to a lunchtime broadcasting awards ceremony to which Chris has belatedly remembered that he was invited. A table has been hastily found for us, but the fuss our three-fold presence seems to be causing is already making this appear to have been a bad idea, and we will shortly offer our apologies and our thanks and leave. Gazza is wearing dark glasses, and he's not really even smiling in the picture, except perhaps rather tensely, because he's a Rangers player and it's not clear that he's even supposed to be in London at this point and the thought of being exposed to his notoriously forthright manager, Walter Smith, is nagging at him. The highly visible bottle neck, conveniently cropped in the later, more incriminating uses of the snap, is actually Highland Spring sparkling mineral water. That's fine: I know how the game works. But you're fighting an uphill battle, of course, because the legend is so much more compelling than the truth.

At worst, Gazza was guilty at this time of a rather gloriously innocent recklessness. Take the night in late March 1996 when England played a friendly against Bulgaria at Wembley. Terry Venables told Gazza in advance that he was going to sub him off after about 80 minutes, and Gazza passed this information on to me and Chris. He also drew us a map of the service roads at the back of Wembley, in behind the industrial estate, and told us to bring a car and be outside a specific metal door ten minutes before the end of the game so that we could pick him up and beat the traffic getting away.

Chris and I hired a people carrier and drove over, listening to the game on the car radio. I don't think either of us really thought this plan would come to fruition, but, sure enough, as we were nearing Wembley, exactly as foretold, the commentator announced that Paul Gascoigne was coming off and being replaced by Robert Lee. So we duly drew up outside the appointed door with the engine running and the game still going on inside the stadium. Moments later the door opened and out came Gazza in his England strip with his street shoes on, and carrying his kit bag. He ran across to the car, jumped in and said: 'Right, where are we going?'

Chris lived in west London at the time and proposed a pub down that way but Gazza was understandably thirsty after his efforts in what would turn out, in the course of time, to have been a hard-earned 1–0 victory, and he was keen that we should get a can of something for the journey. Accordingly, just a few minutes down the road from Wembley Stadium, the car pulled up outside a fairly crowded pub.

Chris jumps out and heads inside to get the beers and, rather to my surprise, Gazza gets out, too. There are clusters of people standing outside with their drinks, because it's a warm, early-spring evening, and, rather to their surprise, these people are now joined by England's Paul Gascoigne, who eagerly engages them in conversation. Through the pub windows, the night's match can be seen continuing on the telly, while here on the pavement one of the players who as recently as ten minutes ago was gracing that match, is standing about in his England strip, minus the boots, with a lit cigarette, chatting to the clientele. Meanwhile, traffic is passing and Gazza is standing with his back to it, and people are no doubt thinking: 'Look at that sad bastard with the number 8 on his back, dressed up in the full kit.'

Eventually, Chris emerges and Gazza is persuaded to get back into the car and continue our journey south, all as if this were entirely regular behaviour – which, of course, it was, or would have been, if one of us hadn't been Paul Gascoigne.

Or there was the time Gazza and I had arranged to meet at Champneys health club in London and Gazza walked into reception smoking a cigar. Now even the most superficial of acquaintances with health club etiquette would inform you that cigar-smoking in the spa environment is frowned upon. But Gazza wasn't trying to flout the rules, or being wilfully controversial. He was just . . . smoking, at the wrong time, in the wrong place. And, being Gazza, as soon as this was pointed out to him, he was immediately full of sincere apologies for his thoughtlessness.

'Gazza! What are you doing? You can't smoke in here!'

'Oh, yeah, yeah, sorry, sorry.'

But what does he then do? Looking around hastily for somewhere to extinguish the cigar (and, for very obvious reasons, failing to see an ashtray), his eyes alight on the electric fan positioned on the reception counter. And before anybody can intervene, Gazza reaches forward and stubs his cigar out on the plastic hub at the centre of the fan's protective frame. Whereupon the air generated by the fan sends a thick spray of smoke, ash and flecks of mashed brown tobacco right across the room.

Welcome to Champneys, Mr Gascoigne.

Again, of course, he is mortified. There was no malice in this act, no pre-meditation of any kind. It was just what he found himself doing. Why would you enter a spa with a cigar on the go? And why, having done so, would you then choose to extinguish that cigar on the nearest available electric fan? If we knew the answers to those questions, we would perhaps be some little way closer to understanding the enigma of Paul Gascoigne. But we still wouldn't have solved it entirely, and I don't suppose anybody ever will.

It was as true on the field as off it: he didn't behave in ways you were expected to behave. He didn't do it like you were supposed to do it. Yet, to the infuriation, I think, of people like Glenn Hoddle, he was still better than everyone else regardless. For many of his contemporaries, I suspect it was like Salieri with Mozart: how could you put this unearthly talent in this apparent child? You would be bound to feel affronted. Players who were great suddenly found themselves eclipsed by someone who appeared, superficially, from certain angles, to be a cartoon.

I sat with him after a game once, when he was playing for Middlesbrough, and he pulled his trouser leg up slightly to scratch his calf, at which point I caught a glimpse of what looked to me like a quite shocking bruise.

'Paul, your leg!'

With that, he pulled the trouser leg all the way up to the knee. I couldn't believe the state of the limb that he thereby exposed: it was a mass of lumps, bruises, stud marks, cuts. I had never seen damage like it. Superficial it might have been, but it looked as though somebody had recently pulled him from a car wreck. And I somewhat naively asked: 'Who did that?' He said: 'Well, it's every game, isn't it?' And he gave me a look that said: 'What do you think happens in football matches?'

When you walked up the street with him, his presence would literally stop traffic. I've never been with a star like it, in that sense. Buses would halt, workers would pause from their labours, pedestrians would change direction and run to him. An extremely self-conscious person, he didn't quite know how to position himself inside that. When he was at Lazio, I went to restaurants in Rome with him, and the place would rise to applaud him as he came in, and the staff would guide him in formation to his table, and great heaving platters of food would arrive at the table unbidden in his honour. And a lot of stars would be perfectly easy with such treatment and even consider it their due. But it bothered Gazza. It embarrassed him and rendered him uneasy, and he didn't know how to accept it, so he would end up in the middle of the restaurant doing tricks, or juggling bread rolls, or playing the part of the waiter for a while and serving the other tables, all in an effort to justify the treatment he was getting, which he couldn't ever quite feel he deserved or understood. And thus the whole 'Gazza being Gazza' thing would snowball.

That self-consciousness could make him a confusing person to meet, too. People would approach him and he would reflexively, almost defensively, say: 'Did you come alone or are you on your own?' And moving on, he would say: 'Moscow! Moustache!' He had a favourite cartoon: it was that one where a child in school draws a picture of his mum, with a huge head and jagged hair and a crinkly smile – a typical child's drawing. And in the next frame we're outside the school where the parents are waiting to pick up their kids – and there's the kid's mum, with the huge head and jagged hair and crinkly smile, exactly as portrayed. Paul loved that joke and told it, with great relish, over and over. '. . . and then you see her outside the school, and she's got a massive heed!' And sometimes autograph hunters would find that, without explanation, he had drawn them a version of that picture and signed it 'With best wishes, Massive Heed'. And people would think 'What's that about?' They thought it was an act, maybe. But it wasn't. It was Gazza being genuinely, magnificently unhinged.

Ironically, given the on-the-town myth that expanded, what he seemed to enjoy most about our friendship was coming to stay at my house in Deptford and getting to share a bit of domestic security: a sense of family life, with the kids, the meals, the noise. I think he drew immense reassurance from the solidity of that. You would suppose, perhaps, that bringing Gazza home would be like inviting a tornado to touch down in your living room – that five hours later you would be searching for your loved ones in a pile of ash and cushion-stuffing. On the contrary, you would hardly notice he was there. He always went to the door when he wanted a cigarette, because he wouldn't smoke in the house. The paparazzi would be out the front, in search, no doubt, of something incriminating, but what they were missing, more often than not, was the sight of Gazza lying stretched out on the sofa watching the telly, and mumbling to himself the constant monologue that he engaged in when he wasn't conversing.

'This is it. Stay in. Staying in. Door's shut. Fook off, that's me in now. Done. Door's shut. Telly's on. Love it. In. IN.'

Sleeping over on our couch, Gazza would crash spark out at about 11.45. An hour later, he would wake up again and the insomnia would kick in. He would then spend much of the early hours watching television, sleeping fitfully. By then, I would have long since gone to bed, rousing him briefly on the way out to point out the water I had left for him, the biscuits, the snacks, the pile of videos – and reminding him, once again, that on no account should he go into the kitchen and disturb the dog.

The dog in question was Twizzle, acquired from Battersea Dogs Home, a wonderful and loving family pet, although, quite frankly, insane and, one had eventually to conclude, more of a missile, really, than a dog. See volume two of my critically well-received memoirs, *Going Off Alarming*, for the full low-down on this canine incendiary device. But in brief, Twizzle would throw himself sideways at doors in his attempts to free himself from closed rooms, and, in a rather alarmingly random manner, had very few qualms about attacking non-family members that he didn't know well. When Paul was around, I would make sure to shut Twizzle in the kitchen. 'England star maimed by Daz man's mutt' was not a headline I was especially keen to read.

One night, I left Paul to his slumbers in the sitting room, pausing only to remind him, as usual, not to go into the kitchen during the night. About an hour later, I awoke with a jump to hear the most tremendous crashing and banging from below, accompanied by frantic barking and, beyond that, terrified shouting.

'Dan! Dan!'

I run downstairs. Twizzle is in the hall, highly agitated, snarling and trying to pound his way sideways into the living room, in keeping with his preferred method of entry. I wrestle him away from the door and throw him, still frothing with irritation, back in the kitchen. Gazza, meanwhile, is in the living room, where he has been holding the door shut so the dog can't beat it down with his flanks and get to him. He is equally if not more agitated than Twizzle, and there is blood running from a wound on his leg.

I hear myself beginning to compose the sentence you found yourself saying to Gazza over and over again in the course of your exchanges with him: 'What is the *matter* with you?'

Gazza has, it emerges, left the sitting room in my absence and gone to the kitchen, where he and Twizzle have stared at each other through the glass panel and where eventually Gazza has, for reasons at this point known only to himself and despite the strictest of instructions to the contrary, opened the kitchen door.

'But what's the one thing I always tell you?' I say. 'Why would you do that? Look at your leg!'

Gazza is, as ever, instantly contrite. But he volunteers the following explanation for his actions.

'It's just that every night you say to me, don't go out there, don't go out there. Don't go near the dog. And I just thought . . . well, how fucking hard *is* he?'

The next night, or very shortly after this, England play. I'm watching on the television as Terry Venables, the manager, is asked to explain the absence from his starting line-up of a certain influential midfielder. 'So, no Paul Gascoigne tonight, Terry?' And Venables says: 'No, he picked up a knock in training.'

News update: he didn't pick up a knock in training. He opened the door to my dog.

That constant, almost Keith Moon-like desire to push the boundaries, to seek the extra dimension, to add something to every moment: how does that not end badly? Sometimes, even then, Gazza would talk about life after football and what it might hold, and his eyes would well up. He knew. He didn't have a clue what he was going to do when football was no longer available to him, when he was ejected from the mothership. Football – the one place he felt comfortable, the closest thing he knew to rails.

Somewhere around 2010 – that would be the last time I saw him. He came to my house, he was sober, we went out to dinner, and he made my son, Sonny, who was only little in the days when Gazza was coming to stay, laugh fit to burst with stories he's heard a thousand times from me, but never told as well as Gazza could tell them.

Nothing since then. There are 12-step courses where they tell you not to get in touch with your friends from the bad old days. I guess it's about that. Which is a shame, because it buys into the myth that we were permanently on the piss, and that is simply untrue.

In one of the last conversations we had, I was urging him to do corporate events.

'What's that?' he said.

'Well, like the Bank of Hong Kong, say. I would be very surprised if they wouldn't give you thirty-five grand to fly out to Hong Kong and do a couple of nights for them.'

'What kind of thing?'

I offered to write him a script. How hard was it going to be for him? People love him – and far much more than he has ever believed. Everyone's going to be on their feet before he's said a word. He'll come on to that goal he scored against Scotland and the whole place will be in the palm of his hand. An hour of telling stories, and then questions and answers.

'Yeah, yeah,' he said. 'Do that.'

Next thing I know he's not answering my calls, and he's changed his phone again. And then I hear he's opening a supermarket in Redcar for £200 in cash. What can you do?

GARY

The thing about Gazza was, he just couldn't help himself. For example, if he was warming up at Wembley and there was a marching band doing its stuff on the pitch, Gazza would invariably try to take out one or two of the musicians with a long ball from distance. The dream, I think, was always to get it into the tuba, which I don't think Gazza ever quite achieved. But high points were certainly available for striking the bloke with the big bass drum – or better still, his drum – and Gazza certainly managed that on a couple of occasions.

He also pinched a Royal Marine's ceremonial helmet just before the band was due to go out at Wembley in 1991, and received a full-bore, military dressing-down from an angry drum major, who came into the dressing room and bawled at him to give it back. And on at least one occasion, the marchers were briefly obliged to double as cones for Gazza's dribbling practice.

And then there was the communal bath. You wouldn't want to find yourself in the bath at the same time as Gazza. Things would appear. Things that floated. Permit me to draw a veil there.

He called me 'Goldenballs' – this was long before David Beckham was given that honorary title by his wife. For some reason, maybe low-lying jealousy, George Best had taken against Gazza and had come out with the line, on a chat show somewhere, that Gazza's IQ was less than his shirt number. This went down very well in the England squad and we spent an entire training session ribbing Gazza about his IQ, with Gazza defending himself against Best's charge and giving back as good as he got.

Afterwards, as we left the training pitch, Gazza sidled up to me for a private word. 'Here, Goldenballs,' he said. 'What does IQ mean?'

Of course, all this stuff about what he got up to off the pitch tends to obscure this point a little, but Gazza was also phenomenally serious about football. He trained really hard, completely investing himself in it and working his socks off. I'm not sure I ever worked alongside a player who trained harder. And then, at the end of a session, when everyone else was getting changed and leaving, he would stay out on the pitch for ages practising free-kicks. Or if kids had been watching, he would play with them – spend literally 45 minutes to an hour dribbling around them and nutmegging them. I might go over for two minutes and sign a few autographs on my way off the pitch. But that wouldn't be enough for Gazza. He was looking for any chance to play football – literally any chance that presented itself, with anyone – because it was the one thing that truly made him happy.

As a consequence of that application, wedded to an astonishing natural gift for the game, Gazza was probably the most talented footballer I ever played with, along with Glenn Hoddle, though in a very different style to Glenn. In terms of pure, raw ability, and the sheer range of things that he was capable of doing, he was quite extraordinary. He could win matches out of nothing when you were really struggling – he would suddenly beat four men, put the goalkeeper on the ground and flick it in the corner. Time and time again. He was a magician.

I have to admit, though, that, speaking as a striker, he could be enormously frustrating to play with. Because the truth is, he wasn't that keen on giving the ball to someone else. He was a little bit like a kid in a playground in this respect. He loved the ball and wasn't entirely happy to share it.

In fact, there were really only two ways that you could get the ball off Gazza. One was if he was exhausted – and England's quarter-final against Cameroon in Naples in Italia '90 would be a good example of that. It was 2–2 in extra-time and Gazza started a run through the midfield and then, when he got just beyond the centre circle, he hit a pass down the middle to me, and I was able to take it on and run into the penalty area, where Benjamin Massing brought me down. I scored the penalty and England won 3–2.

Now, would Gazza have hit that pass to me if we hadn't been deep in extra-time, if he hadn't been running himself into the ground for the past hour and three-quarters and if he hadn't been utterly knackered? I don't believe so. He would have carried on himself as far as his breath would have taken him, I'm absolutely certain of it.

The other way you would get the ball off him – and this was another indication of how clever he was as a player – was if he knew, when he passed it to you, that you had absolutely no alternative but to give it straight back to him. It might have been hard to persuade him to part with it in other circumstances, but if you were backed up against defenders, he was certainly prepared to release it for a guaranteed one-two.

So, we had our fall-outs, certainly – never off the pitch because I got on with him really well, and still do. But on the pitch we had a lot of rows. I could really whine when I wasn't given proper service, as anyone who played with me would no doubt happily confirm, and there would be many occasions when I would be in a good position, but Gazza would set off and beat four men before losing it to the fifth, at which point I would be shouting: 'Gazza! For fuck's sake! Give me the fucking ball!' And he was always very apologetic about it – 'Yeah, yeah, yeah, OK, OK, sorry, sorry.' But still the ball wouldn't necessarily come.

What an entertainer, though. He could bury a free-kick from 30 yards in the top corner (the way he did for Spurs against Arsenal in the semi-final of the FA Cup in 1991), he could shrug off big players, he wasn't scared of anyone, he could take the mickey out of opponents with the skill that he had . . . and he could make you smile with what he got up to, even during matches. Even in World Cups. When we were playing Holland, he was continually pulling Ruud Gullit's dreadlocks – just giving them a gentle tug every time he was passing. It drove Ruud absolutely mad. But, setting all that stuff to one side, he simply had a massive amount of talent, and, to my mind, you have to place him right up there with the best English footballers of all time.

And he's so loved, of course. I saw Gazza come on in one of the special all-star matches they staged in 2019 to test out Tottenham's new stadium before it opened, and he got the loudest and warmest reception from the crowd by far. We all know he's fallible, but it turns out that people actually quite like that about a person. It makes them real to us. And with Gazza, somehow people know, too, that his heart is in the right place. Any of the players who got to know him would say the same: that fundamentally he's a generous man with a loving spirit who would do anything for you.

Except pass you the ball, obviously.

CHAPTER TWELVE

'I'm not sure how much the keeper knew about it.'

In which GARY goes to Spain. With thoughts on Terry Venables, Johan Cruyff, sticking it to Real Madrid in the Nou Camp and talking balls in furniture stores.

At some point in 2018, the *Match of the Day* team discussed the protracted saga of Philippe Coutinho and whether he would move from Liverpool to Barcelona. (Spoiler alert: he did.) During our deliberations about the pros and cons of such a transfer, I think I may have said something broadly in favour of the move – or at least something that was understanding about how such a move might appeal to a player.

This seemed to stir something in Danny Murphy, my esteemed BBC colleague, who drily remarked: 'Not everybody wants to leave Merseyside for the money in Spain, Gary.'

To which the obvious answer would have been: 'Not everyone gets the opportunity, Danny.' However, I allowed the moment to pass. You have to let the pundits score one every now and again or they become dispirited and restless.

Anyway, contrary to Danny's little jibe, my move from Everton to Barcelona wasn't quite like that. I hadn't sought the opportunity to move to Spain for any reason, financial or otherwise. In fact, I hadn't been thinking about going anywhere. It was 1986 and I had just scored 40 goals in a season in which Everton had come very close to winning the Double. I thought I was at a great club with a great chance of the big prizes – a feeling that was borne out the following year when, in my absence, Everton recaptured the league from Liverpool. As far as I was concerned, I was good for a few more years on Merseyside.

Footballers aren't always in charge of their own destiny, though. It may be less true now, but it was strongly the case then. When Howard Kendall, the Everton manager, first mentioned Barcelona's interest to me, at the end of the season, he did so in such a way as to suggest that he wasn't entirely averse to the idea. His advice to me was that I should go away and have a good think about it. He certainly wasn't on his knees saying: 'Please, for my sake, for Everton's sake, for English football's sake . . . don't do this.' And whatever I had gone away and thought, the move would probably have happened anyway. The fee

Gary: A perennial winner, and Pep Guardiola.

Gary: It's coming home! The great man behind England's magical summer of 2018, Gareth Southgate. Also a local triple jump champion.

Danny: Round my house with Gazza. I'm part of a big noisy family and he loved being indoors with us, just being part of it. He'd kip on a couch in the front room so he could watch TV in the night. Sleep for Paul was an elusive state and he'd await first light so he could help our milkman on his rounds. No joke.

Gary: The last time I saw Maradona was in Moscow at the draw for the 2018 World Cup finals. I was presenting it and he was attending as a guest, one of eight star players representing the victorious World Cup nations. Afterwards, Maradona came up and gave me one of the huge hugs that he goes in for, and he complimented me on getting through the complexities of the draw without falling on my face. 'You know what?' he said, 'You were all right as a footballer. But as a TV host, you might almost have been as good as me.' (Top: *Getty/Bob Thomas*)

Danny: I first met David Moyes at the South Africa World Cup and we became good friends. When he was appointed at Old Trafford I remember thinking, 'I can't believe I know Man United's manager!' What a wonderful ten minutes that was.

Danny: As a boy, the only international players I ever met were Eamon Dunphy of Ireland and this man. Nobody remembers him but, at a function in 2010, I did. He was standing alone and was thrilled when I told him he'd signed a bus ticket for me in 1970. This is the great Mordechai Spiegler, former captain of Israel and star of the Mexico World Cup. All fame is fleeting, Gary . . .

Gary: Me and Wayne Rooney, England's record goal-scorer. No Golden Boot, though.

Gary: Me and Tiger. Almost as good as the time I played golf with Samuel L. Jackson and Michael Jordan.

RIGHT
Gary: Me and the other Ronaldo. Also a bloody good player.

Danny: One of my better ideas was inventing The Shirt of Hurt for Sport Relief in 2010, the idea being you would put on your bitterest rival's shirt if money was donated to the charity. Here, Ray Winstone and I do the unthinkable. All over the country, similar sacrifices were made. Everyone has their price (Glasgow excepted).

Danny: While in Southwark Park in the 1980s imagine my surprise to find 'Her Majesty & Prince Philip' looking for a game. Our side took 'the Queen' on and she put in some good crosses before being substituted after 70 minutes. This was her only match for us because 'Sunday morning is usually church at Sandringham'.

Gary: I get a fair bit of stick on social media for speaking in awestruck tones about Lionel Messi. But I'm right. #GOAT

Danny: Signing off on another crackerjack *Behind Closed Doors* episode, congratulating Gary on both his magnificent anecdotal flair and the delicious bowl of peyote-infused pasta, of which I'd apparently had sixteen helpings.

Gary: Not even presenting *Match of the Day* in your underpants will give you the rush you get from scoring – which I'm in a unique position to affirm, of course, having done both.

eventually agreed was £2.8 million. I can only assume that, for people at the Everton end of the deal, it made sense financially.

So, that was that. I was off to Barcelona. But hey, there are far worse places for a player to have to go.

Not that I had ever been there before. I'd had to look on a map to see exactly where in Spain Barcelona was. The deal was signed in a hotel in London and then I flew to Barcelona for my presentation ceremony – driven direct from the airport to the Nou Camp, getting changed into the famous blue and red shirt and then emerging from the tunnel into the sunlight to find 60,000 supporters screaming their greeting. It was the closest I had felt to being a pop star.

Then it was back to England to pack before moving out there properly with Michelle, my first wife. This was exciting, if also daunting. But then, at the same time, it was Barcelona: they were bound to look after us. The club had told me not to worry about accommodation at first. The vice-president owned a big hotel chain and they would happily put us up for as long as we needed at the Hotel Presidente – 10 or 15 minutes from the ground, on the Avinguda Diagonal.

Fine by us. Until we could find a place that suited us, we would just have to live like royalty in a luxury hotel suite. I was beginning to see how signing for one of the biggest clubs in the world had its positives.

So Michelle and I land in Barcelona, with all our possessions stuffed into about 14 suitcases. But not to worry: we are collected at the airport by a limo and whisked to the Hotel Presidente, with our luggage following behind in a people carrier. At the check-in desk, the staff are respectful to the point of worshipful.

'Here's the key to your room, Mr Lineker – room 583.'

Up we go in the lift to the fifth floor, ushered by smiling staff the whole way. I slide my key into the door and open it – and the room is a little square place, not much bigger than the small double bed inside it. The walls are dark brown and so is the bedspread. Further exploration reveals a poky bathroom off to one side with barely enough room to swing a bar of soap. Your archetypal, bog standard hotel room.

The porters now arrive with two trolleys bearing our 14 suitcases. These they solemnly unload into the tiny space available around the bed, piling them three or four high where necessary. After they leave, I sit on the edge of the bed, practically walled-in by luggage.

I'm thinking 'I've just signed for Barcelona. Shouldn't this be a little . . . different?'

It occurs to me that maybe there has been a mistake. Perhaps there are two Gary Linekers checking into the Hotel Presidente this morning, one of them not having recently signed for Barcelona, and the desk has got us muddled. I decide to go downstairs and ask some questions. But on the way I pause to knock on Mark Hughes's door, a couple of rooms away. Mark is the other British player that Terry Venables, the Barcelona manager, has brought in along with me, and Mark has recently checked in, too. (These were the days when a team could have only two foreign players in its first-team squad.) Part of me is wondering whether the door will swing open, and there will be Mark in a towelling bathrobe, fresh from the Jacuzzi on the garden terrace of his penthouse suite, saying 'Got a problem, Gary?'

But no. Mark has been given exactly the same kind of brown-walled box-room. We are both a little disappointed, to say the least. Although I am also a bit relieved to find out that it's not just me.

I go to reception and ask if there is any chance of getting something slightly larger. No, there isn't. I explain that I'm currently sharing my room with my wife and 14 suitcases. The hotel promises to find another room for the suitcases, just as soon as one becomes available. And this they duly provide – five days later.

Michelle and I ended up living in Room 583 for four months. And I suppose you could argue that it was no bad thing, in the circumstances, for me not to be pampered – to be made to keep my feet on the ground. It's just a shame that there wasn't a bit more room on the ground for my feet, on account of the suitcases.

I guess what was surprising was that, when it came to acclimatising, there was no real help from the club – not like nowadays, when foreign players on arrival are given assistance with everything to help them settle in, whether it's their houses, their cars, their bank accounts, the schools for their kids . . . Terry Venables was quite helpful. He introduced me to a guy who sorted me out with a car and who eventually found us a place to rent which we liked – a little villa, with a communal swimming pool. And finally, four months into our stay, we had room to unpack our bags, hang up our clothes and spread out a little bit. Otherwise, the club had left us entirely alone to get on with it.

That's my only gripe, though. Well, that and the training pitch, which was surprisingly terrible – a little scrubby field directly next to the Nou Camp. A whole stellar sports complex sits on that site now, but in those days you would have been hard pressed to distinguish it from a sun-baked public rec.

Ah, but the lifestyle, though. The lifestyle was simply great. I would train for a couple of hours in the morning. And then quite often Michelle and I would head to the Castelldefels Beach Club, where we might find Mark Hughes and his girlfriend Jill. Spot of paella there for lunch, bit of lying in the sun. Then we would return home and, exhausted by the paella and all that hectic lying on sun-loungers, have a siesta for two or three hours in order to gather energy for supper. You couldn't get a meal in a restaurant until 10pm at the earliest, so the evening would start late and end even later. Sleep and repeat.

Friendly, welcoming team-mates, too – relaxed, quietly sure of themselves. I was quick to notice the very different culture around drinking. When you sat with the Barcelona team for your pre-match meal, there would always be bottles of red wine on the table. Most players would have a single glass of it with their food, perfectly naturally, without comment. There was quite simply no English club where that would have happened. Wine on the lunch table? With an English football team in the eighties, it would have been inviting carnage.

I elected to learn Spanish, in what was actually a very calculated decision. I had noticed that, of the English players who had gone abroad, those who had done well had been the ones who spoke the language a bit and immersed themselves as best they could in the culture. And the ones who did less well were the ones who didn't. I couldn't speak a word of Spanish on arrival. The transfer had happened so suddenly that there was no time to pick up anything in advance. But as soon as we got out there I started having lessons at a language school three times a week. I continued doing so for two years, along with Michelle – and with Mark Hughes for the first few sessions, until he gave up. It wasn't his thing. But I really wanted to crack it. I just thought I was giving myself a better chance to succeed.

Of course, there were some early struggles. Shopping in a furniture store, and looking for some bedside tables with drawers – '*dos mesitas con cajones*' – I asked if I could be shown '*dos mesitas con cojones*'. 'Cojones' doesn't mean 'drawers'. It means . . . well, you probably know. I had just asked to see the store's most ballsy bedside tables.

I dropped a bollock, as it were.

But after three months I had attained a basic survival level and could more or less work my way through a post-match interview.

'*Obviamente estoy feliz por eso.*' ('Obviously, I'm happy with that.')

'*Sabiamos que nos lo harian dificil.*' ('We knew they would make it difficult for us.')

'*Lo estamos tomando un juego a la vez.*' ('We're taking it one game at a time.')

After six months, I was OK. After a year I was fairly fluent – without being grammatically brilliant. And after two years I was thinking in Spanish, and sometimes dreaming in it. It came up eventually not to the level of my English, but to somewhere fairly close. Towards the end of my time, I was good enough to be able to do a bit of co-commentary in Spanish on a couple of televised games.

It's still reasonably good, but I get less chance to practise, so my standard dips. These days my opportunities to speak Spanish seem quite limited even when I'm in Spain. When I was living in Barcelona, nobody really spoke English apart from the ex-pats, and I avoided them like the plague because I thought, Mark Hughes and his girlfriend Jill aside, what's the point of coming all this way and hanging out too much with other Brits? All the invitations were arriving for the commissioner's party to celebrate this and the ambassador's party to celebrate that, and I thought: thank you, but no. As much as possible, I wanted to surround myself with Spanish things. The only time Michelle and I spoke English was between ourselves at home. Now I go there and everybody seems to have excellent English – every shop, every restaurant. And then I might get asked to do an interview in Spanish and suddenly I'm fighting for words and semi-translating stuff in my head, which I wasn't doing at the end of my time there. And then I get frustrated with myself because I'm not as good as I was. It's quite a lot like sport, really.

On the pitch, all was great. I was working with Terry Venables, a brilliant coach. He was far warmer, as a person, than I was used to in a manager. In fact, he is the only manager I've ever socialised with. We would go out for meals in Barcelona every now and again and it never felt forced or difficult. But that's not to say he couldn't get angry and have a stern word if he felt he needed to, and, for all the avuncular joking around, he had an extremely driven edge to him. And this was a great period for Terry. He had arrived at Barça two years earlier, in 1984, when the club was underperforming. He brought in this thing called a 'high press' that nobody understood: what the hell is this? The idea was to put pressure on the ball as high up the pitch as possible. You hear people crediting Jürgen Klopp with the invention of this tactic, but Terry was working with it all those years ago. And he was getting slammed for it in the first couple of games. But then Barça started winning and it all changed. They trounced everyone, smashed Real Madrid in the Bernabéu, and the supporters suddenly wouldn't hear a word against him. Terry coached Barcelona to their first league title for over a decade, and took them to the European Cup final – and if he'd won that, he would have been immortalised. (They lost on penalties to Steaua Bucharest in a lame shoot-out recalled elsewhere in these pages.)

I think Terry was, along with Johan Cruyff, the best coach that I ever played for. He was unique in the way that he would pull you out of a training session and ask you to consider possibilities for movement and positioning and whether they would work. He was constantly pushing you to go into different areas of the pitch and try something different. There would be at least three of these suggestions, for you, personally, every week. And maybe only one in five would come off or end up being applied in a game. But you had this sense that he was constantly thinking of things. That set him apart. I'd never had that – that individual coaching, in such detail.

I was given the number 8 shirt, which I had also worn at Everton and Leicester. People sometimes ask why, as a centre-forward, I didn't opt at any point for the traditional number 9. And the motivating factor, not for the first time in my life, was pure superstition. I had worn number 9 a couple of times very early on at Leicester and had bad games while wearing it. Number 8 worked better. However, when Mark Hughes left Barcelona after one season to go to Bayern Munich, Bernd Schuster replaced him as the second foreign player and asked for my number 8 shirt, which he had previously worn, so at that point I took number 10. I was already wearing 10 for England. It's the number you want to be wearing, in my humble opinion.

The big highlight for me from this period would have to be scoring a hat-trick against Real Madrid in the Nou Camp. That's the game, obviously, that the Barcelona fans most care about and the city virtually crackles in anticipation of it. I got two goals in the opening five minutes, and a third shortly after half-time – 3–0 up against the big rivals, with 120,000 fans going nuts. That, right there, was the most blood-tingling moment of my entire career.

And then, agony. Real got a goal back. And then another. No, no! Don't ruin it! Imagine scoring a hat-trick in the Clásico and yet not winning . . .

We held on: 3–2. The relief!

Obviously, when you score a hat-trick you get to keep the match ball as a memento, so when the game finished I went to the referee to claim my prize. I was standing there, smiling, with my hands held out – but he wasn't handing it over to me. In fact, he was giving me a look that seemed to say: 'Why the hell is this grinning Englishman standing in front of me asking for the ball? Doesn't he realise the game is over?'

Ah, I get it. Giving the ball to the hat-trick scorer isn't a thing in Spain. Sometimes you just have to learn these things the hard way.

Other differences to get used to: almost no away fans. I remember going 1–0 up against Real Madrid in the Bernabéu, with 98,000 people present, and assuming that the referee must have disallowed it because the place fell entirely silent. But practically every one of those 98,000 was a Real Madrid fan, and following your team away from home was considered eccentric. Also, booting the ball into touch to solve a defensive problem would earn whistles of derision, even from your own fans. You got a cheer for doing that in England, but Spanish supporters seemed to think it was contemptible – not really football. And – again, unlike in England – winning a corner seemed to generate very little excitement in the crowd. Perhaps the fans just understood the percentages better. Goals are very rarely scored from corners, unless the defence is doing something it shouldn't do. Even so, the first few times Barça won a corner and the place didn't buzz in response, it made me wonder why people weren't a bit more grateful.

The fans were avid for their own players, though. If you didn't know what it was like to be an object of public interest before you signed for Barcelona, you soon found out. Shortly after Mark Hughes and I arrived, Rod Stewart gave a concert at the Nou Camp. We were invited and given seats in the chairman's area. The stage was in front of the opposite stand, facing us, and the pitch was a sea of people.

As Mark and I looked out across it, we couldn't understand why so many people had their backs to the stage and were facing us. We both wondered who had come in. Who was sitting near us that we hadn't noticed? Then we realised they were looking at us.

The hat-trick against Real Madrid pretty much cemented me with those fans. I did wonder briefly whether I might have un-cemented myself again when I scored four for England against Spain in Madrid. On the contrary: that particular feat appeared to make me even more popular in Barcelona. A local newspaper went with the headline: 'Catalan player scores four against Spain.' I travelled to that game from Barcelona with half a dozen Spanish team-mates, and those four goals were scored past Andoni Zubizarreta, my own Barcelona goalkeeper. He came into the dressing room after the game, stood in front of me and said 'Fackin' ew' in a perfect cockney accent, copied very carefully from Terry Venables.

That match (I might as well mention) also marked the beginning of my brief period as a wearer of Quasar boots. Quasar were a brand new company and let's just say they had one or two teething problems with their production, early doors. Running around against Spain, I was thinking 'These feel heavy – a bit flappy, almost.' Four goals, though. I wasn't complaining. But when I got back to the dressing room, the sole of one of my brand new boots was hanging off and came clean away in my hand.

That wasn't my only dodgy moment with a Quasar boot.

In March 1990 England played Brazil in a friendly at Wembley – and beat them 1–0, an extremely rare occurrence which encouraged hopes to grow for that summer's World Cup in Italy. I scored with a diving header from a Peter Beardsley corner. Would VAR have picked up Stuart Pearce's handball on the goal-line after Muller had later made his way around Chris Woods in the England goal and shot? Possibly. Maybe there are some arguments against VAR after all . . .

But that was also the night one of my Quasar boots split before the game, which at least made a change from having one split during it. I discovered that the only person in the squad with some spares available and who had the same size feet as me was Bobby Robson. So if you closely scrutinise any footage from that game, you will notice that I am wearing a Quasar boot on one foot and, on the other, an Adidas boot which actually belongs to the England manager.

An England striker, facing Brazil, in an odd pair of boots: there are levels of amateurism here which would surely induce a fainting fit in the modern game. Then again, I have just seen the lucky boots in which Jack Grealish helped secure promotion to the Premier League for Aston Villa in the 2019 Wembley play-off. Well-worn? The top layer is actually torn off in places. They look like a dog's chew-toy which has been left out in the garden over the winter. The lucky boots that got me through the 1986 World Cup finals were practically box-fresh by comparison with these monsters. So maybe a bit of amateurism continues in the higher echelons. It's good to see.

Quasar boots, by the way, are no longer with us. In the end, they just didn't quite have it in them to take on Nike. I wonder why that is.

And while we're on the subject of endorsements, perhaps this would be the moment to come clean about my spell during this period as the face of Sondico shin pads. The Gary Lineker Sondico Platinum shin pad was available to buy from all good sports shops, bearing my signature halfway up each pad. Perhaps you owned a pair; they were very much the Aston Martin of football-related leg protection, I would suggest. Perhaps you were persuaded to buy some by the magazine advertisement for which Bryan Robson, Ian Rush and myself dressed up as American Prohibition-era gangsters, with dark pinstripe suits, black shirts, white ties, black fedoras and (incredibly) straight faces. Robson and Rush both touted machine guns, while I held an open violin case, displaying the Sondico shin pad range. Slogan? 'When you need protection.' Which would work for certain other products one can think of.

However, it's time to confess. Shin pads were not really a piece of equipment for which I was fully entitled to be an ambassador. For as long as it was possible to get away with it (and this, I'm embarrassed to relate, would include my period as Sondico's stern-faced Mr Protection), I never wore them. I found them restrictive. Something about my circulation means that if my shoes are too tight, I stop feeling anything below the ankle – which is a hopeless situation for a footballer. It's also the reason I can't and don't ski: skis and ski boots are too tight and I immediately lose contact with my feet. For the same reason, I was reluctant to strap anything tightly around my legs if I could get away without it. So, no shin pads. When FIFA made the wearing of shin pads mandatory in 1990, I got round it by cutting out two tiny pieces from a shin pad – literally about a quarter of an inch square – and sticking them to my legs with plasters. For although FIFA had stated that shin pads were obligatory, they hadn't said how big those shin pads should be. So there was my loophole.

Anyway, me and my under-protected shins were having a perfectly nice time, thank you, at Barcelona. I scored 21 goals in 42 appearances in my first season. Terry Venables left and went back to England to manage Spurs, but I stayed put under Luis Aragonés, we won the Copa del Rey, and I carried on scoring – 20 goals in 50 appearances in 1987–88. And that was despite once again failing to nab the role as the team's penalty-taker, which I was always desperate to do because obviously it works wonders for your goal-scoring figures. But who do you have to talk to? With England I managed to snaffle the job – though England then went on a run where they didn't get given a penalty until 1990 – but in club football I never seemed to be able to. At Everton Trevor Steven had the job, and at Barcelona it was Julio

Alberto, who was no slouch. It wasn't until I got to Tottenham that I managed to hold down the appointment.

And then Johan Cruyff arrived and I got hepatitis – facts which were in no way linked to one another, although the experience of life under Cruyff and the experience of having hepatitis would turn out to have more in common than you might think, certainly in terms of the frustration both caused.

Let's start with the hepatitis. I started to notice something was wrong during the European Championships in the summer of 1988. They took place in West Germany, as it was then, and England did not distinguish ourselves. Our opening group game was against Ireland, we lost 1–0 and I felt mostly terrible throughout – really sluggish and incapable. Was it the consequence of a long, tiring season? It seemed a bit extreme if so. In our second game we played, if anything, even worse and lost 3–1 to Holland, which meant we were out of the tournament, and I felt considerably more ill – heavy-limbed and aching. There didn't seem to be any explanation for it. I was also losing weight – about a stone and a half, it would eventually emerge. I quietly wondered if I had AIDS. This was a period when that disease was in the forefront of people's minds, with all sorts of ridiculous and uninformed rumours about ways in which you could contract it. Maybe I had done so. I managed to frighten myself with the thought.

We still had to play Russia – now an inconsequential match for us. I told Bobby Robson, the manager, how bad I was feeling, and asked if I could sit it out. He wouldn't hear of it. Neither would Don Howe, his assistant, who carried on, in training, shouting at me to get my act together. 'You don't want to do it, you don't want to do it.' Both of them thought I was just having a moody and trying to duck a meaningless game, which was so far from true. So I was picked for that third group game. I spent 45 minutes wandering around in a daze – absolutely nowhere. At half-time, Bobby, clearly furious, took me off – which was a relief, at least, but the atmosphere was terrible.

The British newspapers were faxed to our hotel every day and the next morning, as we got ready to fly home from Germany in disgrace, one of them carried a back-page splash in which Bobby had had a go at several players, including me, for not putting in the required effort. That really made me angry. It's not especially in my nature to confront anybody in anger, least of all my own manager. But as I passed Bobby, climbing on to the coach, I rolled up the paper and threw it at him, saying: 'You're out of order.'

Back home, I saw a doctor and had some tests. Verdict: hepatitis A, a liver infection. Shellfish can carry the virus, apparently, if they've been feeding in contaminated water and I'd certainly been eating plenty of seafood in Spain. A dodgy mussel in Tenerife? Who knows? The wrong ice cube could give it to you, too. All I understood for sure was that it would mean a week in a hospital bed in London and four months before I was fully fit to play football again.

Assuming I ever would be fully fit. Jimmy Greaves, coincidentally, contracted hepatitis while he was a player and I read an article in which he claimed he was never quite the same afterwards. Very frightening.

Bobby Robson came to see me in hospital. He stood by the bed and said: 'I've come to see that you're well, and I've come to say I'm sorry.' I don't mind admitting that I cried. I was glad to heal it with him. Bobby was the last manager I would have wanted to have had a lasting rift with.

None of this put me in a very good position when Johan Cruyff arrived at Barça. I wasn't going to be able to take part in his first pre-season. At precisely the point when I would have wanted to be making an impression on the new manager, I was away from the club and convalescing. That made me anxious, inevitably. At the same time, I was excited that he had the job. If you had watched the legendary Dutch 'total football' side of the seventies and seen Cruyff in action, you could hardly fail to get enthused about the prospect of working with him.

However, it became obvious quite quickly that he wasn't going to give me much of a chance. When I was finally fit, around November, he asked me to play out wide on the right of the attack, instead of centrally. That was frustrating. The man he picked to play up front was Julio Salinas. He was a great lad, and definitely a decent goal-scorer. But I genuinely thought I was a better one.

What was doubly frustrating was that I thought Cruyff's

system was perfect for me. He used to play a bit similar to the way Pep Guardiola's teams play now: with two wide men, instructed to get really wide, and with the striker staying pretty much within the width of the box. And every time the wide men got to the byline the striker was to make a run. Bread and butter for me.

But I know what Cruyff was doing during all this. You were only allowed two foreign players and, given those restrictions, I totally understood that he would want two of his own choice, not two that he had been left. So his tactic was to piss me off so that I would kick up a fuss and demand to leave.

Now, if he had known me as a person, perhaps he would have spoken to me and said: 'I want to use other foreign players. We'll look after you and get you a move.' But that conversation never happened. The press would ask him why I wasn't playing centrally and Cruyff would say I was fine on the right – that it suited me because I was quick. Well, I did OK. If you've got a bit of pace, you can play on the wing. And I knew how to cross because I knew how I liked the ball crossed to myself. I made the first goal in the Cup Winners' Cup final with a cross from the right to the far post, so clearly it worked to some degree. But I got no satisfaction playing out there – none whatsoever. I would get home and be fed up. I think I only scored six goals that season, which absolutely killed my ratio, and that was important to me. I knew I had to go.

Still, I wasn't going to squeal about it – not to the press, nor to Cruyff. In fact, I went the other way with it, as much as I could – doubled up on the professionalism, never complained in his earshot, just got on with the job. And I think because I played it in quite a gentlemanly way I was given a lot of respect at Barça, which I retain. At the end of my last season, in 1989, there were massive banners in the crowd saying 'Don't go' and there was a lot of affection for me which I still feel when I go there.

Although you have to be a certain age, of course. People ask 'Do you get recognised in Spain?' and I have to reply 'Well, yes I do, actually. But mainly by the elderly.'

Let me state it clearly, though: Cruyff was a genius, not just as a footballer, but as a coach. It's where the modern game has come from – from ideas set in motion by Johan Cruyff. He was the biggest know-it-all I've ever met in my life – I mean, about literally everything. He would sit behind the bus driver and tell him how to drive. He was pretty relentless in that sense. But about football, he literally did know it all. And what a brain. He would teach you about possession and about play in different areas of the pitch: about seven against five here, and nine against seven there, and how to take advantage of the space that you've got, and all of that was fascinating to me. I wasn't as technical, maybe, as the players that suited him, but I learned so much.

I worked with him two or three times on television after my career finished and there was no problem between us.

Yet not long ago I was given a lifetime achievement award on what is basically the Catalunya version of the BBC Sports Personality of the Year show. They brought a lot of my old Barcelona team-mates together, and we talked about Cruyff and they all said the same: that he was a complex person, hard to get close to, far easier to respect than to like. But he was a brilliant and transformative coach who single-handedly changed Barcelona altogether, and football more broadly.

Eventually, though, he was leaving me on the bench – including for the Clásico in the Nou Camp. It was late in the game, the score was 0–0 and we desperately needed a goal. The crowd was singing my name: 'Leen-ay-ka! Leen-ay-ka!' They wanted me brought on, and I was itching to get out there. Cruyff made a substitution: not me. And then he made another substitution: not me. Still no goal. The crowd was going nuts by this point. It got to about the 80th minute and I shouted at him from the bench: 'You haven't got the balls to bring me on now.' I said it in Spanish, and I used 'cojones' in its correct and intended sense, and not 'cajones', meaning 'drawers'. And I was right: he didn't have the balls, and he didn't bring me on. (And the game ended 0–0.)

It was a bit like Everton again: I didn't want to leave but I had no choice. The next year would be a World Cup year – 1990. I needed to be playing in my best position, and scoring. A shame, but it was time to go home.

Where to, though? During that period, when my number was clearly up at Barça, I was with England for an end-of-season game against Denmark, rooming, as usual, with Peter Shilton, and the phone rang. I was in the loo at the time, but I heard Peter answer it and I could tell from the way he was speaking that he was somewhat in awe of the person on the other end, which was not common for Peter, who was a very confident man.

I heard him say: 'He's actually in the toilet at the moment.'

When I emerged from the bathroom, Peter was holding the phone out to me.

'It's for you,' he said. 'It's Brian Clough.'

This brought me up a little short. Clough's slightly scary reputation went ahead of him. I nervously took the receiver.

'Mr Clough?'

'Young man, have you washed your hands?'

'Yes, I have, Mr Clough.'

'Call me Brian. Tell me, are you signed, sealed, delivered?'

I said I wasn't, that I was still, at this point, a Barcelona player.

'Would you consider coming to Nottingham Forest?'

Now here was a dilemma. How to respond? Be straight. Be honest. Say what you think.

'No, Brian,' I said. 'I don't think I would.'

'Why not, young man?'

We were now clearly on highly delicate ground, and I chose my words as carefully as I could.

'Well, if I was going to come back to England, I think I would like it to be . . . one of the . . . big clubs.'

There was a pause during which I felt the air between us down the phone line grow considerably more thunderous than it had been up to that moment.

Eventually Clough said: 'We *are* one of the big clubs.'

I started scrambling feebly backwards.

'Well, of course, I don't mean to say . . .'

'Only Liverpool have won more than us in the last ten years.'

I continued to scramble.

'Of course,' I said. 'I think, when I say "big" clubs, what I'm trying to say is, one of the bigger *named* clubs . . . I'm sure you understand, Brian.'

'No, young man, I don't understand. Call me Mr Clough.'

And he slammed down the phone.

Oops.

Anyway, that summer I joined Tottenham.

CHAPTER THIRTEEN

'It would have been easier to score from there.'

In which DANNY cheats his way to the semi-finals of the World Cup, but somehow it's not enough and England go out on penalties. With tributes to the magic of showbusiness and that irrepressible American can-do spirit, and with an impassioned defence of the vuvuzela.

When life throws something at you for nothing, you seize it, don't you? Latin speakers are seizing days all the time, I understand. How would you feel about one of your rival's shirts, though? Crystal Palace, say. Life lobbed me one of those for nothing a number of years ago – or, to be more precise, Mark Lazarus, the Palace winger, lobbed me one. Lazarus had just played his heartless part in a defeat of Millwall at the Den and, as he left the field in triumph, his parting gift to the home crowd (perhaps a little gloatingly) was his shirt. And I, standing among that home crowd, caught it, something which has never happened to me in a football stadium before or since.

However, even before I had had time to process this rare triumph, the same shirt had been ripped straight out of my hands by my Millwall brethren and ritually torn into tiny pieces, betokening the high degree of contempt that exists around our way for our south London rivals, especially in defeat.

I got luckier later when life lobbed me a free trip to a World Cup and I was able to leg it with the booty before anyone could shred it. Subsequently, life, noting I was a pair of safe hands when it came to these dream jaunts, has lobbed a free trip to a World Cup not just once, not just twice, but a total of five times.

The first occasion was Italia '90. At this time, I was a reporter for *Six O'Clock Live*, a show fronted by the legendary Frank Bough and which was the successor to *The Six O'Clock Show*, the Friday night LWT magazine programme which had seen me, much to my own surprise, land up on television in the eighties. With England set to face West Germany in the semi-finals and the entire nation hog-wild about it, the producers of *Six O'Clock Live* felt the show needed some World Cup content and someone duly had the following bright idea. What if Danny was challenged to hitch down to Turin for the match? In one of those entirely self-imposed time-trials that television loves, I would have just 24 hours to blag drives to Italy where a ticket for the match (courtesy of ITV Sport) would await me, assuming I made it in time.

We roughed out the journey. Maybe, if I started near the ferry in Dover, there could be a first stage to Paris, then a change of lorry. Then I could find another driver to take me down to the Alps before another switch. There would need to be a lot of glancing at my watch, clearly. And I would need to be beside the road in an unpromising location with my thumb out at some stage, for that all-important element of jeopardy.

Armed with a small video camera and an overnight bag, I was driven to the port at Dover and dropped off in the lorry park to make my first connection. Here I set the camera going and, running alongside a queue of lorries to create the required sense of urgency, I delivered my introduction.

'There's just 17 hours to the big game in Turin,' I explained breathlessly to the lens, 'and I'm at Dover hoping one of these lorry drivers can get me to the first stage of my big journey – Paris! It's going to be *so* tight but what a prize awaits in Italy if I can do it! Fingers crossed for me!'

With this, I got up beside a lorry in the line and reached up to tap on the side window. The driver wound down the window and looked out.

'Where are you headed?'

'Turin,' said the driver. 'Want a lift?'

Ah. Clearly his reply lacked the tension the piece required. However they edited it, a six-minute film of me sitting in the cab of an 18-wheeler Scammell lacked dramatic interest.

That said, it would get me there in plenty of time for a beer and a tagliatelle. So I hopped aboard and thereafter would film myself approaching lorries at various truck stops and petrol stations on the way, so it could then be edited to make it look plausibly like I had a truly complicated job getting to the big match. In Turin, where my man dropped me within view of the stadium, I found a bar, settled in, and later filmed myself running towards the Stadio delle Alpi 'with only seconds to spare'. What a racket.

Anyway, it meant I was in the stadium for Gazza's tears, Waddle's penalty and the spectacular bursting of England's bubble that year. But from what I hear, Gary Lineker was a little closer to the epicentre of those particular storms, so I'll leave that side of the tale to him. What I did know was that, in the whirling emotional cauldron of the Stadio delle Alpi, I had discovered a desire for World Cup football that I would spend at least the next quarter of a century failing to sate.

I got lucky again four years later when I covered USA '94 for, of all places, Radio 1. I flew out to New York in the company of my broadcasting cohort Danny Kelly, where it was our first duty, on a blisteringly hot day, to attend the Ireland v. Italy game at Giants Stadium. Heading across Manhattan on the morning of the match, we stopped for refreshment at a bar on Eighth Avenue, where the big screens were up, the beers were cold and a lively mixed crew of Irish and Italians was already in place in anticipation of the game. It was extremely welcoming. Hard to leave, indeed. Temptations began to hatch in our minds. The Giants Stadium is eight miles outside New York City in New Jersey. Did we really need to trudge all that way in this sweltering heat when the bar we were in was so lavishly appointed and so hellzapoppin? We took another sip of beer and looked around the room. I mean, this, too, was a proper World Cup experience, wasn't it? We were staying.

But then within minutes of taking that decision, our consciences began to prickle and the tickets in our pockets began to burn a hole. Sitting on them just seemed so cavalier when you considered the magnitude of the occasion and what people would have given to get anywhere near it. After all, I had been on the ground in Turin. I had a reputation to uphold. So we finished our drinks and set off for the Port Authority to get the bus out to the stadium.

And it was right there and then that I truly experienced and appreciated for the first time the sheer power and efficiency of America. At the Port Authority, a phalanx of buses stood at the stand as stewards with glowing pointers kept the queues of ticket-holders moving along. As soon as one bus filled, the doors would close with a 'tish!' and out it would move, no stops, no delays. Aboard our bus in moments, we were ferried in air-conditioned splendour to New Jersey and deposited on the tarmac where, but a short step away, escalators stood ready to bear us straight into the stadium past guys with heaving trays of refreshments – 'Buck a beer! Buck a beer!' – and directly to our seats. There, in an atmosphere as frenzied as any I have witnessed, we watched Jack Charlton's Ireland beat Italy 1–0 before emerging in a state of hepped-up wonderment to be ferried straight back into Manhattan as smoothly as we had come.

Those of you who have tortuously shuffled out of Wembley towards the tube station, looking like Napoleon's retreat from Moscow, can only wonder at such organisational genius.

For France '98 it was Talksport (or Talk Radio, as they were known back in those days) paying the bills, allowing Danny Kelly and myself to run our fingers down the fixture list and pluck out the plum, which was Iran v USA at the Stade de Gerland in Lyon – arguably the most politically sensitive game in the history of FIFA, played before a crowd comprising a small clump of Americans, a massive swathe of dissident revolutionary Iranians and an almost equally massive swathe of members of the Iranian secret service, there to keep an eye on the dissidents. Iran won 2–1 to the apparent delight of all but the clump of Americans, though even they might have had cause to be relieved. Some years after this, Danny Kelly interviewed Kasey Keller, who was in goal for the USA that night, and he asked him if he had ever in his career known such a ferociously possessed stadium as the one that night in Lyon. Keller gave Danny a dark look. 'I think you are forgetting,' he said, 'that I spent three years at Millwall.'

For Germany 2006, it was *The Times* newspaper that furnished me with the requisite passes and per diems, enabling me to experience both the barren otherworldliness of a Sunday in Frankfurt and the sheer fat-melting heat of the unshaded upper rotisserie section of that city's Commerzbank-Arena for England v Paraguay. (Your archetypal England group stage performance, that one: won 1–0 thanks to an own goal in the third minute. But the cola-flavoured Calippo ice lolly that I managed to source at half-time, in the absence of other plausible options, was a life-saver.)

And thence to South Africa 2010, where I was working for Radio 5 Live, and privileged to assemble a portfolio of memories, from the bubbling carnival that was Cape Town to the eerily suburban feel of razor-wired Bloemfontein, and from which I was able to bring home in my hand luggage an actual street-legal vuvuzela. I still possess it, and what an instrument it is. It's impressive enough when blown on its own, but when you get 2,000 of them going, you've got yourself something – the noise of a million angry hornets. Yet, of course, the world turned its back on the vuvuzela in the immediate wake of the 2010 World Cup, to the point where you could lose friends merely by appearing around the corner with one.

'Oh, Baker, not a vuvuzela.'

'Yep, a vuvuzela.'

I never lost faith in it, though, and I'm waiting patiently, vuvuzela cocked, for the revival. Let's face it, everything in music comes back around eventually. Hell, it even happened to Queen.

Getting paid to go to a World Cup may just be the sweetest dip in the gravy that a working person can know. Frankly, getting paid to go to any kind of football would be difficult to describe as a hardship. Yet you would never really know as much from that inordinately dreary show they have on Sky Sports on a Sunday morning, when a bunch of football hacks sit around a bowl of fruit and some plastic croissants. That to me is one of the most inadvertently funny television shows that the culture has produced – like something out of Beckett. Here are people who haven't paid to get into a ground for 30 years, yet talk mournfully about the game as if all that time they have been buried up to their waists in sand for no good reason that they can discern. There's a powerful whiff of the scented handkerchief emanating from that show, too. I would love the presenter to say: 'But enough about what's gone wrong at Manchester United. What's the biggest claim for expenses you've ever made in the course of a tournament?'

And the first person up cracks his knuckles and says: 'Right! Well, let me take you back to 1998 . . .'

I've been to tournaments on a newspaper's shilling and . . .

what ho! It's the streakiest gig outside of being a rock critic. At least let a little bit of the high jinks and the joie de vivre colour that show. Look into the camera at least once in a while and wink and say: 'We get paid to go to football matches, you know.' Why so maudlin, everybody? Do you think we don't realise? Why are you pretending so hard that what you do is like deciphering parliament?

I'm not sure those people would be the best ones to ask about it, but take it from me if you don't already know: being in town when there's a World Cup on is like nothing else that sport can offer you. No other football is ever like it. It's a hyper-heightened whirligig reality, wherever you go. I might have been born too late for the Roman amphitheatres, but surely that nutty scene had nothing on this: nothing like, in particular, that ten minutes before a World Cup game, when the colours of everything seem more vivid, the pitch becoming some exotic super-green. And there are dozens of helicopters in the air and the crowd is kicking up a racket to match, and you realise that pretty much everyone in the world is looking at this one spot on the globe at this one moment, and you're there.

And yes, I'm English, so I'm supporting England for as long as they're in the tournament. But it's a completely different dynamic to supporting Millwall. I couldn't name the current England squad if you put a gun to my head. I have no use for that information, I don't absorb it. I'm mystified that managing England could be a full-time job, rather than something a person did in addition to a job, a bit like a paper round. I mean, England hardly ever play and, when they do, the team virtually picks itself, with a couple of exceptions, so what, do you suppose, does an international manager actually do all week? There's only so much time, surely, that a man can spend thinking about Kyle Walker. Yet the months go by. Let's face it, most of the time the manager and their assistants are probably sitting cross-legged on the floor, idly flipping playing cards into a top hat.

And then there's the singing. There's no established hymn sheet at internationals. At England games, who can really join in with the singing? 'Come on, England'? It's just too generic. It sounds like something people shout at Wimbledon. It smacks of obligatory, community-organised fun, or the oral equivalent of the Mexican Wave. No, give me a 2,000-strong chorus of vuvuzelas over that, any day. Blow, boys, blow!

But I do without reservation love a World Cup and unswervingly regard that tournament as the most magnificent of human spectacles, the greatest circus that mankind has ever devised and one of the towering achievements of civilisation. So, if anyone ever offers to pay you and your best friend to go to one, force yourself to attend. Except Qatar. That one already sounds like a nightmare.

CHAPTER FOURTEEN

'This game is by no means over.'

In which GARY revisits Italia '90 and, sadly, Germany
still end up winning on penalties. With meditations
on the place of Rodgers and Hammerstein in the
history of English football, and some more motivational
speaking from Bobby Robson.

Driving back to the hotel after matches, the theme song on
the bus would be 'Do-Re-Mi' from *The Sound of Music*. Normally Chris Waddle, somewhere near the back, would start
it, or it would be Gazza.

'Doe, a deer . . .'

And it would gradually take hold, working its way forward down the aisle until pretty soon the whole bus would
be rattling with it.

'. . . that will bring us back to doe, oh, oh, oh . . .'

And then round again, with clapping and stamping.

It's a little acknowledged fact that England's 1990

World Cup campaign was propelled by the spirit of Julie Andrews.

And how far Julie took us that year: all the way to the semi-finals, where it all ended agonisingly in tears (Gazza's) and then penalties and then tears again (everybody else's). But what a great run. And what a tribute to the powers of the legendary nun-turned-nanny.

If I could change anything about the experience, I would pick only two things, really. Obviously, I would bring Chris Waddle's penalty down by a couple of hundred feet, or in some way alter it so that we won that shoot-out against West Germany and thereby went through to face Argentina in the final.

Actually, ideally, I would change the circumstances by which Chris came to be taking a penalty in the first place, because that wasn't part of the plan.

Either way, though, we would get to the final. And, remember, Argentina were nothing like the same force they were in Mexico in 1986. Maradona was well below par and they were struggling for goals. They had barely scraped out of their group and needed penalties to come through both their quarter-final, against Yugoslavia, and their semi-final, against Italy, after a 0–0 draw and a 1–1 draw respectively. In the course of losing the final, they would become the first World Cup finalists in the history of the competition not to score. Hardly sparkling. I will always think that this was the year we could have had them, redeeming 1986 and all that.

And I would have changed it, too, so that at no point in the entire tournament did I shit on the pitch. Where was Julie Andrews then, eh? Somewhere up a mountain, most probably, and who could blame her?

Ah, Poogate: it's the incident that has haunted me ever since, and I guess it will continue to do so in some form or other until the end of my days. Still, if you're going to suffer diarrhoea publicly at some point in your life, then you might as well do so on the biggest stage of them all. 'Go big, or go home' is a respectable motto.

My digestive troubles began the night before England's opening game, which was against the Republic of Ireland at the Stadio Sant'Elia in Cagliari. I must have eaten something dodgy because I was up a lot in the night. Of course, the professional thing would have been to report this immediately to the medical staff in the morning. But that might have meant getting left out of the team, so obviously it was never really an option – not with World Cups only coming around every four years. The smart move, it seemed to me, was to keep quiet, practise clenching, and take the obvious precautionary measure – which is to say, visiting the dressing-room toilet as late as possible before going out for the match. That should sort it.

In any case: a bout of diarrhoea in a football match – what's the worst that could happen?

And at first everything seemed to be working out fine. I must have managed to push the anxiety to the back of my mind because I scored after only nine minutes, running on to a truly superb pass from right out wide by Chris Waddle, knocking the ball past the advancing Pat Bonner in the Republic goal and virtually bundling it into the net between a sandwich of defenders. All this without my bowels getting involved. I even managed to celebrate convincingly afterwards. So maybe everything was going to be all right.

If only. I spent much of the rest of that half with a sense of what I can only describe as growing unease. I made it through to half-time and got to the toilet again, giving myself, surely, a fighting chance of getting through the second half. But no: in the 54th minute, ten yards into the Ireland half, stretching for the ball, I was fouled and brought to the ground and, in the exertion, briefly let go of the muscles that, up to that point, had been successfully keeping everything together.

Footage of the immediate aftermath of this moment captures me on the floor with a look on my face of absolute anguish, mixed in with a bit of disgust – the look, clearly, of someone who has just suffered one of the greatest embarrassments in the human catalogue, but who, on top of that, has suffered it while representing his country in the world's largest international sporting event in front of a global television audience stretching to hundreds of millions. That said, in all honesty, the broader picture wasn't really in my mind at that point. I was much more urgently focused on, as it were, the job in hand.

Noticing my distress, Gary Stevens ran up to find out if I was OK. And you can practically make this out on the TV coverage – I look up at him and make what was definitely the saddest announcement I have ever had to make to another professional on a football pitch: 'I've shat myself.'

Take it from me, in almost any situation, no matter how dire, there will always be positives. And it was true, even here, at this lowest of low-points. I was lucky that the pitch was damp and therefore could be used, to a certain extent, as a very large, naturally occurring wet wipe. Had this mishap occurred on a hard, crusty surface in Mexico, say, or even on one of those legendary cold Tuesday nights up at Stoke that people are always said not to fancy it on . . . well, it doesn't really bear thinking about.

The fact is (and here, more sensitive readers might care to skip ahead a paragraph) as I sat there, with a speechless Gary Stevens looking on, I was able to reach into the leg of the shorts and scoop out the worst of the problem, and then to wipe my hands clean on the wet grass. This cleared, shall we say, the bulk of the problem.

However, I was now worried about how my shorts might appear from behind. Praise be that we were wearing dark blue that night. Had we been in white, I think I would have been presented with a problem that even one of Danny's knock-down boxes of Daz would have struggled to solve. However, in order to clean myself up as best I could, while trying at the same time to disguise what I was up to and make it look like a sort of extended version of getting up off the ground, I kind of scooted myself along the pitch for a couple of feet, dragging my backside across the grass. Dog-owners will recognise this move straight away. It's what dogs very charmingly do, in the absence of toilet roll.

Behold the glamour and the glory of World Cup football.

All of these things I did as discreetly as possible – which is to say, not discreetly at all. A football pitch with 22 players and a referee on it can suddenly seem extremely exposed sometimes. I felt like I had no hiding place, although it's some consolation to me, in retrospect, that television cameras were quite a lot less numerous in those days. Nowadays, anyone caught short in a World Cup group stage game would, at the very least, have Spidercam to contend with. And then the high-def reverse-angle replays in super slo-mo . . . It doesn't bear thinking about.

Indeed, it's an odd thing to reflect on now, but this entire episode didn't properly come into the public domain for another 20 years. Despite the presence of the cameras and the magnitude of the occasion, the incident remained pretty much hidden until an interview I did with Ian Payne for BBC Radio 5 Live, two whole decades later. Ian gently mentioned that there was this rumour he had heard about me possibly losing control of my bowels during a game in Italia '90, and he asked me if there was any truth in it. And then it all came out. As it were. So I guess we need to think of Ian Payne as Poogate's Bob Woodward. At the time, though, the footage hadn't revealed much. The angles were few, the pictures were grainy, people didn't have the facility to pause the picture and rewind ('Why is he doing that dog thing? Hang on, he's wiping his hands on the pitch . . .'). All those possibilities to explore the footage more deeply only arrived later.

Still, back on the pitch, I had no option but to get up and get on with the game. The old wisdom about 'putting it behind you' has never seemed more applicable. However, the evening didn't get any better when Kevin Sheedy equalised for the Republic of Ireland in the 72nd minute. Just over ten fruitless minutes after that, I was subbed off and Steve Bull came on.

Now, technically, this should have meant my personal nightmare was over. In 99 stadiums out of 100, the dug-outs are next to the tunnel, which would have meant I could have slipped quietly away to the changing room at this point and sorted myself out. Not in the Stadio Sant'Elia, though. The benches were on the opposite side of the pitch from my access to a lavatory and a shower. So all I could do was park myself on the bench and sit there, alone and quietly humming, while my team-mates all bunched up to get away from me and while the players on the pitch continued to fail to beat the Republic of Ireland.

Of course, had we managed to find a winner in those last ten minutes and had everyone jumped off the bench and leapt into each other's arms in delight . . . well, I think I would probably have found myself celebrating alone, actually. As it was, the game finished 1–1 – which was an improvement, certainly, on the opening of Mexico '86, when we lost to Portugal. But these additional factors made it just as miserable from my point of view.

And the agony still wasn't quite over because, on the way down the tunnel, I found myself diverted for post-match television interview duties with Bobby Robson. In what was one of the more muted interview performances of my career, I managed to say something diplomatic about how, hopefully, tonight's draw would mean both teams eventually qualified. And then, finally, I made it back to the dressing room. (Both teams did qualify, of course. The Republic made it all the way to the quarter-finals that year, where they lost to Italy.)

A difficult night, then. Naturally there was a bit of stick from the other players in the ensuing days. Only high-quality stuff, of course: I was called 'shitty pants' a few times, as I recall. However, bear in mind that I was one of the senior players at that time. Seniority counts for a lot in an England squad. People around my age and general caps-level might have felt able to chip in with the odd remark, but not the younger players.

Anyway, as the famous line of poetry says: There is a corner of a foreign field that is forever . . . Well, actually, don't worry because I'm sure they've replaced that area of turf many times since then.

Of course, the Italia '90 experience picked up considerably after that – although not immediately. Indeed, there were shades of Mexico '86 all over again. We drew our second group stage game, against the Netherlands, 0–0, meaning that qualification would once again come down to getting a result in the third game. And worse, in an eerie parallel with the previous tournament, Bryan Robson, the captain, who had struggled so badly with his dislocated shoulder in Mexico, now injured his toe at the same stage in the competition. It was terrible for the team, and terrible for Bryan – his second successive World Cup destroyed early by injury. Anyone would have found that hard to take.

And there was nothing Olga Stringfellow could do about it. You don't know who Olga Stringfellow was? Long before there was Eileen Drewery, there was Olga Stringfellow. A New Zealander, at that point based in Hampshire, and no relation to Peter, Olga was a writer of historical fiction who claimed to be able to heal through the power of touch. I'm not sure what he thought about the historical fiction, but Bryan Robson was very persuaded by her therapy. It was decided that it wouldn't hurt to have Olga come into the England camp in Italy and see if she could do anything about Bryan's toe. The intention was to smuggle her in privately and avoid setting up a gold-plated story for the tabloids, but there's not much private smuggling that can be done when the team is sharing the same hotel as the press. (England stopped making this mistake eventually.)

Consequently, Olga's brief presence duly made perhaps not entirely helpful headlines back in Britain. Of course, had Bryan returned to fitness and captained England to the World Cup, Olga's place in the history of English football would be more secure. Sadly, that's not the way it panned out. For the record – in common with all the players, I think – I was asked if I wanted to have a session with Olga. Not about the diarrhoea specifically, I should say, but just for anything in general. I declined. I mean, whatever works. But it wasn't for me.

Bryan was replaced as captain by Terry Butcher, the role Terry was arguably born to fill. Large and intimidating, and later famous for playing on regardless in a blood-soaked head bandage, Terry liked to impose himself on opponents not only on the pitch but also, if possible, in the tunnel beforehand. Well, you might as well get in early. I remember lining up outside the dressing rooms before one match with Terry and there was a line of metal trollies along one wall. While we waited to walk out, Terry started bashing on the sides of these trollies and bawling: 'Caged tigers, lads! Caged tigers!' Eyes widened with terror – ours, perhaps, as much as the opposition's.

Morale among the players at Italia '90 was great – the best I knew in an England squad, off the pitch as well as on it. Steps have to be taken to alleviate the boredom of these World Cup spells because obviously there are only so many hours of the day you can spend training and seeing your faith healer, and you are bound to spend quite a bit of time twiddling your thumbs in the hotel. Our headquarters in Italy – the Is Molas in Sardinia – had its own golf course, which helped greatly. But additionally, very much in the Victorian spirit of creating your own entertainment, we hatched the idea of staging race nights.

Now, we had no horses, we had no jockeys and we had no course. But we weren't going to let little things like that become a barrier. The FA's largesse had extended to equipping us with a lounge area and a VHS player, and Channel 4 kindly agreed to send us out some tapes of recent race meetings, which we could then play in the room during the evening as if they were live. As a kid, at Leicester racecourse, I had learned how to run a book and do the necessary sums, so I was made the official course bookmaker, along with Peter Shilton. We had a white board on which to write up the odds and a bag for the cash, and we called ourselves Honest Links & Shilts, because honest was what we were. As honest as the day was long.

If only the same could be said for some of our customers.

One evening we were working our way through a recent six-race meeting from Cheltenham. Five races in, Honest Links & Shilts were doing just fine, thank you very much, as bookies generally do, and we started to take bets on the sixth and final race. A few people came forward and bet little bits and pieces – a fiver here, a tenner there – on a wide spread of the horses in the field, but otherwise the betting activity was strangely flat. And then suddenly, in the final seconds before the off, all the big hitters came in – Gazza and Bryan Robson foremost among them – and weighed in large on this one particular horse, which had drifted out to 12/1 on account of a complete lack of interest in it up to this point.

I was already thinking: this smells a little funny. But the bets were on, the money was in the bag and the horses were under starter's orders.

Needless to say, the big hitters' last-minute favourite romped home amid suspiciously universal cheering and shouting from the punters. They all knew. They were all in on it. Gazza had found out the result of the race from somewhere and set up the sting. Ruin for Honest Links & Shilts. Gazza stood in front of us, gleefully shouting: 'Pay 'em out, you bastards, pay 'em out!' We did. But we knew we had been royally mugged.

Away from the racecourse, we beat Egypt in that third group stage game, defeated Belgium with a cracking David Platt volley in the round of 16 and pushed past Cameroon in the quarter-finals with that penalty in extra-time, which I wrote about in the pages on Gazza. Whatever now happened, the tournament was turning into a massive vindication for the managing of Bobby Robson.

I was once on the bench when I heard Bobby issue the instruction: 'Garth – warm up.' We all looked at each other. Who the hell was Garth? We didn't have anybody called Garth. Then I realised he meant me: Garth Lineker.

But then Bobby was notorious for muddling names or accidentally reinventing them. He was responsible for calling Peter Shilton 'Shilly' – perhaps accidentally, perhaps not, you simply didn't know, but we all happily took it up and ran with it anyway, and Shilts became Shilly for a little while. The presence of Gary Stevens and Trevor Steven in the same squad seemed specifically sent to baffle Bobby. And sometimes he would forget names entirely and end up standing in front of you, snapping his fingers and desperately trying to retrieve them from his memory.

'You know . . . you know . . .'

'Neil Webb?'

'Yes!'

At the peak moment for these kinds of confusion, Bobby addressed Bryan Robson as Bobby Robson.

'No, you're Bobby,' Bryan had to explain. 'I'm Bryan.'

I was once in a television studio with Bobby when he mislaid his phone. 'I'm sure I had it a moment ago,' he was saying. I said I would call his number so that we could listen out for it ringing anywhere. Sure enough, a few moments later, while we all waited quietly, a dull buzzing could be heard. It seemed to be coming from the vicinity of Bobby's jacket.

Slightly annoyed by the distraction, Bobby reached into his inside pocket, pulled out his phone and answered it.

'Could I ring you back?' he said. 'I'm just busy looking for my phone.'

He was an idiosyncratic figure who seemed to have an

appreciation for everything. He once took me around St James' Park, and he was talking about the quality of the woodwork in the doors to the boardroom. I'm not sure many managers pause to notice those kinds of things. And I mentioned at the beginning of this book his eccentric team-talks and his love of the white paper flip-chart. In Italy, the evening before the semi-final against West Germany, Bobby brought the team together in the conference room at the hotel for the usual pre-match meeting. Bobby, as he often was, was a little late, and the flip-chart was sitting there temptingly at the front of the room, and I found I couldn't resist. I turned the top page over, and on the page below it I wrote: 'Even money he mentions the war.' Then I concealed it with the top page again.

Sure enough, Bobby walks in and his opening line to us is: 'Well, we beat them in the war . . .'

The whole room roared with laughter, to Bobby's bafflement. When he eventually turned the page on the chart, he understood why.

'You bastard, Lineker.'

But none of this obscures the key point about Bobby, which is that he was an absolutely superb football manager. This wasn't so much a matter of his coaching, which was fairly basic, really – certainly nothing out of the ordinary. But he understood footballers and he was very loyal to them. When you're England manager you're under enormous and constant pressure to change things – to react to every little setback with a major upheaval and a top-to-bottom rethink. That's just the overheated nature of the debate around the national side, where things are either entirely brilliant or entirely terrible and very rarely anywhere in between. But Bobby was very calm at the centre of all that, and he understood that, when you had world-class players, you perhaps didn't need to panic at the first sight of trouble: that you could stick with them and see it come good. And in Italy, in the shape of the best tournament performance by an England side since 1966, it did.

How close it was to being even better, though – the ultimate vindication. The semi-final in Turin still rolls through my mind every now and then. And unfortunately the outcome is always the same. West Germany go ahead through that free-kick that takes a freakish deflection off Paul Parker and loops like a balloon over Peter Shilton. Maybe we should have known whose side fate was on, right then. My finish for our equaliser remains one of the goals I'm most proud of – cutting the ball from wide on the left into the bottom right-hand corner. Unusually for me, I'm actually outside the six-yard box at the point of scoring it, too. Maybe it should have counted double.

Then comes extra-time and the second booking in the tournament for Gazza, which means no World Cup final, whether we get there or not. He knows, of course, as soon as he completes the tackle. He knows what's coming and he's waving his arms at the referee but really at that point he is trying to rewind time. As he walks past me, away from the ref, I see his face dissolve and that's the moment where the television camera catches me alerting Bobby Robson on the bench to the tears, urging Bobby to have a word with him. It's a fluke that the cameras caught it, in a way, because they're tracking Gazza, who has turned his back. But that then became the image which told the story – me with my finger to my eye, looking worried.

No further goals. The final whistle. Penalties.

Four of us definitely wanted to take one. David Platt was bursting to do it. Platty had come up to me before the penalty against Cameroon and said: 'If you don't fancy it, I'll take it.' Well, if you don't ask . . . But I very much did fancy it. Turn down a chance to get my goal tally up? That wasn't going to happen. So file me, too, under 'ready to take one'. Peter Beardsley was fine about the prospect. Stuart Pearce definitely wanted it. The fifth taker should, of course, have been Gazza, but Gazza wasn't in any state at that point. So Chris Waddle put his arm up – very reluctantly. He didn't really want to take one and people weren't exactly pushing themselves in front of him. I've no idea even now who penalty-taker number six would have been, had we got down that far.

As we got ready to head out to the centre circle and wait our turns, Bobby Robson came to the five of us and issued a few last words of encouragement and inspiration.

'There's 30 million watching this at home,' he said. 'Don't let me down, lads.'

Peter Beardsley and I caught each other's eyes after this and actually laughed. No pressure, then.

I was up first, which suited me fine. Get it done. I felt pretty calm about it. I've said it before: for better or worse, I didn't really get nervous. Something inside me actually embraced the opportunity. I went low and to the left and actually didn't hit it very close to the corner, but the goal-keeper, Bodo Illgner, didn't move so it didn't matter.

Germany equalised.

Beardsley hit the perfect penalty, no problem.

Germany equalised.

David Platt possibly got a bit lucky because the keeper was on to him, but there was enough power in it.

Germany equalised.

But Stuart Pearce struck it low and down the middle and watched it bounce almost back to him off Illgner's legs.

Germany went ahead.

Chris, who hadn't wanted to take one in the first place, now found himself kicking to keep us alive.

I'm guessing you'll know what happened next.

In an alternative version of this match, Gazza doesn't get booked, Gazza takes his penalty, Gazza scores. Because I know he would have done. As Bobby Robson said about him: 'The bigger the game, the better he got.' But you could be rewriting these things in your head for ever, until you went mad with it.

People ask what was said afterwards. The truth is, nothing

was said. There was nothing to say. We all just sat in the dressing room, numb, staring into space or down at the floor. To rise up close enough to the peak of a World Cup final that you can practically smell the air up there, and then to sink back down again . . . for all of us, that was a kind of deflation beyond words. I think Bobby went round the room and ruffled everybody's hair, and told us all to be proud of how far we had come. But otherwise it was silent. Desolation.

Eventually, still silent, we got changed and climbed on to the coach to head back to the hotel. A few cans were passed around, and the bus moved away.

And then it began.

It would have been either Gazza or Chris Waddle, as usual, just quietly.

'Doe, a deer . . .'

Then a couple of others picked it up.

'Ray, a drop of golden sun . . .'

And now the singing was gaining volume.

'Me, a name I call myself . . .'

And gradually it built and built until, amazingly, emotionally, everybody had joined in and the song was right round the bus.

'That will bring us back to doe, oh, oh, oh . . .'

Julie Andrews was back, working her powerful magic again.

I stayed out in Italy after the team flew home. This meant I wasn't on the open-top bus tour of Luton, where Gazza inspired a heated national debate by choosing to wear a pair of plastic boobs. My loss, I guess. Three hundred thousand people turned out on the streets for the losing semi-finalists that day, which gives some indication of the extent to which the country had engaged with the experience.

Instead, I remained in Italy with Bobby Robson to do some punditry with ITV for the final. I had a terrible, terrible suit on, but despite that it seemed to go OK. I was even tempted to wonder whether there might be a future in it at some stage.

CHAPTER FIFTEEN

'He's got to be doing better there, surely.'

In which DANNY takes a reasoned and entirely dispassionate look at video-assisted refereeing, its pros and its cons, and ultimately decides that, on balance, despite the delays and the unfortunate disruptions to the game's flow, what's important for the integrity of the sport going forward is that the correct decision is reached. Oh, wait – no he doesn't.

We saw it again during the Women's World Cup in 2019: the battle over rights to the big telly. Typically, forces loyal to myself (me) will have taken control of the big telly in an unopposed manoeuvre around about kick-off time at 8pm (the end-title music of *Emmerdale* being my cue). Typically the opposing forces, under the command of my wife, or one of the daughters, will arrive in the room at around 9pm, commonly when *Love Island* is due on, and the skirmishing will then begin.

The first question is always: 'Are you watching this?'

In response to which I will commonly suggest that I am, indeed, 'watching this', relying on the secondary evidence (the fact that the telly is on, the fact that I am sitting in front of it) to support me in that assertion.

The second question, which may or may not come after a short pause, is: 'Is it an important game?'

Now, I'll be honest: sometimes I have to massage slightly here. When it comes to football matches, there are, one appreciates, degrees of importance. But with a view to simplicity, and with one eye on the longer battle ahead, I will usually claim that the match currently unfolding is indeed important. Important enough, at any rate, that I am watching it.

And now the conversation deepens slightly.

'I thought you said we'd had the last game of the season.'

'When?'

'The other Sunday. You said the FA Cup final was the last game of the season.'

'Well, no: that was the last game of the FA Cup.'

Another short pause may occur here.

'What were those other ones after that, then, on that Sunday?'

'Those were the last games of the season – Premier League.'

'So that was the last game.'

'Of the season, yeah.'

'But last Saturday, what was that?'

'That was the Champions League final.'

'Right. And what's this?'

'It's the Women's World Cup.'

'When does it finish?'

'This game? In about 40 minutes.'

'No, the whole thing.'

'In about three weeks.'

'So it isn't over, then.'

And so it goes on, as members of my family ruthlessly try to pin me down on the exact 20 minutes in any summer when the football season isn't on – that period of time we used to refer to as 'the closed season' but don't any more, on the grounds that football, or rather its paymaster, TV, has taken the decision never to close if it can help it.

I suppose I could go in another room and put the radio on. Tom Waits said his favourite music was a ball game on the radio, and I can entirely relate to that. Pootling around filing old LPs on shelves while football is on the radio – Eden could not have contained such delight.

On the other hand, if it's on the telly . . .

There were things I saw during the Women's World Cup of 2019 that made me glad I had stood my ground in the battle for the big telly. And when I say 'stood my ground', I mean everyone was out anyway. The USA thrashed Thailand 13–0 in the group stage, and one of the things I loved about it was the way in which every single one of those

13 goals was celebrated by the players as though it was the first and possibly the only goal they would be scoring in their lives. Bravo, and why wouldn't you?

Now some observers later complained that they found this relish disrespectful – that even if they hadn't eased off on the goals, at least the USA could have eased off on the celebrating. Imagine telling that to the supporters! 'One should temper one's elation commensurate to the moment.' Pipe down, sour puss!

The USA, in their ebullience, seemed to me to be showing Thailand exactly the respect that should be shown to any opponent, no matter how deeply you are ploughing them into the grass. Indeed, what would have been disrespectful, and possibly even disgraceful, would have been *not* celebrating. I speak as a Millwall fan here: I can think of no scenario more universally degrading than one in which Manchester City, say, arrive in our humble home, score after 20 minutes and just jog back to the centre with a shrug. That would be patronising balls, and a teeteringly haughty thumb in the eye. The USA scored their 13th and were all over each other. That's how you do it.

Unfortunately, what I also saw on the big telly during that tournament was a string of nonsense arising from the application of VAR, which clamped its ice-cold hand around the beating heart of so many critical moments involving goals, offsides, handballs and the movements of goalkeepers at penalties. During the game against Nigeria in the group stages, the South Korea forward Lee Geum-min was given offside when the video analysts in their remote studio revealed that the arm she had raised to signal that she was available to receive the cross was ahead of the defensive line when the ball was played. Not any other part of her body, just her raised arm. You would have thought such boggling pedantry would have brought people out on to the streets with rough-hewn clubs and vengeance in their eyes – not just in South Korea but everywhere that people had a pulse. But no. All the weasels, the do-gooders and the joy-sucking vampires simply sighed and said: 'Well, technically, as the law stands . . .'

I have a better idea. Let us hear from the people who made that law. Let's drag them into the light to explain themselves to the rest of us. Tell us why a goal shouldn't stand because a player put her arm up to call for the ball. Why? Why are you skewing this global game? What lies at the heart of your desire to do this? These are the people who voted to change the handball rule, and who are happy to see a goal ruled out because a player called for the ball. I would have them on the end of a phone at every game. 'Come on. Tell us why you spoiled another game.'

Yet nearly everyone accepts it. Sell-outs bow to the tyranny of television, saying: 'Ah, well, that's just the way the modern game is going . . .' Even the television pundits rally round the flag, apparently undeterred by the fact that, by speaking up for VAR, they are arguing themselves out of a job – Tesco cashiers voting for the self-checkouts. Because ultimately what will be left for the pundits to talk about, apart from VAR itself?

Who knew that in 2019 we would find ourselves soberly scrutinising a straight line drawn in digital marker pen across a frozen photograph which has revealed that somebody's toe was offside? For, without exaggeration, it has come down to this. Or that we would compliantly see the joy unleashed by goal-scoring slightly suspended every time, pending the possibility of review – all our pleasure nervously compromised while the bully that is VAR stands on the sidelines, menacingly slapping a cosh against its leather-gloved fist.

And as for this idea that 'at least we've got the correct result' – well, forgive me, but fuck the correct result. Football has always been chaos. It's a football match, not a murder trial. The idea that Almighty TV is going to fix everything for us, at this stage in the game's endearingly pockmarked history, and smooth it out for us is worse than presumptuous.

Now, Gary would say: 'Yes, but you've never been in a World Cup quarter-final where someone has punched the ball into the net.' And I get that. I can't play laugh-along-a-Maradona any more than any other England supporter. At the same time, I don't doubt people in Argentina feel very differently about it. In the quarter-final of the 1970 World Cup in Mexico, when England were 2–0 up against West Germany, Geoff Hurst had a good and possibly decisive goal ruled out. England lost 3–2. How far back do you want to go about all this?

But, of course, in 1970 television merely covered football, it didn't govern football. Now football is entirely owned by television and the inevitable consequence is that cameras and screens are swallowing the game. TV tells football when to kick off, it tells it when a goal has been scored, and now it's telling it what the rules are. It's a liberty and an impertinence and it makes supporters extras in their own film, there merely to add a dash of atmosphere to someone else's small-screen entertainment project. 'Thanks, guys. Can we do that again?'

Smash the cameras, I say. Smash all the cameras. I want that on T-shirts. I want that to trend as a hashtag: #smashthecameras. Let's remind television: you're not here to *be* the game, you're here to transmit it – *whatever happens*.

I look forward to the first club that says, punk rock style: 'No – we're not being televised. You're not coming in here.' If I were Bill Gates, I would have bought a football club and then barred television from it, just to make the point. 'We might let you have the goals for *Match of the Day*. On the other hand we might not. I shall ask our paying supporters what they say.'

And people will say: 'But there's so much at stake.' Well, there shouldn't be. Stop being so craven. When it's flawed and chaotic, we like it more. I once witnessed a Millwall goal against Gillingham where the ball was punched back into the penalty area from a yard over the touchline. So, not just out of play, but actually handled in the process of returning it. And Millwall then scored. Never a goal in a million years. Except, no – a goal right then, that afternoon, and a precious memory forever more. We have had goals against us like that, too. Otherwise, there is nothing to talk about aside from dreary record-book facts.

I say again to these people: why are you using electronic geometry to eliminate the flaws? And if the flaws are so utterly unbearable for you, then would you not be happier playing a computer game – perhaps, for perfect symmetry, a bad one, where the chip takes a small age to process the information?

Of course, you're looked at as some kind of Luddite for mounting such arguments. But surely not all of us can simply stand on the pavement, waving meekly as television's occupying tanks continue to pass through. Surely at least some of us have got to step into the road at some point soon and accept the risks. Because it's only going to get worse. How can anybody conclude that partial use of VAR makes any sense? What about the mistakes that VAR is, as yet, not allowed to correct: the incorrectly given throw-in or free-kick, some moments earlier than the goal, but inevitably connected with it because everything that happens in a football match follows from what has just happened? The people who high-mindedly explain that what takes place on the pitch is intricately interdependent and that 'playing it out from the back' might look fiddly and dangerous to the untutored eye, but is actually part of an organic process designed to cause spaces to occur further up the pitch – these are the same people who somehow don't mind that VAR doesn't necessarily care what happened as little as six seconds ago.

And rest assured, soon enough the managers will notice this and begin to press for wider and wider use of the system. And soon VAR will be ruling on everything, while those of us still watching drum our fingers sorrowfully and hope that at some point the action will be allowed to resume and that, when it does, it will be allowed to flow for more than 15 seconds before the next marginal call needs reassessing. That's the logical end of this argument and those who have forced it upon us will be in no position to complain.

Smash all the cameras, I say. #smashthecameras.

In the meantime, you'll find me calming down in the lounge, where I believe there's some football on.

'What's this?'

'This? It's the Africa Cup of Nations.'

'I thought you said . . .'

CHAPTER SIXTEEN

'The referee thought about blowing up.'

In which GARY analyses the work of a certain Lionel Messi of Barcelona and Argentina, and decides that, relatively speaking, he's no slouch. Includes a full explanation for the night Gary ended up in the arms of Rio Ferdinand.

A little statistic for you: at the time of writing, Lionel Messi has made 76 appearances as a substitute for Barcelona. And in those appearances as a sub, he has scored 34 goals. In other words, practically every other time he comes off the bench, in the usually fairly small amount of time remaining in the game, Messi scores. There are first-pick strikers who wouldn't mind a strike-rate as high as that. And no doubt Barcelona would be minded to use Messi as an 'impact sub' more often than they do, if it wasn't for what happens when he's on the pitch from the start.

As I write this, Messi has just made his 450th La Liga appearance. He scored 417 goals in those games. That's a ludicrous rate of conversion. I'm pretty proud of my goal career average – 238 goals in 460 appearances, making a scoring rate of 0.51 per game. That's not too shabby. I'm even prouder of my international record, which is slightly better: 48 goals in 80 games for an average of 0.6 per game. But Messi's 417 goals in 450 appearances makes an average of [hastily taps at calculator buttons on phone] . . . 0.92! And that's before we add in the 111 goals he has scored in 134 European appearances. These numbers are off the charts. There are whole La Liga clubs who haven't scored as many league goals as Messi *in their entire histories*.

Which is all another way of saying that he's really quite good.

Now, I get a fair bit of stick on social media for speaking in tones of awe about Lionel Messi. Some people like to accuse me of being far too attached to him. (They put it in slightly more robust terms than that. But that's Twitter for you, especially late at night.) And as I know from experience, one of the sure-fire ways to bring a digital storm down on yourself at this point in the 21st century is to drop a casual remark about how far superior Lionel Messi is to Cristiano Ronaldo, or vice versa. Talk about divisive. This really does seem to have become the Blur v Oasis of our time. Or the Leave v Remain, if you prefer.

The thing is, I genuinely rate Ronaldo – and you would need to be blind or a fool not to. Indeed, I regard it as a testament to how good Ronaldo is that he's considered to be up there as Messi's chief competitor. And here's the key thing, of course: it is possible to enjoy both. Pleasure in one does not exclude the possibility of pleasure in the other. So, lucky us. What a time to be alive. But if the comparison is going to be made and if it's going to be turned into a head-to-head, hand-to-hand, fight-to-the-death kind of thing – and clearly it is – then I think you would find that most ex-players and people who really get the game will come down pretty firmly on the side of Messi.

And personally, I would go a little further. I honestly believe that there is no comparison, really: and that's not taking anything away from Ronaldo, who is a player I admire enormously. It's just that I have come to the conclusion that Messi is in a category of his own.

Ronaldo is a phenomenal player – a brilliant talent and one of the best goal-scorers the world has ever known. And his goals-to-matches ratio is pretty similar to Messi's, although Messi's numbers in that area are slightly better. But Messi, to my mind, has many things over Ronaldo. For instance, he's got the most unbelievable spatial awareness and vision. He sees things that other players, including Ronaldo, simply don't see: approaching opponents, moves made by his team-mates. He's quite possibly the best passer of a football that you will ever see, with the most beautiful feel for the ball, enabling him to strike the most deftly weighted passes.

He's as good a free-kick taker as you are likely to find.

(Consider, as a prime specimen, the one he scored against Liverpool in the semi-final of the Champions League in 2019, his 600th career goal, fittingly enough – hit from an implausible distance, swerving around the wall and ending up practically in the top corner. Glorious because just so plain inconceivable. There aren't many things with the power to drive me into the arms of Rio Ferdinand but, that night in the BT Sport studio in the Nou Camp, that impossibly refined strike did so.*) And, on top of that, he's probably, along with Maradona, the best dribbler of a ball I have ever seen – and possibly slightly better, in fact.

The one thing Ronaldo clearly beats him on is heading. He's half a foot taller than Messi, so you would expect him to be better at that aspect of the game, but there's also the

---

* A brief explanation of that embrace between Rio and myself, if I may. After those images emerged, I got quite a lot of blow-back from Liverpool fans who didn't take entirely kindly to the sight of me and a former Manchester United player leaping around in apparent delight after their team had received an almighty Champions League setback. The reason we look quite so happy, though, is that, as Messi was standing over that free-kick, I said to Rio: 'What's the betting he sticks it in the top left corner for his 600th goal?' And Rio replied: 'That would be amazing, but I think it's too far out.' Next thing: boom, swish, goal. So it wasn't Liverpool's discomfort that drove us into each other's arms so much as the fact that we had just predicted it, and then doubted it, and then seen it come true in front of our disbelieving eyes. Anyway, I did used to play for Barcelona, you know. I think I get a pass, don't I?

fact that Ronaldo has that astonishing ability to spring off the ground as if using rubberised calves, and get uncannily high. You're not getting that from Messi, it's true. (Official height: just over 5ft 5in.) But does that outweigh all of Messi's other advantages on the pitch? Handy though the ability to climb several miles into the sky in the opposition's penalty area clearly is, I don't think so.

I played at the top level and I played against the Messi of my time, who was Diego Maradona. Yet there will be at least two or three occasions in any match that I see Messi play where I will be looking down at something he has just done and thinking to myself: 'I don't know how he did that. How did he manage it? How?' It's not even like he seems to be busy a lot of the time – and this is probably the art to it. He doesn't run around the way that other players do, and he certainly doesn't run himself out of steam. He stands and he watches and he waits and then he seizes his moment. And presumably it's what he is seeing and planning and calculating while he is watching and waiting that makes the difference. He is applying this unique level of intelligence to it all.

I never thought I would live to see Maradona outperformed, but I genuinely think that's happened and is continuing to happen. You'll be watching and, all game long, you'll be muttering to yourself: 'Give him the ball, give him the ball.' And when he's got ball, you're alight with excitement about what he might do with it – even in the least promising circumstances, surrounded on the wing, crowded out in the centre, in the circle with his back to goal. No scenario seems to preclude the possibility that he might produce something amazing, a moment of danger, an opportunity conjured out of what appeared to be nothing.

I've talked about him to other pros, and they feel the same. It's gobsmacking what he does. If I'm in the stadium, as opposed to watching on the telly, I'll take the chance to watch what he gets up to when he doesn't have the ball. I know it's hard in the course of a match, but it's worth doing if you ever have the chance. Look where he is at certain times, and what he does. He stands still, he walks about. He'll randomly walk out wide at some point, stand on the touchline for a bit. He'll have a little look around and then wander into the middle. It's as though the game is going on and he's just a mildly interested observer.

And then he'll find himself a bit of space – often by standing still because it's amazing how many people run away from you if you stop moving. And then, finally, he gets the ball. And when he gets the ball, things start to happen and keep on happening – a run through a gap between players that didn't seem to exist, a pass that you hadn't remotely anticipated, a shot that had never seemed on. His peripheral vision is absurd. It's as though he's watching the game from above, on his own personal Spidercam feed. Or he's got some kind of Google eyewear, which is granting him streamed monitors of the view behind and all around him in real time.

And consequently he seems to have no blindside. Somehow he knows where that challenge is coming from, where that team-mate is running to, where that gap between those three, or four, or five defenders is. And suddenly with one surging run, or one quick pass, an entire defence is in ruins.

Best player ever? I think he must be.

Now, his critics, such as they are, will always raise the World Cup at this point. Messi has had the slight misfortune to be playing at a time when the Argentina side has been pretty average on the whole, and by no means the permanent and dire threat that it represented 30 years ago. And it's true that he hasn't always exactly sparkled in World Cups, and he certainly hasn't won one. And, for a lot of people, not winning the World Cup would actively disqualify you from being regarded as the Greatest of All Time, with no further discussion necessary.

But I just don't think I buy that argument any more. For one thing, you're ruling George Best out of consideration straight away, which feels like a mistake. And, in any case, you have to think about what a World Cup actually is. We're talking about a knockout tournament, for which teams are thrown together by accident of birth, packed off to a corner of the globe that they may not be familiar with, and made to compete in a short and intensive burst of action in the middle of the summer. Which is great, of course, and we all love it. But that doesn't mean that it's entirely immune to the operation of the random and bizarre forces which can affect all knockout tournaments, nor, by extension, that it's a completely reliable meter of one player's form and ability. The World Cup might well represent the pinnacle of a player's career. But that's not necessarily the same thing as being wholly representative of that career.

Similarly, I disagree with this argument regarding managers, which you see gaining a bit of traction now: namely, that we should judge them, ultimately, on their success in the Champions League. When Manchester City were knocked out of the tournament in the quarter-finals by Tottenham in the 2018–19 season, a few people raised their eyebrows and tutted a bit about the merits of Pep Guardiola. Hasn't won the Champions League for ages! Only did it when he had Iniesta and that wonderful Barcelona side!

But knockout competitions are precarious. You only need a slight off-day or a freak moment of misfortune, and that's it: you're gone. Again, that's why we love them. But if we're going to be ranking players and managers, and trying to hand down some kind of ultimate judgement on them, we probably need a more solid basis on which to do so. And that more solid basis seems to me, fairly obviously, to be league football, with contributions to cup competitions and international football taken into consideration on top of that. Show us your medals, yes. But also show us what you got up to, week in week out, over a period of years, with your club.

So, on that basis, I'm handing it to Messi. I go on about

him, I know. But watching him brings me joy, and it will be a devastatingly sad day when he quits because we have never seen the like of him before. We really haven't.

Of course, I have appeared alongside Messi and consider myself very fortunate to have done so. I also like to think – without wishing to boast or appear to be over-reaching myself – that I held my end up pretty well on the day, and arguably more than matched his input. You will almost certainly remember the occasion. It was in an advert for crisps.

In fact, there have been two adverts graced simultaneously by me and Lionel Messi, although I suppose the one that has gone down in cinema history, and is still talked about wherever people gather to discuss major advertising campaigns for salted snacks, is the one where Messi, in a fetchingly casual crew-neck jumper, is trying to play table football in an apartment, while I try to put him off by loudly munching on crisps. Has anyone tried this in a real game? It's got to have as much of a chance as anything else.

Anyway, I'm sure you'll agree that the on-screen chemistry between the two of us during that 30 seconds or so is pretty special. Natural. Unforced. The clear product of a natural human sympathy which the cameras couldn't help but pick up on and record for posterity. Particularly the bit where I end up with a trophy on my head.

Let me tell you something about that chemistry, though. We were never together on the set. Not for one single second. Not in either of the ads that we did. The word is that Messi is pretty shy and quite introverted. I'm not sure that he likes to be around lots of people anywhere. And he certainly didn't want to be around lots of people on the set for those crisp commercials. He shot his part in front of a green screen, I filmed my bit separately, in a completely different place on a completely different day, and the two of us were brought together by technical wizardry in the editing suite.

Apologies if I'm shattering your illusions here. What can I say? Stevie Wonder and Paul McCartney weren't in the same room as each other when they recorded 'Ebony and Ivory'. That's just the way of things in showbusiness, I'm afraid. Indeed, that's why they call it 'showbusiness' in the first place.

However, for the sake of absolute clarity, please note: this kind of trickery has never been employed in the making of the *Behind Closed Doors* podcast. No smoke, no mirrors, no crafty business in the editing room. In that case, without exception, what you hear is what you get, with Danny and myself genuinely together at the microphones, separated only by my kitchen counter. And even if we were tempted to do it over the phone (which might be a handy way to save some time, now I think about it) we couldn't, because Danny doesn't have one.

Anyway, don't let this revelation detract from Messi's performance in the finished piece, though. There's that spatial awareness again – the ability to pick the individual crisp out of the bag without drawing other crisps out at the same time. Pros will understand what I'm talking about. You can't learn that kind of thing. Either it comes naturally or it doesn't come at all. I've made crisp adverts with some of the truly great performers in my time. I'm thinking of the likes of the Spice Girls, Ulrika Jonsson, Lionel Richie . . . But Messi was quite simply in a different class.

Go ahead. Slaughter me on Twitter for saying so.

CHAPTER SEVENTEEN

'I'm not sure what he was thinking there.'

In which DANNY offers any youngsters just setting out in the professional game, and harbouring dreams of hitting the heights, the benefit of his immense wisdom in ten key footballing categories. It may be the first time that Kim Jong-un of North Korea has been mentioned positively in a discussion pertaining to football.

1. TATTOOS

There's not much space left on many of today's players, what with the passages of scripture, the inspirational phrases and sayings, the Chinese pictograms, the heartfelt and permanent tributes to loved ones, the illuminations. Memphis Depay alone now runs to three volumes. Clearly, footballers are going to end up like the Sunday papers, and we'll be saying: 'How am I supposed to find time to read all that?' My word to the next generation is that in football, as in life, only two tattoos are really allowed: either an anchor or the word 'Mum'. And, ideally, you should have come by those tattoos in one of only two locations: prison or the navy. Do people realise that they will never come off? Would anyone decide at 17, 'this haircut I have now is amazing! I'm keeping it for life'? That's what a tattoo is.

2. HAIRCUTS

Footballers' haircuts, like talking about pies on sale at various grounds, is a bit of a cliché these days. However, let a bald man have his say. It's the sheer range of options that is the devil here – all that elaborate plaiting, chiselling and carving. I'm more instinctively in favour of the North Korean approach to men's hairdressing, where, essentially, there are two haircuts to choose between and that's it. Now, don't get me wrong: Kim Jong-un and his direct predecessors in the Pyongyang hot seat have taken some rum and unacceptable approaches to the business of governing a country down the years. But he's on to something with the haircuts, isn't he? Any more than two and suddenly there's choice and extended deliberation involved and, frankly, that's why nothing's getting done.

3. HAIR REPLACEMENT THERAPY

Supplementary to the above, and even within my two-haircuts-only strictures, we sympathise with any young player who, in due course, and with the money coming in, elects to seek 'help up top'. To do so is merely to join an impressive list of talents who have gone down the rethatching path at some point or other: Wayne Rooney, David Silva, Andros

Townsend, Ashley Barnes, Dimitar Berbatov, Antonio Conte . . . we could go on. But if Frank Sinatra couldn't get a good rug, nor Paul Simon, despite all their connections, well, what hope is there for you or me? We might as well give up and go naked-headed into that good night. Alternatively, I once acquired from a Florida truck stop, for the bargain price of $1.99, a bandana with a built in grey/blond hair attachment, which I can confirm, from employing it to cover my own now thoroughly vacant pate in various broadcasting scenarios, does a serviceable job over the short-to-medium term. Then again, I have never attempted to wear it while playing football, so clearly further testing is required. I'll get back to you.

4. BIN LINERS

Now sadly in abeyance at the highest levels of the game, bin liners were once considered an utterly indispensable accessory for pre-season training. Ripping head and arm holes in a black binbag and then putting it on in order to create your own dark plastic steam-room was for many years considered a reliable method to re-achieve match-ready leanness after a summer at ease. The likes of Peter Reid and Graeme Souness as good as swore by the bin liner come July. True, the question always hovered: are you actually removing fat by this method or merely collecting liquid? Sports science is notably silent in this area, and it is possible that there is no more truth in the alleged efficacy of bin bags as a fat-burning tool than there was in the rumour which took hold during my youth that if you were to cut open a golf ball, the special liquid inside it would blind you. No matter. My feeling remains that if you're not doing those long-distance pre-season runs while clad in a bin liner, you're not doing them properly. Incidentally, I once saw Gazza entirely lose the toxic and depleting effects of a previous late night by skipping with a rope, very hard, in the necessarily fetid climate provided by a leisure centre's boiler room. This, too, apparently, will do the trick. Though, never go running in a recyclable bin bag. New laws mean local councils can legally throw you in the back of the dustcart.

5. ROLE MODELS

Be most wary in your selection of a role model, for people are not always as they seem. Hear now the parable of the prodigal footballer. There was once a player who could do no wrong. Apparently flawless in his conduct and ever-professional in his attitudes, he was held up as a shining example to the young. Yet one day, in training, the prodigal footballer was dispatched with his team-mates on a cross-country run. This was a hateful prospect for the squad almost unanimously. Yet they recognised, as a unit, that theirs was not to question or take lightly the methods of their masters, so they all buckled under and submitted to the task, as instructed. All, that is, except the prodigal player. Part way through lap one of this cross-country ordeal, the prodigal player took it upon himself to leave the course and hide in a bush. There he quietly waited. When his team-mates eventually came by on their final lap, the prodigal footballer emerged from his hiding place and nonchalantly joined them for the final jog home. Moreover, with the attention to detail that marks out the truly devious from the mere amateurs of the deceit game, rather than joining the race leaders, where he might have drawn attention to himself, the player carefully inserted himself in a modest position in the middle of the pack. Despite this precaution, though, and a mid-placed finish, he was rumbled. Informed of the prodigal one's behaviour, the team's devastated manager summoned him to his office, where he explained to him in sorrowful tones that he had let his manager down, that he had let his club down, and that, saddest of all, he had let himself down. Was the trust ever there again? It's hard to imagine that it was. Young players: behold this flouting of authority by the seemingly impeccable and reflect deeply. Choose your role models with enormous care. (The manager in this tale was Terry Venables, the squad was Tottenham Hotspur's, and the prodigal player was Gary Lineker.)

6. GLOVES

Absolutely not. Sorry. Notwithstanding Gary Lineker's surprisingly extensive circulatory problems, amply documented elsewhere in this volume, gloves are for boxing and for boxing solely. No place for them in football. That said, I would have no problem at all with players seeking to insulate parts of themselves that actually hurt when struck by the ball. Thighs, for example. Then there's testicles. And, of course, ears. If you want to protect your lobes from the worst of a sharp winter's evening, you'll get no argument from me. Ear protectors will come in S, M, L, XL, and Gary Lineker.

7. GOAL CELEBRATIONS

... should be conducted wholeheartedly, always, without exception – and especially when the goal is against your former club. Fans know that there are two kinds of returning player: Lion Judas and Chicken Judas. Chicken Judas is the player who is due back at his old ground with his new side but then mysteriously picks up a tweaked calf muscle or a lightly bruised toe, or some other probably entirely bogus injury, and thus never makes it out on to the pitch. Or if he does make it on to the pitch, and by some further freak scores, he resolutely refuses to celebrate the goal – a display of cravenness for which, incredibly, he is praised in sappier quarters for having shown 'respect'. Lion Judas, by contrast, is the player who comes back to your club and takes a spectacular amount of pleasure in running your defence ragged and sticking the ball into your net over and over again, grinning wildly the while. And quite right, too. It is not 'respectful' to fail to celebrate a goal against your old club; on the contrary, it is marginally disrespectful to your new club and wholly disrespectful to the spirit of football. It also arises from a misguided desire to 'do the decent thing', of which there is far too much in the modern game. Young players: it is your duty as the next generation to resist the siren call of 'the decent thing'.

8. ABUSE

You're going to hear some strong stuff coming from the stands under the cover of that revolting term 'banter', it goes without saying. But my very strongest counsel would be that you don't 'banter' back, because that rarely goes well. Note the following cautionary tale relating to Lee Dixon, the former England full-back. While playing for Arsenal at West Ham, Dixon was receiving treatment near the touchline when a large West Ham fan took advantage of his proximity to address the player, directly and at volume. 'You're a fucking useless c***, Dixon,' the West Ham fan suggested. Now, in ordinary circumstances, this would have been so much water off the back of a player of Dixon's vast experience and mature temperament. But on this occasion Lee couldn't help noticing that the fan had, beside him, a young boy who couldn't have been anything more than six or seven years old. And this unsettling detail prompted Dixon to react. 'Very nice, talking like that in front of your boy,' said Lee. To which the fan replied: 'Don't you worry about him. He thinks you're a fucking useless c***, too.'

9. CAPS

No doubt, like me, as an upcoming youngster, you dreamed of representing your country and thereby assembling your own personal collection of those satisfyingly strange pieces of tasselled headgear with which a football association rewards its chosen ones. Furthermore, on taking receipt of it, I would immediately pose before a full-length mirror, nude, wearing just this sacred hat. I would certainly wear it while out and about, which, as it happens, a disappointingly small number of players seem to do. Heed this, though – a shocking and under-reported fact about England caps. Gary Lineker, as we know and celebrate, made 80 appearances for England. But how many actual tasselled caps do you suppose the former goal-scorer has in the specially built, glass and silver 'cap cabinet' that dominates the sitting room of his London home – or in the black bin bag under the bed in the spare room, whichever applies? The answer, shockingly, is just 40. Why so? Because apparently any one-off game for England, be it a friendly or a qualifier, will earn you a cap, and rightly so. But a tournament (a World Cup, a European Championship) in which you have played, say, five or even six games, only earns one cap with all the teams you've met in the course of that tournament lamely written around it in a token gesture to completeness. That is lamentable stinginess on the part of the FA. 'One game one cap' is surely the law. And if you only got on for 45 minutes? You get half a hat. This way, everyone knows where they stand.

10. FAME

When I was newly arrived as a presenter at the radio station GLR, a young and energetic production assistant walked in to the studio, held out a hand and said: 'Hello, I'm Chris Evans.' It was the beginning of a permanent friendship. One evening, early in our acquaintance, the pair of us were having a soothing drink after work when a woman approached me and asked me for an autograph, which I duly signed. Chris was astounded. 'Wow, what was all that about?' Having never seen my London-only TV shows, it seemed to boggle Chris that he was in the company of someone whom people might recognise. Now flash forward 18 months – which have been 18 very busy months in Chris' broadcasting career. The pair of us are photographed emerging from a media whizz-bang and in the newspaper in which this important documentary image appears, the caption below it reads: 'Chris Evans and one of his hangers-on out on the town.' From the only public attraction in that particular friendship to bootlicking entourage member in merely a year and a half. And from that, we must once again dwell on the greatest proverb the Bible has to offer: There is no business . . . liketh show business.

CHAPTER EIGHTEEN

'You've seen them given.'

*In which GARY presents the 2019 Champions League final
for BT Sport and somehow manages to stay awake. And with
some further gripping ruminations on jousting for glory
with Ian Wright, being given surprisingly small medals,
and breaking into stadiums dressed as cleaners.*

End-to-end play, outrageous goals, unlikely twists, enough tension to have you biting the arm of your sofa, an outcome in doubt until the very end . . . Everything that you could possibly want from a football match, the Champions League final of 2019 wasn't.

Such a shame. Two English teams in the reckoning, a nation agog – it could have been one of the great broadcasting nights. Instead it turned into one of the greater broadcasting challenges. On BT Sport, we gave the game two hours of build-up and then set more than an hour aside for discussion afterwards. The latter, particularly, ended up looking a touch optimistic, given the lack of talking points generated by the game. 'Casting around a bit' doesn't begin to define it and I guess it's a tribute to the resourcefulness and professionalism of everyone on the panel that night that we didn't resort to asking each other how our kids were getting along or talking about our holiday plans. Good job there were the celebration scenes to look at.

I suppose we should always have known it would be anti-climactic. The semi-finals, in which both finalists, on consecutive nights, completed ludicrously unlikely come-backs, Liverpool against Barcelona, Tottenham against Ajax, were a kind of double lightning strike, and what's the old expression? 'Lightning never strikes thrice.' The com-petition had peaked right there and, predictably enough, the final had the feel of a warm-down.

On top of that, with the expectations piled high, the game was killed stone dead in the first minute by the penalty awarded against Spurs for handball. If it had been the other way around, Tottenham scoring first, it might have been dif-ferent. Liverpool, when they need to go for it, are pretty dynamic. But once they're ahead they become extremely hard to break down. Tottenham played reasonably well in the circumstances, but it looked to me like both teams had suffered from the unhelpful three-week break that ended up being inserted between the end of the league season and the game. That unusual pause seemed to have taken some momentum out of them, and they both had the slightly baggy appearance of teams who hadn't played in a while – perhaps since the 1980s, in fact. The game certainly had a slightly eighties feel about it: long balls getting humped up, people giving possession away all over the place.

Glenn Hoddle, on the BT punditry team, was properly disappointed. He thought Spurs were the better side. He wasn't having it that it was a penalty and he made his case very firmly in the show. And fair enough. In the days when we played, getting struck on the arm as Moussa Sissoko was by Sadio Mané's cross wouldn't have resulted in a penalty in any circumstances. On the other hand, the way the handballs have been given in this Champions League – the one late in the PSG v Manchester United game for example, and the one that Danny Rose was done for in Tottenham's first leg against Manchester City – you would have to say it was consistent.

Big miss by the scriptwriters, though. It was all set up, wasn't it? Glenn Hoddle has a near-death experience, is saved by the smart intervention of a bystander, returns to health, goes back to work and, in the final reel, sees his beloved Tottenham win the European Cup. Cue music and roll credits.

But no. In this version, the scriptwriters blew the big finish. Do they not test these things on the public before they release them?

What a season for Glenn, though. It was on his 61st birthday, in October 2018, that he collapsed at the BT studios from a heart attack and he might well have died right there if there hadn't happened to be someone on the production staff, Simon Daniels, who had had medical training and was able to use a defibrillator. Glenn then underwent surgery and spent a month in hospital before going home to recuperate and he didn't get back into a television studio until the beginning of March. I guess, in the end, that's the kind of experience that will put something as trivial as the outcome of a mere football match firmly in perspective.

Or maybe not because, boy, was Glenn gutted in Madrid. You should have seen him. Absolutely hollowed out. The power of football, eh? No matter what life shows you, football will still find a way to get you.

I was disappointed too, of course. Not to Glenn levels, clearly. But definitely disappointed. I spent three years at Tottenham and it's a club I continue to care for. OK, a Tottenham result is never going to be able to change my mood the way a Leicester City result will. But there's still an affinity there and I would have loved to see them win the Champions League that night.

I arrived at Tottenham in 1989. I had just spent three years playing in Spain, so there was a certain amount of re-adapting to be done, certainly with regard to defending. At Barcelona, the first time I chased after a full-back, the coaching staff were like, 'What are you doing?'

And I had to explain. 'Well, that's what we do, in a 4–4–2 line-up in England. If it goes out to the full-back, the forward chases out to them and slides in, or tries to tackle them.'

'Nah, nah,' they said, shaking their heads. 'Not here. You

just stay in the middle up there, find holes, look for chances to score.'

I didn't take much persuading.

'Oh. Well, all right. If you insist.'

It wasn't like I exactly had a reputation for defensive excellence. I can still recall the time at Leicester, quite early in my career, when we were playing Manchester United and Gordon Milne, the manager, instructed me to come back at corners and man-mark Bryan Robson. Apparently, they had watched United and noticed that they were putting Robson on the edge of the penalty area to look for the second ball. It was now up to me to cut him off.

Which rather seemed to surprise Bryan when United got their first corner and I jogged back and appeared at his shoulder.

'What are *you* doing here?' he said, as if we had just run into each other on the other side of the world.

'Marking you, mate.'

Bryan laughed – a touch unkindly, I felt.

Anyway, at the corner, Bryan stormed away from me into the box, rose up and headed the ball smack against the bar. At the second corner, the same thing happened, although this time I went with him and jumped underneath him. And this time the ball ended up in the back of the net, and so did I.

At half-time, Gordon Milne, said: 'Gary – stay up for corners, OK?'

And that's pretty much where I remained at corners for the rest of my career – at least until I reached Japan, where they would say: 'Bring back the big man.' By which they would mean me – all 5ft 10in of me. In Japan, I was respected for my heading prowess in defensive situations. In other parts of the world, not so much.

Anyway, when I got back to Spurs, I was very set in my Spanish ways. I had grown almost completely out of the habit of doing even a limited part of the defensive side of things. So I had to pick it up again, start tracking the full-backs – and perhaps, at getting on for 30, with not quite the enthusiasm and energy that I had for it when I was 22. It might sound odd but it was probably harder to re-adapt to English football than it was to adapt to Spanish football in the first place.

The stand-out time from my years at Spurs was the 1991 FA Cup run, with Gazza almost single-handedly pulling us through at certain times – certainly in the fifth-round tie against Portsmouth, a game in which I missed an absolute sitter of a header in the first half and in which Portsmouth led for a while, only for Gazza to score twice, having created numerous chances which the rest of us squandered.

And, of course, the semi-final against Arsenal was amazing, with that now legendary and endlessly re-shown Gazza free-kick – 35 yards, into the top right-hand corner, with steam coming out of it all the way. Before he took it, I ran across to him and said: 'Don't try one of those bendy ones. Just smack it, man.' Because he was so far out. And he kind of smacked it, and he kind of bent it. An incredible strike.

Incidentally, I got the two goals in that match that no one remembers. And I wouldn't mind but, for one of them, I actually beat someone with the ball, running in on goal from distance, which was an extremely rare occurrence in my career. Ah, well. My historic moment was eclipsed by Gazza's historic moment.

That was the first year an FA Cup semi-final was held at Wembley, instead of on another neutral ground, a break with tradition which seemed to upset a lot of people, including, as I understand it, a certain Mr D. Baker from south London. I hear the argument – that Wembley should be reserved for the truly special occasions, such as the FA Cup final, American football and Take That concerts. But I have to say, packed to the rafters for a north London derby, Wembley felt like a perfectly appropriate venue that day. I certainly enjoyed it, anyway, tradition-busting or otherwise.

And then came the final against Nottingham Forest, when it all seemed about to go badly wrong again: Gazza getting carried off after 15 minutes following one of his less controlled performances, damaging his own knee ligaments with his second over-committed challenge of the afternoon, and Forest taking the lead from the resulting free-kick. I felt my first-half performance was as good as any I had ever given in a big game and at half-time I couldn't believe I didn't have a goal to show for it and that we were losing. I had had a perfectly good strike disallowed by the linesman's flag, when I knew, with absolute certainty, that I wasn't offside. VAR would have given it: roll on VAR. And I had missed a penalty – or rather, had a penalty saved, which I think is the right way to express it in this case. I hit it sweetly enough, but it was a brilliant stop by Mark Crossley. By way of revenge, I did him the following season with a dinky Panenka number. But that was in a Rumbelows Cup tie, which I suppose wasn't quite the same.

Eventually, Paul Stewart got our equaliser, although I was nearly on the end of it and I could have nicked it off him with a little bit more foresight. And then, in extra-time, Forest's Des Walker knew the feeling of scoring the winner in a Cup Final at Wembley, but in his own goal, which you wouldn't wish on anyone, least of all someone as genuinely nice as Des Walker.

Still, I took it – and I took it gladly. I hadn't won much in my career, really. I could have won the Double with Everton and didn't. I ended up at Barcelona during a period when Real Madrid were practically unstoppable and we finished second three years running. True, we won the Spanish Cup and the Cup Winners' Cup in that time, and that was great. But to come back for my final years at the top level and not win anything in English football would have felt deflating. So a lot of what I was feeling at the end of that Cup Final, in among the obvious joy, was relief – relief that I had actually got my hands on something substantial in England.

And, finally, here it was: an FA Cup winners' medal, handed over in the little blue, square jewellery box that you would see everyone clutching as they came back down the Wembley steps. The medal is tiny, by the way: no bigger than a ten pence piece, with barely enough room for the inscription: 'Football Association Challenge Cup Winners.' Good enough for me, though. And to this day it's one of a very small number of trinkets from my career that I can instantly lay my hands on at home. (A certain gold-coloured facsimile of an item of football-related footwear is one of the other ones.)

Almost exactly a year after that Wembley triumph, I was playing my last game in English football, away at Manchester United. Yes, perhaps it would have been nice to bow out on the biggest stage of them all – Filbert Street – but the Theatre of Dreams wasn't a bad substitute. People have often asked me what I was feeling on that monumentally emotional occasion. Actually, as it might no longer surprise you to learn, what was prominent in my mind was the destination of that season's Golden Boot.* I had been in an

* For the elimination of all doubt, permit me to clarify the distinction between the Premier League Golden Boot and the World Cup Golden Boot. The Premier League Golden Boot is the trophy you receive for scoring the most goals in a single top-flight season. The World Cup Golden Boot, by contrast, is the trophy you receive for scoring the most goals at the 1986 World Cup in Mexico. Hope that helps.

intense competition all season long with Ian Wright for top Premier League goal-scorer. It had been a tight contest, with the lead changing hands several times. But going into the last game, I was one goal ahead of Wrighty, on 27.

So when I suppose I could have been musing on the end of my career and time's fickle passing, the questions that were actually prominent in my mind that afternoon were: would one goal be enough? Could I add to it? And what would Wrighty manage for Arsenal at Southampton?

Come half-time we were 1–0 down and I hadn't even looked like scoring. In the dressing room, I nervously checked the other scores. To my immense relief, Southampton v Arsenal was goalless. So my lead was still intact, but also still precarious. Obviously, it would be handy if I could increase the gap and make sure.

Unfortunately, Tottenham were getting a bit of a kicking. This was second in the league versus 15th, and it felt like it. United scored two goals early in the second half to go 3–0 up. But then glory be: we mounted an attack, a cross came over and I headed one in. I remember getting a kind reception even from the home fans for that goal. Of course, United were 3–1 up, so they could afford to be generous. But even so: for that, and the applause I received at the end of this match, I have had warm feelings about Old Trafford ever since.

Of course, the really important thing about this goal was that Wrighty would now need to score three times in the second half at Southampton to beat me. A bit of a stretch.

Clearly, I was going out with the Golden Boot for the fourth time, which would be a nice way to say goodbye to English football.

I returned to the dressing room feeling, inevitably, emotional, but also elated. And what do I go and discover? Arsenal have won 5–1 and Wrighty has scored a hat-trick in the last 20 minutes: a 70th-minute penalty, a goal on 90 minutes to draw even with me on 28 goals, and then a third one, nudging his total ahead of mine and clinching top scorer, three minutes into injury-time. Talk about absolute theft. He should have been arrested when he left the pitch.

I phoned him from the bus.

'You bastard!'

He was, of course, laughing his head off.

'I love you, man.'

For the Tottenham that I played for – in a bit of a pickle financially, and always a few players short of a title challenge – a European Cup final was a distant dream. Still, I like to think the history books will show that I played my small part in laying the groundwork for a proper tilt at Champions League glory just . . . er . . . 27 years later.

And at least there were some consolations available that night in Madrid. For one thing, I really like Jürgen Klopp, the Liverpool manager – he's smart, has an infectious personality, and is fun and unpredictable in interviews, which is what you want and what you rarely get. I could find it in my heart to be pleased for him. And I love the way that

Liverpool team plays – the speed, the flair, the commitment to attacking.

Plus, there was a degree of justice about the outcome, in the grander scheme of things. It would have been very cruel if Liverpool had come out of the 2018–19 season and won nothing. Imagine getting 97 points in a Premier League campaign, and still being beaten to the league title. To be relentlessly superb for an entire term, only for one other team (Manchester City) to be that fraction more relentlessly superb – that's ridiculous. But 2018–19 was a ridiculous season. And perhaps the mere fact there was an all-English Champions League final (with an all-English Europa League final featuring Arsenal and Chelsea on the undercard) was a fitting climax to that ridiculous season, even if the match itself wasn't.

In Madrid before the game, I was stopped a couple of times, as usual, by fans of both sides, wondering if I had any tickets I could give them. Clearly lots of people had decided to travel and take their chances – although I must say, I encountered nothing quite as extreme in this area as I had back in March, on the plane out to Munich with Rio Ferdinand for the away leg of Liverpool's round of 16 tie against Bayern. That time, just before take-off, a Liverpool supporter came alongside our seats and asked if we had any tickets at all that we could spare for him and the group he was travelling with. As usual, we didn't.

I asked the bloke: 'Do you not have any at all?'

He said: 'We've got three.'

'And how many are you?'

'Eighteen.'

Just 15 short, then. Anyone got 15 together for the match? Not me or Rio, unfortunately. We wondered if any of them were going to make it into the ground.

The following day, at the airport waiting for our flight home, Rio showed me his phone.

'You won't believe this.'

It was a photo, posted on Twitter, of the guy we had spoken to on the plane. He was dressed up in orange overalls and holding a broom – a full-kit ground-sweeper, you could say. Heaven knows where he had blagged the outfit from, but as the photo and the giant smile on his face made clear, he was inside the stadium for the match. What can you say? Nothing really, except well played.

I wonder if that guy made it to Madrid. I hope so. Quite apart from anything else, when we left at the end of the night, it looked like there was lot of sweeping up to be done.

CHAPTER NINETEEN

'You can't say they haven't given it everything.'

In which DANNY undergoes a miserable but ultimately affirmative experience of the kind it's always nice to read about near the end of a book, with some thoughts on shower gels, penalty shoot-outs, and the soulless concrete bucket which is Wembley Stadium.

At 3.05pm on Tuesday 26 February 2019, Tottenham Hotspur issued an all-media news bulletin to announce something that was clearly of great importance to the club and which they felt would also excite all who cared for the club and its history.

After months of rumour and speculation, they announced that Molton Brown were indeed their new official toiletries partner. Needless to say, this news broke like a thunderclap above the soccer terrain, blindsiding even seasoned pundits, myself included.

Many of us had to read then re-read the press release from Spurs announcing this horizon-tilting news, and were attempting to process the dizzying new reality in which the London company's 'expertly blended collection of signature fragrances, bath and shower gels' would now be available 'at the Club's Training Centre, Head Offices at Lilywhite House and premium spaces in our iconic new stadium'.

Premium spaces only, note. No fine liquid handwashes available in the cheap seats. After all, the great unwashed are known as such for a reason.

'Molton Brown's home and handcare products have attained iconic status thanks to their vibrant colours and bold scents,' the press release proudly told us. 'Each creation is intricately composed by some of the world's best perfumers for a truly indulgent, memorable experience,' it added. Indeed, as Spurs were excited to communicate, 'Molton Brown is proud to hold a Royal Warrant for the supply of toiletries by appointment to Her Majesty the Queen.'

And lo, at a celestial garden party far beyond Heaven's gate, Dave McKay embraced Henry VIII whispering, 'We are now one, my deodorant bro.'

This epoch-making development at the game's front line – unarguably a major breakthrough in the nationwide push for a more fragrant football experience – set me pondering a tale once told me by Clarke Carlisle, the retired defender who went on to be chairman of the Professional Footballers' Association. In the middle of a game, while waiting for a corner to come in and all a-jostle in the penalty area in the accepted manner, an attacker whom Clarke was marking took a moment to ask him, apparently in all seriousness: 'What's that aftershave you've got on?' Clarke told him the name of the brand (a detail now lost, alas, to time's mists), to which the curious attacker offered a discerning 'Nice', and the game moved on.

It was hard not to drink this tale in without being tempted to wonder whether, in the heat of combat, these kinds of humdrum exchange went on between players from opposing teams all the time. If you could get below the crowd noise and the sound of angry battle and move among the players as they played, would you discover that casual questions such as 'What you having for supper tonight?' and 'How much do you think I paid for three avocados yesterday?' were actually the norm?

Clarke, sadly, suggested that his experience was otherwise. In his entire career, which had encompassed 13 years and nine clubs, only one opponent had asked him, mid-match, about his aftershave. According to Gary Lineker, the occasional barbed or otherwise satirical comment between opponents is not unknown. Why (and here the scales fall from one's eyes), by his own confession, even the very barometer of fair play, Lineker himself, has been known to instruct a goalkeeper, coming off his line and offering a helpful word before the taking of a penalty, to 'get back in your goal and get ready to pick it out'. Do as he says and not as he does, kids.

However, if we're talking about casual conversations on more general themes (clothing, cinema, neighbourly enquiries after the dog), apparently it doesn't really happen, even during the longer breaks for serious injuries, and Clarke's eau de cologne-spotter turns out, disappointingly, to be the exception rather than the rule.

Anyway, that broader matter aside, Clarke's experience did set Gary and me briefly wondering who, in the broadest of all polls of the professional game, would be ranked football's most fragrant player ever. Would Clarke feature? It's notoriously difficult to compare eras, of course. Yet with the investigative vim for which Gary and I are justly famous, we asked around.

David Beckham, it almost goes without saying, was very quickly ahead in the running, his high-end and no doubt carefully sourced musk earning high levels of approval from people who had, literally, rubbed shoulders with it. A draught of Cristiano Ronaldo, caught somewhere around the halfway line during a warm evening fixture, apparently smells even more lovely, and this would be one category, I guess, where the Ronaldo v Messi debate wouldn't even be worth drawing breath over.

But possibly the loudest acclaim of all (perhaps surprising the judges) was for David Luiz, largely courtesy of someone who had somehow come by a T-shirt worn by the large-haired Arsenal defender and who reported enjoying a draft of the great smell of David whenever she inhaled in its proximity. It was, this person claimed, the most gorgeous smell she had ever encountered coming from a man, though in my experience this is not quite the boast it may seem.

So the benchmark is set. May we now look eagerly forward to daring new sensations from Molton Brown such as 'Harry Winks' Post-match Whiff'.

Meanwhile, it might just be that Tuesday 26 February did not stand entirely alone as the high point for football in 2019. For me there was a day that was, if possible, still more momentous than that declaration of the heart-stopping amalgam of Spurs with its toiletries partner, which left the Vice-President of Sales and Operations at Molton Brown Global (and, again, I'm quoting from Spurs' press release here) 'beyond excited [to be] giving people the opportunity to experience our fragranced luxuries during the week and on those all-important match days'.

The date I'm thinking of is Sunday 17 March. Which, as it happens, was an actual 'all-important match day'. At any rate, records will confirm that on this day in 2019, Millwall faced Brighton in an FA Cup quarter-final at the New Den. And let me state this clearly: the effects of what happened on that withering afternoon were as profound as any that football has made on me in whole decades.

This was Millwall of the Championship versus Brighton of the Premier League – so not the most forlorn of mismatches, yet with Millwall certainly as the underdog. In fact, Millwall made Brighton look bloated and sluggish for the best part of the match and, in nine glorious minutes in the middle of the second half, scored twice, surely ending the argument.

The argument still looked as good as over even after Brighton had managed to pull a goal back in the 88th minute. Nothing could go wrong now ... And frankly, the argument was still looking finished when, in the fifth minute of injury time, an overhit Brighton free-kick, travelling high and slow, floated innocuously in the direction of David Martin, standing unchallenged in the Millwall goal. Brighton fans were already rising to their feet and getting ready to leave as their team's last chance swirled away limply down the drain. All Martin had to do was catch it, hold it a moment, boot it upfield – game over. Semi-finals here we come.

But no. The Gods, it appeared, were bored. Suddenly time seemed to slow. Martin reached above his head for the ball, but somehow omitted to bring his hands together. The ball dropped gently through the gap and into the net for 2–2. A five-star blunder, an utter calamity – and all on live television, courtesy of which all enemies of my club (there are a few) would now bust a gut. For them this was soccer succour of the ripest stripe.

At moments of individual embarrassment like these, while the captain is gripping the emotionally ruined player by the arms, looking closely into his eyes and urging him to look beyond the devastation he has wrought, I'm afraid I'm entirely with one of those six or seven players you will usually see in the background, looking disgruntled and thinking:

'Fuck's sake. Couldn't you have palmed it? Couldn't you have headed it? Couldn't you have done absolutely anything other than what you just did?' So, yes, David Martin looked distraught. But in my view, he was entirely right to look distraught. I, too, was distraught. My father's ghost was on the pitch kicking his arse for him.

The equaliser meant extra-time. And extra-time, as so often, meant not very much. There were no further goals, although Millwall did manage to get a player sent off, who just happened to be Shane Ferguson, who just happened to be Millwall's first-choice penalty-taker. Which would prove significant because now, deadlocked after 120 minutes, the game would be settled with a penalty shoot-out. Everyone loves a penalty shoot-out, right?

Well, actually, yes. Indeed, by my reckoning, mankind will never produce another drama so intense within the bounds of sport. Even a bad penalty shoot-out – lots of confident strikes, no wobbles – has value that most other forms of entertainment can only dream of. So, in fact, why even let extra-time get in the way? I have known – certainly while watching as a neutral – that sense of outrage which is produced when some spoilsport scores in the 119th minute, meaning you've sat through all that tired play and you're not going to be rewarded with some penalties. It seems almost cruel, not to say uneconomical. Extra-time, we can surely agree, is quite literally a waste of extra time. Why not cut straight to the good bit, as standard? Penalties after 90 minutes. In end-of-season dead rubbers, we don't even need the 90 minutes.

Not that I wouldn't have taken a 119th-minute winner for Millwall against Brighton that afternoon, thus robbing gloating West Ham fans of their sudden-death fun. But it hadn't arrived, so here we were, still alive and with David Martin in goal getting an instant shot at redemption. He had dumped us in this mess; now he could get us out of it by saving a few penalties. Or even one penalty.

And what do you know? Brighton missed at the first attempt, someone or other whose name escapes me smacking the ball against the post. It couldn't still come right, could it?

As our sixth penalty sailed over the bar confirming Brighton's victory, the remote control left my hand, was launched into our front room wall and broke into a million pieces.

Reader, trust me: I believed I was over feeling football at this depth, the way it can kill you. I was too experienced for that now, surely; too wise to its ways. I thought I had outlived the point where any of this game's torture implements could still break me like a twig. I certainly thought I was past the point where it could cause me to, if not actually cry, then pull that face that makes you look like you're going to.

Here is the truth, though: I had not felt as decimated since the day David Bowie died. On the day of Bowie's death, I thought hard about what I could put on Twitter that would mark my feelings about it. Realising that I had no words, I ended up posting a single full stop. And that is exactly what I did after the Brighton game: a tweet containing a single full stop. Which might sound melodramatic, and indeed was melodramatic, but was a genuine reflection of how I felt. I had not been that way after football for decades: defeated, angered, hollowed out with a spoon. Flat. Punctured. Fucked.

But why this extreme reaction? For what reason? Obvious explanations were slow to present themselves. It was Brighton: Millwall have no particular grudge to bear there. Nor was there any greater prize lying in wait for us beyond this result – not really. A shot at the FA Cup? Fairy tale, Lions? Hmm. In the semi-finals we would have met Manchester City, and I don't think I'm going out on a limb here when I suggest that Millwall would not have asked too many questions of City. In fact, we would have asked only one question of them, and that is: 'Would you mind stopping scoring against us now, please?'

Also, getting to the semi-final would have meant going to Wembley and thereby no doubt enduring an eternity of patronising nonsense about our 'big day out at the home of football'. Away with this myth. Wembley is no more the home of football than B&Q is the home of horticulture. Wembley is a soulless, corporate Nowheredome, where any atmosphere generated by the crowd gathers in a thin goop and rapidly departs for the skies. If I may adapt PJ O'Rourke (who was talking about communist eastern Europe at the time): it's like Disney World, without Disney. And without the world.

Any magic or mystery that the venue might have retained has been blitzed by purely finance-driven over-use. Everyone has grown fed up with it. A slick, unfeeling conference centre. What are the semi-finals of the FA Cup doing there in the first place? They should be on a neutral ground anywhere else, as once they were. And let's not get into a discussion about convenience. Even people who live in London find Wembley just as inconvenient to get to as St James Park – and I mean the St James Park at Exeter. Being deprived of a trip to Wembley? Hard to place this in the 'loss' column.

Yet the hurt that defeat to Brighton imparted, by virtue of its unique rottenness, the brooding mood it brought down upon me in the hours afterwards . . . it was so peculiar. And yet what I realised was that for a long time I had been playing down my connection with Millwall, declining the opportunity to talk about the club in public forums, slightly worried about my image as the club's 'celebrity fan', a concept which, quite rightly, can tax people's patience. And frankly, as a consequence of those efforts, I imagined I had removed myself to ground slightly off to one side, where Millwall and things connected with Millwall no longer had the power to reach so deeply inside of me.

What a dope. What a hope. Like that moment in *Young Frankenstein* where Gene Wilder, as Frederick, having spent the entire film denying his connection with his notorious, mad grandfather and insisting that his name is pronounced Fronkensteen, finds himself alone with his appalling creation and finally, in a bellow, cathartically embraces his heritage: 'My name is FRANKENSTEIN.'

And in as much as anything positive could come out of that miserable FA Cup match, I guess it was this crystal-clear realisation: that I am a Millwall supporter, like my father was and like his father was before him, and like my son is now, and that this would always be the case. Up The Loins! Yes, LOINS!

CHAPTER TWENTY

'The referee has clearly seen enough.'

In which GARY loses a yard of pace and gains a career in television. With thoughts on turning Japanese, learning the broadcasting trade at the silky smooth knee of Des Lynam, and the sheer volume of Alan Shearer.

When you're a footballer, eventually you feel it go. You try to kid yourself a little bit that it's not happening, but you've got a three at the front of your age, which is a hard sign to overlook, and then something happens that makes it unignorable. I can remember the exact moment. I was playing in Japan for Nagoya Grampus Eight, a ball came over the top of the opposing centre-half, and I thought, I'm in. And I turned and set off after the ball, away from the defender, leaving him for dead, surely – only then to be aware of him right on my heels. And then drawing alongside me. And then getting ahead of me. A straight sprint for the ball, and I lost. And right there I thought: that's it, time's up.

Players talk about it afterwards – that awful, incremental process, realising that you are just fractionally less electric than you were, that you're getting old and that there's nothing you can do about it. Rio Ferdinand told me there was a moment, at QPR, when he found himself getting outpaced by Peter Crouch and he realised his race was probably run. But we don't talk about it at the time. It's a taboo subject. Too painful. Too worrying.

Retirement hits a lot of players hard. They're used to being well paid, comfortable, revered. And that stops, and the money stops and the self-esteem evaporates. Suddenly you're not playing, you've not got people cheering you every week, you're not being driven in training. It's psychologically hard to adapt to. That's when you see the drinking start. That's when people start to flounder, go looking for things to fill the gap, make bad choices. But it's hard. After football, nothing is going to be better, is it?

And your life up to that point has been so structured. People tell me 'You're always on time' and seem surprised about it. But I was a footballer. Of course I'm always on time. Nearly every footballer I know is punctual. Turn up to training at a certain time; be on the bus at a certain time; be down for dinner at a certain time. Everything is by the clock. It's a highly disciplined life. And then that entire structure gets dismantled overnight. How is it going to be when you're running that stuff for yourself?

And, of course, there's so much of your life left to fill after football – more than half of it if you're lucky. Alan Hansen said he never thought about what he was going to do after he had finished playing. He just thought the phone would ring with offers. And it didn't. Eventually his wife told him he had to get out and find some work or he would spend the rest of his life sitting in an armchair. And he was lucky because he managed it.

I've been lucky similarly. I've found something else to do that's different from what I did before, but enjoyable. It's kept me engaged and offered me a purpose, and it's filled that void that a lot of players stare into.

And no, I'm not talking about Twitter, although, now I come to think about it, tweeting does have quite a lot in common with my day-job presenting football on the telly, actually. As with composing the scripts and lines for the show, you write something and it's got to be quite succinct and you hope that it's perhaps vaguely funny. And then you put it out there and see what happens. Plus, there's scope for cheesy puns, and I've always been keen to embrace those. As everyone knows, cheesy puns are the purest form of wit. They're certainly the cheesiest form of wit, anyway.

Could I live without Twitter? I believe so. On the other hand, you look at a feed like SteveBruceatWeddings (basically, pictures of weddings with Steve Bruce Photoshopped into them) and you think: well, this is a form of entertainment that I really wouldn't want to be missing.

Also, without Twitter, I might never have learned about

the guy who, in 2017, while on a lads' holiday, had the slogan 'GARY LINEKER SHAGS CRISPS' tattooed very
neatly around his left nipple. As I replied at the time, urgently
seeking to nip this crude and unflattering rumour in the
bud, as it were: 'I'm not sure it's even possible. Goodness
knows, I've tried.'

I must have convinced him. The guy went on the TV
show *Tattoo Fixers* eventually and got 'GARY LINEKER
SHAGS CRISPS' converted into a large picture of an
angel. Very resourceful, those tattoo-fixing people. But this
whole saga would have passed me by if not for the miracle
of Twitter, and my life would have been poorer for it.

Then again, in a world without Twitter I would possibly
never have heard Peter Shilton express how 'impressed' he
was by Jacob Rees-Mogg and, in particular, the member for
North East Somerset's thoughts on Brexit. Oh, Shilts: really?
From a keeper to a kipper. Maybe it's true what they say:
you should never read a tweet from your heroes.

Anyway, at the point at which I was trying to work out a
second career for myself, both Twitter and presenting
Match of the Day still lay in the future. I was approaching
34 and I had returned to England from Japan after my two
years playing for Nagoya Grampus Eight in the newly
launched J.League. I knew I was done as a player at the top
levels. Even in my last season in England, at Spurs, I had
begun to notice little indications that I was starting to slow
up. To be perfectly frank, those feelings were one of the

reasons for accepting the move to Japan. There was an offer in for me from Blackburn Rovers in 1992, but I didn't want to stick around in England if I was now entering the phase where I was going to be struggling a bit. I would rather enter the inevitable decline elsewhere, in front of crowds that weren't always making painful comparisons. So I chose Japan.

Blackburn, incidentally, had to settle for Alan Shearer and their fans have no doubt been rueing what might have been ever since.

Except briefly on a pre-season tour with Tottenham, Japan was a country I had never been to before. My first wife Michelle and I were given a two-bedroom apartment in a suburb of Nagoya. You wouldn't describe it as luxurious, but it was clean and safe and quiet, if completely alien to us. We had been living in St John's Wood in north London, so to descend into a world in which litter and petty crime didn't seem to have been invented was quite a stretch. We had extremely nice neighbours – Ryuichi and Hiromi – who helped us a lot. The language, though, was difficult. I managed to study it a little bit before we left. With Spanish, as an English-speaker, you can read it and hear it and begin to get along with it quite rapidly. Japanese was obviously far harder. But I did my best. I could ring up and book a restaurant, I could tell a taxi which way to go, I could have a very basic, polite conversation with somebody. I could get by.

What I couldn't do was stay fit. I had problems with a broken toe that eventually required surgery and it meant long periods on the sidelines in both my seasons with Grampus. The first time the injury properly flared, the club doctor took some X-rays and, after a good look at them, announced that there was nothing visibly wrong. So I went out and played. By half-time, I was in agony. In response to the pain, my foot had basically scrunched up and turned into a claw inside my boot.

The club doctor and I had another look at those earlier X-rays. Leaning over his shoulder, I pointed to a dark mark across one of my toes.

'Do you suppose that could have been something?'

The club doctor agreed that yes, on reflection, maybe it could.

Hmm. Anyway, up to a point it didn't matter, because I had been signed to be an ambassador for the new J.League as much as I had been signed as a player, and I could still hop around being ambassadorial at the various dinners and events that were required of me, sitting cross-legged and eating freshly killed octopus with the president of Toyota, for instance. But, for all that I enjoyed the golf which I took up properly over there, it frustrated me that I wasn't spending more time on the pitch. I only played 18 times, and I only scored four goals, and I would like to have done better on both counts. Still, I'm glad I had those years. My second son, Harry, was born then. I still think of it as a happy time. Just one without much football in it.

When I came back from Japan, I filmed an advert for Walkers which was on a 'welcome home' theme: me wandering around the centre of Leicester, greeting people, and then, in the pay-off, stealing a kid's crisps, which was the beginning of a trope that, though we didn't realise it at the time, would run and run. Near the end of a long day of filming, we were outside Leicester train station, trying to get a shot right which was taking a fair bit of time to set up, which meant that, eventually, quite a large crowd of onlookers formed. I was standing around on the fringes somewhere, waiting to be called back in front of the camera, when an elderly lady approached me.

'It's Gary Lineker, isn't it?'

'Yes!'

'So, what's going on here, then?' the lady said, gesturing to the crowd. 'Are they expecting someone important?'

Clearly it was time for me to get off my backside and make a bit of a mark on the world.

I had some offers to go into management, which is the obvious next stage for many players. I was asked a couple of times if I would consider managing Leicester, and I was sounded out by Aston Villa. But the conversations never got far down the line because I knew with some certainty that management wasn't my thing. I found training was bad enough when I was the one doing the training, but the idea of watching other people train . . . that would have been purgatory.

I suppose if I had gone into management I could have exacted my revenge for all those times managers stood on the touchline and bawled 'Hold it up!' at me. Those three little words used to drive me to distraction. And I heard them even from the managers I loved.

'Hold it up!'

You would be on a dodgy pitch in freezing weather with the ball coming at you at great speed and at knee height and threatening to bounce right off you if you weren't careful, and you would hear the shout almost before it happened.

'Hold it up!'

What did it even mean? Control the ball, keep the ball, don't give the ball away. Well, yes, obviously, in an ideal world. But the ball is dropping out of a rainy sky and I'm running backwards to get under it, and it looks like I'm going to have to take it down on my chest, and I've got a defender so tight behind me that he's practically doing the conga with me. So, yeah, *you* hold it up.

I guess screaming 'Hold it up!' at hapless strikers would have brought me a bit of compensation for those times. But I'm not sure that this, on its own, constitutes a reason to go into football management and I suspect that if you asked, say, Sir Alex Ferguson, he would agree with me. Which would be a first.

On the other hand, I had a very clear idea that I would like to work in television, and I also thought I had spotted a possible gap in the market that I could exploit. I watched other sports and saw how well ex-players were doing as presenters – David Gower in cricket, Sue Barker in tennis. And I wondered why that wasn't happening with football. Jimmy Hill did some presenting, of course, but he was better known for his punditry. Bob Wilson, formerly of Arsenal, had done some presenting on *Football Focus*. But he was a goalkeeper so, of course, he doesn't really count as a footballer. Overall, I thought that there might be a niche there for a player-turned-frontman, and maybe, if I could crack it, it would give me a few years' work – possibly even a second career.

For a while it seemed highly unlikely to me that I would crack it, though. I did some work for radio at first, presenting for 5 Live, and I was pretty hopeless, if I may say so myself. I was also picking up television work as a pundit, often on *Match of the Day*, and, to be perfectly frank, I was pretty hopeless at that, too. I knew about the job I had done as a player – I understood goal-scoring – but what I knew about defending wouldn't have covered the back of my own hand if I had written it on there before the programme in marker pen. Alan Hansen, who was often next to me on the show, was brilliant at that job. He would say things all the time that made me stop and think 'Oh, yeah. I see that now' – and he could be enlightening about stuff happening anywhere on the pitch, not just the defensive areas that he had excelled in for Liverpool. But I just knew my own little world, and pretty quickly I realised I had finished giving the nation the benefits of my wisdom about it. How many more times was I going to be able to look at a clip and say 'He's got to be timing his run better there' or 'What he should have done is go round him'?

But the BBC were very supportive. They nurtured me and encouraged me and they gave me some voice training so that I could start introducing a bit more colour into my tone, because my Leicestershire accent was naturally rather flat. And then, in 1996, they gave me the job presenting *Football Focus*, the Saturday lunchtime preview show. Was it a touch too soon? It felt like it to me. I spent six months or so scrambling for a foothold. Getting used to what live television demands was so hard: remembering the links, going from a question into a link, working with countdowns and, above all, coping with talkback in your earpiece, which, ironically enough, is a bit like having someone on the touchline shouting 'Hold it up!', except they're a producer rather than a manager, and they tend to be more softly spoken. All in all, I was a rabbit in the headlights for a while. Maybe it didn't look quite as bad as it felt; clearly not, in fact, because I would have been plucked from the airwaves within about five minutes if that had been the case. But there were so many times when I drove home from Television Centre on a Saturday afternoon, thinking to myself: 'This just isn't working. Just do punditry. Just do punditry.'

Still, at least criticism wasn't likely to throw me. One thing that surprised me when I began working in the media was how sensitive broadcasting people were to reviews.

I walked into the office one day and Des Lynam and Brian Barwick, who was the BBC's head of sport at the time, were hunched over a newspaper looking extremely anxious. Seeing the expressions on their faces, I wondered briefly whether news had broken about the imminent end of the world. In fact, they were poring over a review that hadn't been entirely in favour of some programme that they were involved in.

I thought 'Is that it? Someone writing for a newspaper doesn't like what you did very much? Are you really going to let that spoil your day?' In football you're hearing criticism from day one, normally voiced in the strongest available terms. Stuff pours at you from the stands constantly – and the very worst of it, very often, will be coming from the stands with your own fans in them. You can't be thin-skinned. You would last about five minutes if you let it affect you. So you arm yourself against it pretty fast. As such, football may be the greatest preparation there is for criticism in other walks of life, and also for weathering the stormier aspects of social media. Water off the duck's proverbial.

Anyway, one Saturday afternoon in 1997 I had a breakthrough moment. I was sitting around at the BBC with Alan Hansen, drinking the BBC's coffee and eating its sandwiches, and keeping an eye on the football that was being played that day because we were both due on *Match of the Day* later in the evening. *Grandstand*, the BBC's Saturday afternoon sports show, was at Aintree, covering the

Grand National, and Des Lynam was presenting the programme live from the course.

Suddenly a production assistant ran into our room. 'There's a bomb scare at Aintree, Gary. They're moving everybody off the course. We need you to present *Grandstand* from this end.'

Fortunately there was no time to think about it too hard. I was mic'd up, daubed with make-up and thrust next door into the studio, right into the heat of one of those difficult moments when a sports story becomes a news story with far wider implications. Des, of course, on the ground at Aintree, had handled the bomb scare superbly. Even the prospect of an explosion in the vicinity didn't seem to cause his voice to rise or his pace to change. He had stayed at his post for as long as he possibly could, while the course evacuated around him, but the police moved him out eventually. Two hundred miles away, in the safety of a studio, I was by far the more ruffled of the two of us. No one has ever gone back over the tape and conducted an exact count, but in my improvised explanation to the viewers of what was going on, I think I said 'It's a sad day for sport' about 473 times.

Well, I wasn't wrong: it *was* a sad day for sport. You can't overstate it. Unless you say it 473 times, that is.

Eventually I was able to stop talking about the events at Aintree, in all their sadness, and instead cue in a time-filling recording of some snooker (a pun to 'break' the tension for you there). While that was on, I was given a crash course in talking over the vidiprinter, which the football results used to come rattling in on. So, after the snooker (by which time the police had carried out two controlled explosions at the course) I went live again and did the incoming football results, and then I interviewed Des Lynam down the line from Aintree (or to be precise, a safe place near Aintree) to wrap up the show. The experience had been fully immersive and, in many respects, terrifying. But I also realised that I absolutely loved it and would be very happy to do more of it – though perhaps without the added interest of a bomb scare next time.

Des Lynam, by the way, was the doyen of sports presenters, the absolute and unparalleled master of that role, and he was massively helpful to me in those early years. I sat by him being a pundit when he was presenting *Match of the Day* and tried to watch and learn – his authority, his calmness, the richness in his tone, and, always, his inclusivity. When Des presented football and introduced the panel, he would always say 'joining us tonight' – never 'joining me tonight'. He told me that he did it very deliberately, to include the audience and establish a connection. They might be at home, but that doesn't mean they're not part of it and you should let them know you realise that. I've followed his advice on that ever since: always 'us', never 'me'.

We talked about closing lines, too. He told me not to worry if I had thought of something that felt a bit silly: just go for it. Des would tell you that most presenters are frightened and will just do the job as straight as they can. He was all in favour of trying something quirky. I tried to take that on board. Sometimes my closing lines have worked, sometimes those cheesy puns haven't. But I'll try to be brave enough to attempt a quip. And if it dies a death, well, there's always next time.

Unless it's a really terrible quip, of course, and you get fired. But those are the risks.

At the 2018 World Cup in Russia, the BBC were given England's quarter-final against Sweden. That was our big knockout game in the World Cup of 2018 – ITV showed the semi-final – and it was clear that the audience at home was going to be massive. I was sitting in my hotel room on the afternoon of the match, trying to think of how I could open this show, and, much to my alarm, nothing was coming. I was totally blank. I was thinking about those lines that Des Lynam had managed to come up with on big England tournament occasions – like when England played Tunisia at France '98, in a midweek afternoon kick-off, and Des arched an eyebrow at the camera and said: 'Shouldn't you be at work?' Or his opener for the England v Germany semi-final at Euro '96. 'Glad you tuned in. You've probably heard there's a football match on tonight . . .' How was I ever going to come near that? I thought to myself, where's Des Lynam when you need him?

And then, as a little lightbulb popped in my brain, I thought, hang on . . . that might work. So that's how I opened.

'Good afternoon. Where's Des Lynam when you need him?'

That day went really well – for England, of course, who won 2–0, but also for the show. I remember saying straight afterwards: 'We ought to put that one forward at Bafta time.' It just felt like it had been a good programme. It had some beautiful pre-filmed pieces in it. The punditry, by Rio Ferdinand, Alan Shearer and Jürgen Klinsmann, had been really tidy. There were some nice montages. The broadcast even generated good feedback on social media, which is really unusual. And people seemed to like me nodding to Des at the beginning of it all. Most often you will end a programme thinking something could have come off better. It's incredibly rare that you come off air and say: 'That was actually really slick.' This was one of those times.

The production ended up getting nominated for a Bafta in the Television Sport and Live Event category at the ceremony in 2019. I couldn't be there because we were in Salford doing the last *Match of the Day* of the season, covering the down-to-the-wire race for the title between Liverpool and Manchester City. To be perfectly honest, I didn't mind having an excuse. Award shows are not my absolutely favourite way to pass an evening. In fact, I would rather shut my fingers repeatedly in a drawer. All those hours of sitting still and listening to speeches, while preparing your special 'thrilled for you' face, ready for that moment when your award is up and you lose . . . You need an extremely high boredom threshold. And very strong facial muscles.

I went to the Baftas in 2013 when the BBC's coverage

of Super Saturday at the London 2012 Olympics was nominated – our programme from that amazing day of gold medals for Britain, with Jessica Ennis and Mo Farah pounding their way to glory and the BBC offering every thrilling minute of it in a seamless production that simultaneously employed ground-breaking red-button innovations. I'm not going to deceive you: we fancied our chances at the Baftas that night. We thought the trophy was as good as in the bag, frankly. But no. We were beaten by Channel 4's Paralympics coverage. I mean, nice job, too, clearly. But even Graham Norton, who was doing the compering, seemed a little startled.

What do you know, though? In 2019, the England v Sweden coverage actually won. We were able to parade the gold statuette the following weekend during the FA Cup final coverage at Wembley. Amazing scenes: Alan Shearer getting his hands on a trophy at Wembley at last. The nation was in bits.

And, on that subject, that was also the show where we were able to take the long-running joke about Shearer's record in the FA Cup to a whole new level. I have been carefully mentioning the fact that Al owns no FA Cup winners' medals while introducing distinguished panels of guests since time immemorial, but it was Richard Hughes, our producer, who had the idea of escalating the warfare by getting Wembley's giant video screens involved.

We couldn't rehearse this prank, because we would have

risked revealing it to Al in advance, which would have ruined it. So, early in the programme, when the cameras innocently panned around the stadium and the massive sign popped up ('BBC FA CUP WINS: IAN WRIGHT 2, GARY LINEKER 1, ALAN SHEARER 0'), it was the first time I had seen it, too. I had no idea the screen was then going to start flashing – 'SHEARER'S NEVER WON THE FA CUP'. The sign was funny in itself, but the flashing . . . well, that was the absolute cherry on it, and I practically corpsed.

I'm not quite sure where we can take it from there. But I have a feeling the joke about Al never having won the FA Cup will go on until the end of time. Or until he wins one, whichever comes sooner.

At the centre of what I do on television, and even more central to it than pranking Alan Shearer, is *Match of the Day*. I just love that programme. If you're a football fan, *Match of the Day* is in your DNA, and it can still strike me as bizarre that I have been presenting it since 1999. That said, technically my first appearance on the show was in 1980, playing for Leicester against Aston Villa. I marked the occasion by blazing an absolute sitter over the bar from five yards out. To sit at home later that night with my parents and run through this experience again was a mixed pleasure, for sure. But it didn't put me off *Match of the Day* and I can't really think of anything that would.

It's still the most watched football programme by a

country mile. Its viewing figures have bucked the trend. The combined audience for the Saturday and Sunday night shows is around seven million. Who watches sporting highlights any more? We're thought to live in a world where sport is live or it's nothing, and highlights shows are meant to have gone the way of horse-drawn carts and oil lamps. But there it is. It's been through a couple of rocky spells where people have fallen out of love with it, but I think we've given it a shake every now and again and got it back.

A gig watching football all day? Frankly, it's quite hard to make that seem like work. My routine has been pretty much the same since the show moved to Salford in October 2011. I was settled at the BBC by this point and I had just bought a house in London, which seemed like the most convenient place for me to be. Three weeks later, the BBC announced that they were moving the show, and the rest of the sports department, to Manchester. It seemed an odd thing to do, just a few months away from the London Olympics, but there it was.

So, I'll take the train from London up to Manchester on a Saturday morning. And then afterwards, when everything is wrapped, I'll be driven home in a car. Back by 3am and off to bed. It's amazing how many people don't realise the show is live. We have a look at the first editions of the Sunday newspapers at the end of the programme, which is a bit of a clue, but even so people think we've taped it earlier in the evening. I suppose it's a compliment that it comes across as so honed and polished and doesn't have any of the sweat and panic of live television about it. But live television it most definitely is. This is largely because we're on directly after the news, and if a manager has lost his job or some other seismic football story has broken, it's going to look a little odd if we don't mention it. This happened one evening to the Sunday night edition of the show. Paolo Di Canio got sacked as manager of Sunderland on a Sunday evening but the show had already been taped and everybody had gone home so there was no mention of it. That was the end of pre-recording *Match of the Day*.

But the best bit for me is probably Saturday afternoon when you're sitting on a sofa in front of six tellies with the rest of the team, watching the live feed from six matches – bantering, shouting, talking nonsense and, at some point, ordering food in from the local takeaways. (Nando's, Wagamama. I'm a little sick of the menu now, if I'm being honest. I've been eating that food a long time.) Maybe that's the part that should be on telly, although I don't think any of us would remain employed for long if it was. Ian Wright is enormous fun to watch a game of football with – thoroughly invested in it all. Al Shearer has the loudest voice in the world. At least two or three times in any afternoon I'll be wondering whether he has just tipped me in the direction of a heart attack by reacting so loudly. Martin Keown's incessant talking is . . . interesting. Jermaine Jenas is fun. Danny Murphy is . . . Danny Murphy, exactly the same off the television as on it. It's a really good bunch.

Only four other people have held the main presenting job long-term: Kenneth Wolstenholme, David Coleman, Jimmy Hill and Des Lynam. I'm very proud to be the fifth on that list. It seems unbelievable to me but, at the time of writing this, I've done it for 20 years. We lost the rights to ITV for three of those. But it's 20 years since Des Lynam left. And I've been doing the Sports Personality of the Year shows for even longer than that. How is this possible? But it's the case.

A lot of the things I got from football I get from *Match of the Day*, and from television generally. A bit of camaraderie, a bit of banter, some dressing-room nonsense, some public attention – it's on a smaller scale, but it's still there. You get a bit of a buzz of adrenaline from going live, and even more so from the big live games. It's not as pressured as football, clearly, but it's still pressure. Apparently Alan Hansen, while he was a player, was regularly sick with nerves before matches. He would actually throw up in the dressing room. I never saw Al throw up before *Match of the Day*, but he definitely got tense. You would hear the shuffling of his feet on the studio floor before he took his first question. After that he would settle down, but television was clearly doing something to him, and perhaps something he needed. Something we all need.

Just about the sole thing it can't come near replacing is the rush you get in the moment of scoring a goal. But then, unfortunately, so far as I am aware, there is nothing in the afterlife of footballers to match that – not even presenting *Have I Got News For You*, which I've done three times now. They really make you put the hours in on that show: in at 9 in the morning, out at 10.30 at night. You've got this enormous stack of cards to work through, with lines and jokes and set-ups written on them. And the glasses are on and off because I can't see the cards without them and I can't see the autocue with them. Who knew comedy was such hard work?

Good fun, though. Once on my watch, Nicky Morgan, who was then the Education Secretary, didn't show up because she was embroiled in a spat with Downing Street over some comments she had made about the Prime Minister's leather trousers. Her place on the panel was taken by a brown leather handbag. Again, it wouldn't happen on *Match of the Day* – although maybe we could think about it, the next time Alan Shearer steps out of line.

Not even presenting *Match of the Day* in your underpants will give you the rush you got from scoring – which I'm in a unique position to affirm, of course, having done both. Ahead of that landmark moment for sports broadcasting (the first *Match of the Day* of the 2016–17 season), a number of underwear brands got in touch and offered to dress me for the occasion – much as the major fashion houses approach the big stars before the Oscars, I guess. Very kind of them, I'm sure, but it probably wouldn't have been in keeping with BBC guidelines on advertising for me to have completed this self-inflicted stunt in sponsored keks.

As it was, I appeared in a pair of my own white boxers, with a Leicester City badge embroidered on the right leg as a token of my affiliation. And even then there were complaints that this garment didn't comply with the definition of pants as understood by the underwear police (with my BBC colleague Dan Walker prominent among their ranks).

But I refer you to my original unguarded tweet of December 2015: 'If Leicester win the @premierleague I'll do the first MOTD of next season in just my undies.' Undies, note. At no point was any promise made to appear in tighty whities or novelty pants with 'Pull Down in Case of Emergency' written on them, or whatever would have satisfied Dan Walker on this occasion.

Despite the relatively generous coverage afforded by those boxers, the show's wardrobe people applied tape to the inside of the garment to keep it all together and thereby remove all risk of the kind of exposure the BBC prefers to avoid, even after the watershed, and definitely in its sports shows. Fussy of them to go to the trouble, you might think. But, on the contrary, I would say it was a sensible precaution. I'll confess: at the sight of Alan Shearer's bald pate gleaming at me softly, late in the night, across a hot studio, I can sometimes become a little aroused. But what man wouldn't?

If I've got an ambition in television, apart from ensuring that I keep my clothes on in future, and apart from continuing to wind up Alan Shearer about his lack of FA Cup medals, it's to work on a show where England win something. No, don't laugh. Instead ask yourself: is it getting more likely as time goes by or less likely? Answer: more likely, definitely. At the 2018 World Cup, I actually thought that ambition was going to get fulfilled. England were in the semi-finals and playing Croatia. One step from the pinnacle.

That semi-final was the only game that I actually went to at the World Cup. I was in the studio in Moscow the whole time otherwise. But that night, with the match going out live on ITV, I was free to go. I sat in the stadium with Alan Shearer, and when England went ahead and the place erupted, we both looked at each other and thought: 'This could be it – England in the final.' It was an electrifying thought. On top of being an England supporter, there was the glittering prospect of being at the front of this massive national television event – as big as it comes, surely. England in a World Cup final!

Of course, Croatia turned it around and England went out. I was gutted – doubly gutted in fact. Gutted as an England fan and gutted as a television presenter. I genuinely haven't been knocked flat like that by a football match since I was a player. The biggest show of them all had felt close enough to touch and then it had been snatched away.

One day, though.

APPENDIX

In which GARY offers a small selection of the recipes with which he has personally nourished Danny, thereby making this the first football-related non-fiction publication in history to include a fail-safe method for perfect boiled rice. And in which DANNY counters by setting down the hitherto secret methods behind his own patented tomato omelette sandwich, which you seriously won't regret making either, even though it sounds as though you might.

GARY'S CACIO E PEPE

Serves 8–10

700g spaghetti
2 large handfuls of grated pecorino
Fresh black peppercorns
Olive oil
Unsalted butter

I first had this dish in a restaurant in New York, late at night after going to a concert, and I immediately thought: I've got to learn how to cook that. It's very simple, with some slight trickiness at the end, where it all comes together very quickly and you've got to get the mix right at that point or it can go a bit dry on you.

Practice will be your friend here. And it's worth it: this is one of my favourite meals to make because it's quick – a 15-minute job, max – and delicious and I'll sometimes just do it for myself if I come in late and hungry.

Set the spaghetti to cook in a pan of well-salted water. The salting is important because you're going to be using some of that pasta water to make the sauce. I plan to give the spaghetti two minutes less than the instruction on the packet because it's going to continue cooking in the pan with the sauce, and I like it al dente.

While the spaghetti is boiling, crush a handful of black peppercorns in a pestle and mortar. You can buy it ready done, but it's better if it's freshly cracked. Then, just before the pasta reaches its time, melt a knob of butter with a couple of glugs of oil in a large pan over a low heat and add the pepper.

Scoop the cooked pasta out of the water and add it to the oil and pepper and then directly add a ladle-full of the pasta water. Give it a minute of mixing over the heat, whooshing it around to coat the pasta. Then take the pan off the heat and add the grated pecorino. Whirl that around until it has mixed in and then add another ladle of the starchy pasta water and stir again. This should emulsify everything so that it has a nice shiny look. Grate on some extra pecorino and serve in bowls straight away.

GARY'S ASPARAGUS RISOTTO

Serves 8

5 celery sticks
1 large onion
Bunch of asparagus
250ml white wine
2 litres of vegetable or chicken stock
500g risotto rice
Grated parmesan
2 lemons
Mascarpone
Olive oil
Unsalted butter
Salt and pepper

This is a basic risotto dish which you can easily adapt, using mushrooms instead of asparagus, say, or throwing frozen peas in there or whatever you fancy. The key thing for this method is to heat your stock in two separate pots: half a litre of stock in one pot, one and half litres in the other. This makes your life easier later on. Also, you're going to be busy doing a lot of stirring during this process, so it's a good idea to get all your preparation done while the stock warms.

Chop the asparagus, keeping the tips whole and cutting the stalks into 1cm chunks. Grate a couple of handfuls of parmesan. Grate the zest from two lemons and squeeze the juice from one of them. Cut 100g of butter into small chunks. And finely chop the celery and the onion.

When those things are ready, melt another knob of butter and several glugs of olive oil in a pan over a very low heat and then toss in the celery and onion and soften them as slowly as you can without browning them – maybe for 15 minutes. Then, when they're properly softened, whack the heat right up and throw in the rice along with 250ml of white wine. Keep stirring and stirring until the wine evaporates.

Now drop the heat to low-to-medium. From the pan containing the one and a half litres, start adding the stock, one ladle at a time, and each time stirring until it has mostly disappeared. Repeat this, stirring all the time, until the rice is just starting to soften – probably about 15 to 20 minutes.

Now you're going to make sure that your second pan of stock, the one containing half a litre, is simmering. Drop the rice into that half litre of stock, throwing in the chopped asparagus at this point. Immediately turn the heat up high to bring the liquid to a boil and then turn it right down again. This is where the asparagus gets cooked.

You'll be thinking you've made a soup at this point, with the amount of liquid in there, but it's going to gradually cook down. You've still got plenty of stock in the other pan, too, so, when the liquid does eventually disappear, you're going to restart the process of adding stock, one ladle at a time, stirring until it diminishes, as before. Stir, stir, stir, and keep tasting until the rice is done. You're trying to get to the point where it still has some bite, but before it goes gloopy on you, which is a fine line, I'm afraid, but keep on it. The first time I tried this, it was like wallpaper paste, but I got better.

When you think the rice is finally cooked, throw in the parmesan, the lemon juice and most of the zest, the chunks of butter, and also three big tablespoons of mascarpone cheese, which will really lift it. Add salt and pepper if you need to. Give the whole thing a big mix-up and then turn the heat off, put a lid on the pot and leave it to settle for a couple of minutes.

Serve it up with a bit more grated parmesan and the leftover lemon zest for a garnish. One problem about the constant tasting involved here: you may be full before you've sat down to eat it. But your guests won't be.

GARY'S VEGETABLE SRI LANKAN CURRY WITH RICE

Serves 8

2 sweet potatoes
1 large butternut squash
1 large red onion

4 cloves of garlic
Red and green chillis
Mixed peppers
100g baby spinach
Coconut oil
Coconut sugar
2 400ml tins of coconut milk
Turmeric
Two teaspoons of cumin seeds
Two teaspoons of black mustard seeds
Cinnamon
Paprika
Chilli powder
Juice of 1 lime
Maple syrup
500g basmati rice

I once forgetfully added chilli to a dish that I served to Danny and his head practically exploded. He was charging around the room, tipping water down himself and for a little while it looked as though we might need an air ambulance. The emergency passed eventually, but Danny, it turns out, is not partial to the stronger spices. So if I cook this dish for Danny, I leave out the paprika and the chilli elements. And it works even without them – a lovely sweet curry, the maple syrup perhaps being the key to it.

Heat the oven to 200C. Chop the sweet potatoes and the

butternut squash into roughly 2.5cm cubes. Put a big spoonful of coconut oil on the bottom of a baking tray and throw in the potatoes and the squash. Put some more coconut oil on the top of the vegetables and sprinkle in half a teaspoon of turmeric, half a teaspoon of cinnamon, a pinch of paprika and a pinch of chilli powder. Bung the tray in the oven, where it's going to need 30 minutes. For the last 10 of those 30 minutes, throw in the sliced peppers – one each of the red, green and yellow.

Meanwhile, warm a tablespoon of coconut oil in a pan and cook the cumin and the black mustard seeds for 30 seconds on a medium heat until they start to pop. Add the chopped red onion and the four finely chopped cloves of garlic, along with a couple of green chillis and a red chilli, again finely chopped. Cook all that for five minutes on a medium heat.

Add two tins of coconut milk, making sure to give them a shake first, and a big tablespoon of coconut sugar. Continue to cook for about ten minutes. Then add the juice of a lime, a couple of glugs of maple syrup and the baked vegetables from the oven, and cook it all together for five further minutes. Chuck in 100g of baby spinach at the end, just until it wilts.

For the rice, my trusted method is as follows. Soak the rice in a colander under a running cold tap until the water doesn't run cloudy any more, which will probably be after about two minutes. Meanwhile boil up a pan of salted water. Add the rice and, from just when the rice starts to move slightly in the pan – usually after about a minute – give it exactly five more minutes of boiling. Then drain the rice through the colander and put silver foil over the top of the colander to create a lid. Place the sealed colander on top of a pan with an inch or so of boiling water bubbling away at the bottom of it. Steam the rice in the colander for eight minutes. Comes out perfectly every time.

DANNY'S TOMATO OMELETTE SANDWICH

2 eggs
1 fresh tomato
Butter
Sliced white bread
Hammonds Chop Sauce
Olive oil
Milk

People ask me whether Gary Lineker truly is a good cook, or whether that's some kind of joke between us. No, it's not comedy. He genuinely is a good cook, to a standard that I'm astounded by.

At the same time, I am not without innovative kitchen skills myself. I don't like people who say: 'Oh, I can't even cook an egg, me.' You should be able to. It's like saying you can't get yourself dressed. And it's not as though cooking has to be difficult. Take, for instance, the simplicity of my very own patented tomato omelette sandwich.

Now, I know this sounds downmarket and proletarian, and like I'm trying to harvest the low-hanging fruit here. But bear with me. I cooked this dish on a television show where the chef Gary Rhodes was the guest and I would urge you to try it, as he was obliged to.

It requires buttered white bread – sliced for preference. Again, this is not just me playing the prole card: it's about texture, and your sourdough or your pumpernickel simply wouldn't do it.

Break two eggs into a bowl and beat them together with a splash of milk – just a splash. Put a frying pan with a little oil in it on a medium heat. Roughly dice the tomato and toss it into the pan for about 30 seconds. Then pour in your egg and milk mixture. Stir it around with a fork until the eggs are scrambled, but not dry. Ladle this out thickly on to the already buttered white bread, and then add some Hammonds Chop Sauce. Other brown sauces are available, but I recommend Hammonds Chop Sauce, from Yorkshire. Squash down the top of the sandwich, cut it into four and away you go.

OK, to say that Gary Rhodes' highly trained eyes lit up in anticipation of this feast would be an exaggeration. Indeed, as the sandwich neared his lips there was an expression on his face which can only be described as the grimace of a man obliged to undergo a forfeit in a particularly ugly game of spin-the-bottle.

True, it's a slightly sloppy sandwich which turns into one of Salvador Dali's watches when you pick it up. But then the sandwich reached his mouth, his taste buds took over, and what can I tell you? The grimace slowly dissolved. And from Gary Rhodes came a low moan. 'Oh. Oh! Oh, yes!' Exactly. It is a mouthful of ambrosia. And one day at Gary Lineker's, it's going to be me doing the cooking.